Encyclopædia Britannica

The Book of Fascinating Facts

PUBLICATIONS INTERNATIONAL, LTD.

PICTURE CREDITS:

Encyclopædia Britannica
310 South Michigan Avenue
Chicago, Illinois 60604

8 7 6 5 4 3 2 1

ISBN: 1-56173-929-4

CONTENTS

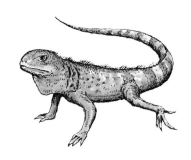

INTRODUCTION · 6

ANIMALS · 8

Captivating information will have animal lovers learning something new with each turn of the page. From antelopes to yaks, you'll read about almost every creature you can think of and some you can't. It's better than a trip to the zoo!

DINOSAURS · 38

Journey back in time to discover the amazing era when our planet was ruled by the dinosaur. Experience the world as it was millions of years ago when flying reptiles and plant-eating mammals fought for survival with terrifying meat eaters.

HUMAN BODY · 68

Our body—the most amazing machine of all—is the subject under consideration here. You'll learn where the smallest bones in the body are, why your hair is straight or curly, and just how long your intestines are. It's a great way to learn about yourself.

NATURE · 98

This chapter will take you on an incredible journey through the beauty and the fury that is the world we live in. Natural wonders, meat-eating plants, coral reefs, and much more that make up Mother Nature's universe are at hand.

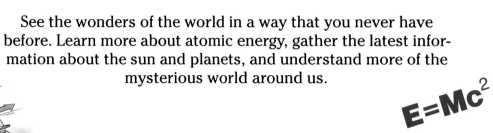

SCIENCE · 128

See the wonders of the world in a way that you never have before. Learn more about atomic energy, gather the latest information about the sun and planets, and understand more of the mysterious world around us.

$E=Mc^2$

HOW THINGS WORK · 158

Take time out to understand what makes everyday gadgets tick. Simple things like door locks, soap, and boomerangs are explained along with more complex objects such as car phones, VCRs, and helicopters. You'll be guaranteed to learn something new and fun!

TRANSPORTATION · 188

From the early beasts of burden to planes that are capable of vertical takeoff and landing, this chapter has it all. Bicycles, trains, cars, trucks, sleds, ships, and tanks—you'll find every conceivable way to get there in here.

GEOGRAPHY · 218

Whether you're a globetrotter or an armchair traveler, this section will show you more of the world. Mine for gold, climb the highest mountain, discover the North Pole, or swim in the saltiest sea. It's all right at your fingertips.

HISTORY • 248

The past becomes the present in this journey back through the ages. Egyptian mummies, Pilgrims, and the heroes and heroines of the past come to life in this amazing chapter where yesterday becomes as real as today.

SPORTS • 278

Discover what people do for fun, exercise, and competition all around the world. You'll no doubt be fascinated by world-class Olympians, the "games people play," and the intriguing "behind the scenes" stories about your favorite sports heroes.

PEOPLE, PLACES, & THINGS • 308

Within this chapter you will discover that truth is often stranger than fiction. Would you believe a fish that flies, a spider that spits, or a bark that sails? You'll be delighted with all kinds of hard-to-believe facts.

CULTURES AROUND THE WORLD • 338

Take a trip around the world without leaving your home. Learn what Germans eat, how the Chinese write, and ponder the smile of the Mona Lisa. Here is your chance to discover your roots and learn more about people from other countries.

INDEX • 368

INTRODUCTION

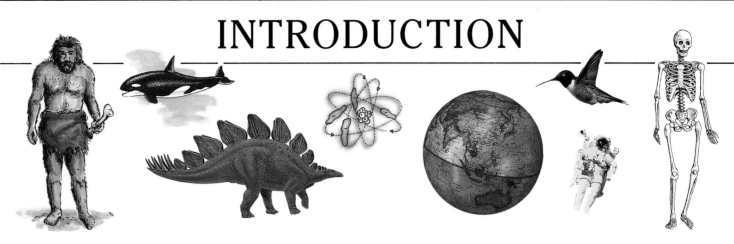

There is nothing more amazing than the world we live in: natural wonders, inventions, the differences and similarities between the peoples of the world. From the first cave dwellers to modern society, we have discovered and rediscovered things about ourselves and our world that are truly astonishing. Who would have thought that someone would invent an airplane, a way to replace a human heart, or a house made of rice paper? And yet, all of these accomplishments are real. What's even more amazing is that we have just touched the tip of the iceberg in the process of our discoveries.

The Book of Fascinating Facts takes you on an incomparable journey into the world around you. This 384-page book, full of color photography, covers dozens of topics of interest. "Animals" is brimming with facts about the animal kingdom. From the undersea world to the barnyard, this chapter provides interesting information about any animal that you can think of and quite a few that you may not have heard of. Did you know, for example, that the Komodo dragon of Indonesia is not really a dragon, but the world's largest lizard? Usually about 11½ feet (3½ m) long, it has led to many stories about fire-breathing dragons and monsters.

Next, move on to those amazing creatures that roamed the earth millions of years ago. They are the subject of "Dinosaurs." This section really takes you back in time. Experience the world as it was then, with flying reptiles, mouse-like mammals, and huge plant-eating dinosaurs fighting for survival with smaller meat eaters.

What do you think is the most intricate and amazing machine of all? It's the human body, of course,

and we have pages and pages of fascinating information about it. About 8 to 16 pints (5 to 8 liters) of blood move through the body of the average adult every minute. All human stomachs do not look alike. Some are shaped like the letter *S* and others like the letter *J.* The variety of interesting information in "Human Body" is endless.

"Nature" will enlighten you to the existing phenomena of the universe. From weather to volcanoes to diamonds and gold—a myriad of wonders is presented. It's truly amazing what nature can do: The biggest volcanic explosion was on Rakata, an island in Indonesia. The noise of the blast could be heard 3,000 miles (5,000 km) away, and over 36,000 people were drowned by the waves set off by the eruption of the volcano!

The mystery of science is at your fingertips in our "Science" chapter. You can read about nuclear reactions, find the latest information about the sun and the planets, and understand the ways in which light travels. Did you ever wonder how scientists can figure out how old something is? They do so through a process known as carbon-14 dating. Carbon is present in all living things. When a plant or animal dies, carbon-14 breaks down steadily enough for scientists to measure exactly how much of it has disappeared over time.

For the mechanically inclined, we have "How Things Work." In this chapter, you will learn how many well-known gadgets operate. We take many conveniences for granted, but it truly is interesting to know the intricacies behind many household objects. Written in a way that is easy to understand, you'll find out about the workings of musical instruments, soap, hearing aids, photography, mirrors, and so on. Did you know that the

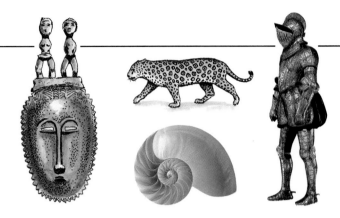

motion picture camera takes hundreds of separate, slightly different photographs to make a movie? We see them as one smooth, moving picture through a wonder of the eye called "the persistence of visual movement."

"Transportation" covers bicycles, automobiles, trains, trucks, sleds, snowmobiles, skates, ships, and planes in fantastic detail. Can you believe that today's average car is made up of over 14,000 separate parts? These range from simple knobs to complicated electronic circuit boards and are made of everything from plastic to steel to silicon.

Did you know that the the planet we live on weighs 6,600,000,000,000,000,000,000 tons? That's the kind of information that you will find in "Geography." Look in awe at the Pueblo cliff dwellings, some constructed over 1,000 years ago. Read all about the tallest mountain, the deepest part of the ocean, the saltiest sea, and many more statistics. What could be more incredible than the natural wonders of the world?

A large portion of what we know and are today is the result of what has happened in the past. People through the ages have amazed the present-day world with inventions, customs, and decisions that still affect us today. Browse through the pages of "History" to learn about the people and cultures of old. Egyptian mummies, the Golden Age of Greece, Europe's discovery of the New World, and the devastating effects of war are all subjects that we should know about. The most interesting tidbits of history are condensed for you in this chapter, and it will give you a better understanding of why the world is the way it is today.

And what person isn't interested in knowing more about sports and their favorite sports heroes? You'll find everything from the first Olympic games to the intricacies of modern-day football. If you ever wanted to know what "love" means in tennis or what a "sticky wicket" is, just turn to "Sports"—you won't be disappointed.

What do you call a chapter that has a little bit of everything? We call it "People, Places, & Things." From marshmallow plants to flying fish to a bark that sails, you'll learn all kinds of intriguing information. You'll get an introduction into why we call certain things by the names that we do. Chopsticks, for example, mean "quick ones" in Chinese. And a sulky is a two-wheeled cart used for trotting horses. The doctor who invented this cart was so prone to bad moods that to this day the word "sulky" is used to describe a person who is in a bad mood.

You don't have to leave your favorite chair to travel the world. With "Cultures Around the World," France, Germany, England, Spain, Italy, China, Japan, and Africa are all at your fingertips. And if you want to learn more about the music, culture, folklore, and literature of the United States, you'll find that, too. How's this for a staggering statistic: The best estimate is that slightly more than one billion people live in China. This means that almost 25 percent of the population of the whole world lives in this one country.

The Book of Fascinating Facts is a unique publication. It is amazingly full of amazing information that is great fun to read. Start reading *The Book of Fascinating Facts* and you won't be able to put it down. Pick a chapter or pick a page. Chances are you will be absolutely amazed!

Animals

An elephant's trunk has thousands of muscles in it, and it can bend in just about any way the elephant wants it to.

Cows supply us with an amazing amount of milk. During the 250 to 320 days each year in which a cow gives milk, it can produce over 4,200 quarts (4,000 liters).

Now That's a Lot of Fish

There are over 30,000 kinds of fish in the world. The largest is the 50-foot (15-m) whale shark and the smallest is the dwarf goby of the Philippines. This tiny fish is less than $^1/_2$ inch (1 cm) in length.

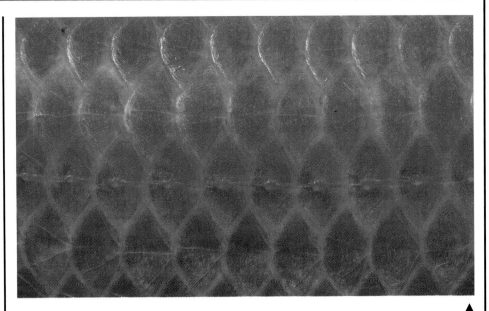

Scaly Creatures

The bodies of most fish are covered with scales. These vary from the teethlike scales of sharks to flat, platelike scales of salmon. In bony fish, scales can be used to determine their age. Usually, scales of bony fish have a fixed arrangement on the body that can be used to identify the species.

Keeping In Balance

Just like in humans, the ear of a fish plays an important part in balance. In the inner ear of a fish, there are three canals that are lined with a sensitive tissue and filled with a fluid. These canals contain ear bones, which are produced from a substance given out by the walls of the canals. They increase in size as a fish grows. At the end of each canal there is a very sensitive swelling. When a fish turns on its side, the ear bones roll and touch the sensitive tissue. A message is sent to the brain—the fish then knows that it is not upright.

A Sense of Taste

Fish have taste buds scattered all over the surface of their bodies. In some fish, they are widely scattered. In others, they are concentrated in the area around their mouths.

The Art of Breathing Underwater

Fish breathe through their gills, which are always found between the fish's mouth and the place where its food goes down. Most of them get oxygen from the water that passes through their gills. Carbon dioxide is then passed out of the gills when the fish breathes out.

Fish That Build Nests

Some fish are called "bubble nest builders" because of the strange nests they make. The males make these nests by blowing bubbles of air and slime, which they push together to form a mass of foam that floats on top of the water. The female then lays her eggs and puts them in the nest. The male stands guard, catching any eggs that fall out and making sure that they get back into the nest. Gouramis and fighting fish are two of the best-known bubble nest builders.

Friends and Enemies of the Deep

Many fish recognize each other underwater by their colors. Since the bright colors of many fish are in definite patterns, they seem to be able to recognize other fish that have the same colors and markings. These identification marks are also used by fish as a way to hide from their enemies.

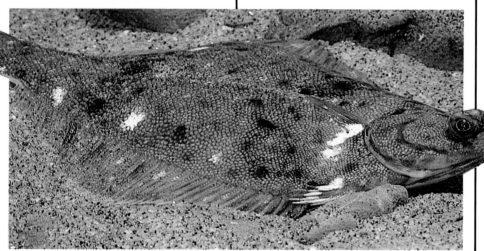

Changing Colors to Suit Fishy Needs

Surprisingly, almost all fish can change their colors to suit their environment. For fish like trout, this can take a long time. Some tropical fish can change from black to white or from bright yellow to scarlet almost instantly. Flatfish like flounder can change colors so successfully that they can be almost impossible to see when they are resting on the bottom of the sea.

Learning Under the Seas

You probably never thought of fish as being very smart or highly developed. The truth is that they can learn. For example, fish memorize smells and colors. This knowledge is especially useful to them when they hunt or when they try to remember where they are going when they travel long distances.

You *Can* Talk on Fishing Trips! ▲

According to most scientists today, it is not very likely that fish can hear, at least not in the same way that we can. However, they are sensitive to vibrations coming through the water, and if a noise is loud enough to make vibrations, the fish are likely to notice it. So, you don't have to keep quiet on a fishing trip—a nice quiet voice is just fine.

Underwater ▲ Kangaroos

Like kangaroos, sea horses have pouches in which they carry their babies around. But, unlike kangaroos, it is the father, not the mother sea horse, who carries the young. In fact, the "daddy" sea horse even carries the eggs around in his pouch until they hatch.

11

The Biggest Creature of Them All ◀

As far as anyone can tell, not even the largest dinosaurs were as big as the blue whale. Up to 98 (30 m) long and weighing as much as 143 tons (129 metric tons), these giants are really the biggest animals ever to swim or walk on this planet.

Thar She Blows!

▼

When a whale returns to the surface from a dive under the water, it blows the used air out of its body through one or two blow-holes on the top of its head. This used air goes out with so much force that the noise can be heard far away. Since that air is loaded with water vapor, a smoky mist usually comes out of the blow-hole(s) at the same time. Old stories recount that sailors shouted "Thar she blows!" whenever they saw this.

Whales on Land?

▲

Unlike sharks, whales are mammals. They have warm blood, their young are born alive rather than in eggs, and they nurse their young on milk. Strangely enough, it is quite likely that the ancestors of whales did not come from the sea. Inside whale flippers are bones arranged very much the way they are in animal paws. Many scientists believe that whales' ancestors first lived on land and then moved to the sea.

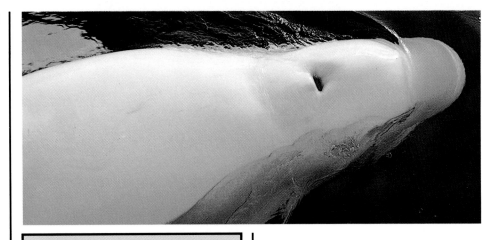

Coming Up for Air

Whales breathe air like land animals; they do not have gills. In fact, they must come to the surface every once in a while to breathe. Whales usually come to the surface every five to ten minutes, even though they have been known to spend as much as an hour at a time beneath the surface.

Eating Like a Whale

Whales usually eat *plankton*, microscopic sea creatures and tiny plants that are eaten by many different sea creatures and small fish. They do not have to hunt down their food. Instead, whales open their giant mouths as they swim through a field of plankton or a school of fish. When the whale shuts its mouth, its meal is trapped inside. All the whale has to do in order to eat is force the water out of its mouth.

Whale-hunting for Profit

At one time, ships from many countries hunted whales. Their blubber was melted down into oil that was used for lamps. Whalers also took *spermaceti,* a waxy substance that was used in perfumes and makeup, and ambergris, which was also used for perfume.

Protecting Whales from Man

Today, whales are protected by most countries in order to keep them from disappearing from the earth. Five different types of whales cannot be hunted at all, and the International Whaling Commission has set limits on the number of other kinds of whales that can be killed.

Killer Whales Do Attack

Killer whales are the only whales that attack other warm-blooded creatures, and they often eat penguins and seals. They sometimes group together in hunting packs in order to attack other whales and people. Most whales are quite harmless. In fact, most of the famous incidents in which whales attacked ships or boats were the result of people hunting whales.

The Smartest Creature of the Sea

Dolphins are very smart. They can be taught to do complicated tricks at aquarium water shows. In nature, they communicate with one another using a wide range of sounds. At present, scientists are giving them many different kinds of intelligence tests. In fact, there are some people who think that dolphins can even be trained to carry out fairly complicated underwater jobs.

Cousins to Dolphins

Porpoises are closely related to dolphins, but are stockier in shape and smaller in size. They also have blunt noses instead of beaklike ones, and their color and markings are different.

Whales That We All Know

Dolphins are mammals. In fact, they are whales, and they belong to the same family of toothed whales as the giant sperm whales. Dolphins breathe air, give birth to live young, and nurse their young with milk. There are 32 different kinds of dolphins; most live in the sea.

Swimming Like a Porpoise

The strange rolling motion that a school of porpoises makes is caused by their need to return to the surface for air about four times each minute. Their swimming actually takes them up and down as it carries them forward through the water.

On Land and in the Sea ▼

Seals are amazing creatures underwater. Once a seal plunges underwater, its heartbeat drops, so that each lungful of air lasts a long time. Seals can even sleep underwater, coming up to the surface every ten minutes or so for a breath of air. Seals come back to land to breed and to raise their young for their first few days of life.

Those Quick-learning Seals ▲

No one really knows how they do it, but baby seals are able to swim almost from the time they are born. Seals not only swim well along the surface of the water—they are also excellent divers.

Ever-popular Sea Lions

Sea lions are what are known as "eared seals," meaning that their ears stick out from the sides of their heads. ("Earless" seals have ears as well. They simply don't show as much because they don't stick out.)

The Bendable Flippers of Sea Lions ▼

Sea lions can bend their flippers forward, so they can use them to steer as well as paddle themselves along. These bendable flippers also help sea lions scramble over rocks when they come onto land.

Traveling Sea Lions

Sea lions, like many other creatures, migrate back to certain areas when it is time for them to have their young. For example, some sea lions return to the Pribilof Islands, off the coast of Alaska, every May and June to breed and have pups. Then, they take off, spending over half a year swimming around the Pacific Ocean. They manage to travel as far south as California during winter, probably in search of food and warmer water.

15

Brown Bear Family ◀

Brown bears include the giant Kodiak bear of Alaska and the brownish, yellow-colored grizzly bear of the Rocky Mountains and Canada. Other types of brown bears were once found all over Europe, but have become rare except in remote parts of Eastern Europe.

Just an Ordinary Bear

The black bear is generally thought to be the most common bear in the United States. It is found coast to coast, even in relatively settled areas, where it can be seen sifting through garbage dumps looking for a meal.

Clever as a Fox ◀

Foxes are amazingly cunning and smart. When chased by dogs and fox hunters, for example, a fox will wade across streams to make dogs lose its scent. It will also ride on the backs of sheep in order not to make footprints. Foxes may even pretend to be dead if there is danger nearby.

Foxy Diet

Foxes eat just about everything small enough for them to catch—birds, rabbits, mice, chickens, ducks, and frogs. They will also eat berries, fruit, worms, and bugs.

Shooting Porcupine Quills ▶

A porcupine uses its sharp quills to protect itself. It usually smacks an attacking animal with its strong tail, driving the quills into the animal's face. The quills stick in the enemy and stay there, quite painfully, until the animal can get them out.

Soft as a Baby Porcupine

Porcupines are born with soft quills. Over time, they grow harder and harder, until they become the dangerous weapons that equip fully grown adult porcupines.

Smelly as a Skunk

A Skunk in the House

Before adopting a skunk as a pet, people sometimes have its smelling devices removed by a veterinarian. Unfortunately, without its weapon, a skunk is helpless in the event of an attack by another animal.

Skunks are not unusually brave; it's just that they know that very few animals are willing to attack them. The terrible-smelling liquid that skunks shoot out is so powerful—and so unpleasant—that the only enemy they really have is the owl. Owls can swoop down on them so fast that skunks may not have time to shoot their foul-smelling liquid.

The Story Behind Antlers

Deer lose their antlers every year, and every year they grow back. At first, the new antlers are covered by a hairy skin called "velvet." Once the antlers have grown back to their normal size, the deer begins scraping off the velvet by rubbing the antlers against trees and rocks. In the spring, the deer shed their antlers, and new ones begin growing in their place.

This deer has already lost one antler and will soon lose the other.

Deer with No Antlers

For the most part, only male deer have antlers. Certain types of deer have no antlers at all. The Chinese water deer, for example, doesn't even have tiny stumps on its head. What it does have, though, are two teeth that are longer than the others. These look like tiny tusks as they come out of the deer's mouth and point downward. Another deer without antlers is the musk deer, which makes its home on the lower slopes of the Himalayan Mountains.

America's Common Deer

Two types of deer are common in North and South America. The white-tailed deer is found all the way from Canada to Peru in open woodlands and farming areas. The mule deer lives in mountain and desert areas from Alaska to Mexico.

White-tailed fawn

Antelopes Come in Different Sizes

North American antelopes are generally a little larger than deer. In Africa, antelopes come in all different sizes. The Derby eland, for example, often stands 6¹/₂ feet (2 m) high at the shoulders and weighs 1,500 pounds (700 kg). In contrast, the tiny royal antelope is about the size of a rabbit, not more than 10 inches (25 cm) high, and about 4¹/₂ pounds (2 kg) in weight.

North American antelope

An Elk by Any Other Name... ▲

The wapiti is one of the names given to the North American elk, a giant deerlike animal that once roamed freely all over the continent. Today, it lives mainly in the Rocky Mountains and in southern Canada. It is the second largest member of the deer family. Adult males stand over 5 feet (1¹/₂ m) tall and weigh up to 650 pounds (295 kg).

Big as a Moose

The moose is the largest member of the deer family. A full-grown bull moose stands about 6¹/₂ feet (2 m) high, weighing in at a full 1,800 pounds (820 kg). Its large, leaf-shaped antlers can run 5 feet (1¹/₂ m) across.

Fierce as a Wolf

Wolves are excellent hunters, and there is little doubt that wild wolves are fierce. The stories about them attacking people are, for the most part, greatly exaggerated. According to most people who study them, wolves attack people only if they have been attacked themselves or if they are extremely hungry. Otherwise, they prefer to be left to their own diet of deer, moose, caribou, and other wild creatures.

Big Cats with a Little Voice

Even though pumas are generally 10 feet (3 m) long, they make a noise almost exactly like that of a housecat—just a little louder. The high-pitched scream that you hear mountain lions making in the movies is a mating call. They rarely use it when they are angry or about to attack.

Wolf Communications

Wolves are extremely intelligent. They are able to live in packs in a highly organized way. They also communicate with each other using a complicated system of barks and calls, facial movements, and body movements. They even use a system of smells to mark off the land claimed by each wolf or wolf pack.

Another Name for a Mountain Lion

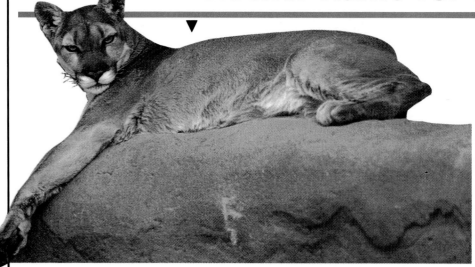

Puma is the real name for the wild catlike creature we sometimes call a mountain lion, panther, or cougar. It is found in North, Central, and even South America, although it is rare in the United States except in Rocky Mountain areas.

The Sharp Eyes of a Lynx

For many years, people believed that the lynx, or bobcat, had the sharpest eyes of any animal. Although scientists are no longer sure that this is true, "lynx-eyed" is still used to describe anyone or anything with extremely good vision.

Prize-winning Hunters of the Night ▲

The lynx is one of the animal world's best hunters. It hunts only at night, when it catches all sorts of birds and small mammals. Lynxes enjoy hunting, and they often seem to break the rule that animals never kill more food than they can eat. In fact, they often get themselves far more food than they could possibly eat, leaving most of a whole sheep or goat behind for other creatures to finish.

A Cat's Largest Relative ▶

The jaguar, America's fiercest and largest cat, is found mostly in the forests and *pampas* (grass-covered plains) of South America. Years ago, jaguars were common in the southern United States and Mexico, but they have become very rare in those areas today.

Spotted Jaguar Coats

Although they are not really closely related, jaguars do look quite a bit like leopards. Jaguars are heavier, shorter, have stronger legs, and larger heads. Most jaguars are golden-brown with black spots. There are jaguars with white coats and black spots as well as extremely rare ones that are almost completely black.

21

The King of Beasts

◄ For thousands of years, people considered the lion to be the "King of Beasts" because of its strength and fierceness. It is also thought that the lion has a regal manner as it lays watching what is going on around it.

This lion couple has a stately air.

The Many Homes of the Lion

▼

Although we usually think of lions as being one of Africa's most famous animals, they once roamed the plains and forests of Europe and were found as far east as India. In fact, they only disappeared from Europe around the year 500 A.D.

Male and Female Hunters

For many years, people have been told that only female lions hunt. The truth is that both male and female lions hunt. The males are by far the stronger hunters—they can drag an animal the size of a horse quickly to the ground using only the strength of their jaws.

Beware of the Lion

Lions are not interested in attacking humans. At times, however, old lions find themselves too slow to attack fast-running antelopes, gazelles, and zebras. Some of them turn their attention to people, who seem far easier to catch. Such cases are rare, and lions have faced far more danger from people than the other way around.

Tigers Are Swimmers▲

Even though we usually think of tigers as animals of the hot jungles of India, many tigers actually live as far north as southern Siberia and northern Korea. They are quite happy living in rocky mountain areas as well as in swamps and forests. They don't particularly enjoy heat, so they tend to hide themselves away in cool, high grass whenever it gets hot. Unlike most cats, tigers are good swimmers. They will often cool themselves off by lying in shallow pools of water.

Tiger Disappearance

Some types of tigers—including the dark-colored tiger off the island of Bali—have already disappeared from the earth. Others, like the South Chinese tiger, are in great danger of extinction. There are probably only 50 to 80 of these creatures left. Scientists fear that of the eight original subspecies of tigers, only three or four will be left by the end of the twentieth century.

The Lonely Life of a Tiger ▲

Except during the mating season, when tigers get together to have their young, they generally live a lonely life. Females have their cubs about once every two or three years, and except for the two years or so when she is raising them, she lives alone. The males also live alone most of the time.

Leopards by Other Names

Leopards are found in many parts of the world, but they are called panthers in both India and Pakistan. There are several kinds of leopards, and they are all excellent hunters.

A Rare and Beautiful Animal

Snow leopards are among the world's rarest and most beautiful animals. They make their home in the Himalaya Mountains, often as high as 18,000 feet (5,500 m) above sea level. Their thick undercoats keep them warm, as do their pale gray outercoats that were once prized as expensive furs.

Disappearing Cheetahs

Today, cheetahs are found mostly in East Africa and Namibia, although a few may survive in northern Iran and Turkestan. They once roamed Africa, Arabia, the Middle East, and the Indian subcontinent. Slowly, they were driven from these lands. In India, the last cheetah was killed in 1948. In Africa, the animals are being driven from the open grasslands they used to live in, as more and more of the land is used for farming and raising cattle.

The Fastest Animal in the World

Exactly which animal is the fastest in the world depends on how you measure it. Cheetahs are certainly the fastest over a short distance; they can reach speeds of up to 60 miles per hour (100 kph) in just a few yards. Over a long distance, most race horses would beat even the swiftest-running cheetah.

The Value of Ivory ◄

Elephant tusks are made of ivory. Ivory is both rare and valuable. The value of ivory has led elephants almost to the point of extinction.

▲ The All-purpose Trunk

An elephant's trunk is a very handy instrument, since the elephant can use it as nose, lips, hand, and arm, all in one. The trunk has thousands of muscles in it, and it can bend in just about any way the elephant wants it to. At the end of the trunk is a small "finger" so sensitive that an elephant can use it to pick up something as small as a pin.

Drinking by Squirting

Without their trunks, elephants would find it hard to get a drink of water, since it would be almost impossible for them to bend over far enough to get their mouths into a river, lake, or stream. Instead of lying down completely in order to drink, elephants simply fill their trunks with water and squirt the liquid into their mouths.

Elephants Are Not All the Same

African elephants are different from Asian elephants in several ways. First of all, they are much larger. They also have bigger ears than Asian elephants do. In addition, African elephants have two little fingers at the end of their trunks. Also, both male and female African elephants have tusks; only male Asian elephants have tusks.

Magical Rhino Horns

Rhinos have almost completely disappeared because hunters and poachers slaughter them for their horns. Many people in Asia believe that the horn has magical powers and rhino horn—whole, ground, or even powdered—commands a great price. Hunters will take great risks to kill rhinos and take their horns.

A Very Muddy Bath

Although an entire rhinoceros species has been called "white," they are almost exactly the same color as the more famous "black" rhinoceros. The name probably came about because these rhinos liked to give themselves baths in pools of mud that were light in color.

Rhinos Need Glasses!

Rhinoceroses have a great deal of trouble seeing things that are far away. However, their senses of smell and hearing are excellent.

Move Out of the Way!

Rhinos can be very dangerous. Most keep as far away from people as possible, but once in a while, a bad-tempered rhino will get it into its head to charge just about anything. There is really nothing quite so frightening as the sight of a 10,000-pound (5-metric-ton) rhino charging directly at you.

A Living Dragon ◀

Iguanas are lizards living mostly in North, Central, and South America. Some are small, barely an inch or two (less than a few centimeters) long, while others grow to over 6 feet (2 m). Most of them are green in color, and they look quite a bit like old-fashioned pictures of dragons. Most iguanas live in trees and eat leaves, fruits, and insects.

An Iguana That Swims

The marine iguana lives on the Galapagos Islands off the coast of South America. Unlike other iguanas, it seems quite at home in the water, going there regularly to fetch its favorite food— seaweed.

Leaping Lizards, It Looks Like a Dragon!

Although the Komodo dragon of Indonesia is not really a dragon, it is the world's largest lizard that looks like a dragon. Usually about $11^1/_2$ feet ($3^1/_2$ m) long, it has led to many stories about fire-breathing dragons and monsters. For many years, travelers heard these fascinating stories. In 1912, naturalists were sent to investigate. They brought back stories of lizards growing up to 23 feet (7 m) long. The biggest ones they brought back in the flesh, however, were less than 10 feet (3 m) long.

Lizards Like Meat

Like all monitor lizards (of which it is the most famous and biggest), the Komodo dragon is *carnivorous*—it eats meat. Small mammals, birds, deer, and pigs can all end up as the Komodo dragon's meal.

27

Bald As An Eagle

◄

The North American bald eagle is not really bald—it just has white feathers on the top of its head that make it look that way. Strangely enough, these birds are not born this way. In fact, it takes them until they are about three years old before their head feathers are white enough to give them this bald appearance.

Electricity Pole Nests ▲

Ospreys are large fishing hawks whose main food is fish, and they make their nests as close to the water as possible. When telephone and electricity poles first came to many outlying areas, ospreys decided these would make wonderful nesting places. Unfortunately, the birds ended up banging into wires, pulling them down, and even putting nests right on top of important electrical equipment. As a result, many of these rare birds were killed and electric power was disrupted often. Rather than fight the birds, electric companies in many areas simply put up empty poles for ospreys to use.

Birds That Like to be Social ▲

Unlike other birds, sea gulls are extremely social. They go around together in flocks, and when it is time for them to breed, they form giant colonies. They also raid people's garbages for food, so they hang out in large numbers around garbage dumps, reservoirs, and even rooftops.

A sea gull waits patiently for its flock.

Vampire Bats Do Feed on Blood

Vampire bats do exist, especially in South America, but they do not turn into human beings, nor do they wear capes and fancy clothes. These tiny bats feed on nothing but blood, which they get by biting animals. They are not a serious problem, since there are not many of them and they live in areas with very few people.

Animals That Fly in the Dark

Bats can fly in the dark because they do not use eyesight when they fly. In fact, experiments show that they can get around just as well blindfolded as with their eyes uncovered. Instead, they use a kind of radar. Bats send out high-pitched sounds that bounce off objects around them. Their sensitive ears are able to pick up the echoes of these sounds—and figure out exactly where things are.

The Changing Diet of Sea Gulls

Gulls were originally hunters. Only in recent years have they learned to eat the leftovers people leave around. In many parts of the world, gulls still hunt fish, shore animals, and crabs. The large, black-backed gull, which may be up to 30 inches (75 cm) long, has even been known to eat mice, lambs, and birds.

The King of Birds

Just as the lion is the "King of Beasts," the eagle is the "King of Birds." Roman soldiers used eagles as symbols of their power, marching into battle behind statues of eagles placed on the tops of poles. Kings and queens of Europe and Asia put eagles on their coats of arms, and many flags and national insignia still show them today. The eagle has even been chosen as the symbol of many air forces.

A Beautiful Feathered Friend

Egrets are large, white birds of the heron family. They were once found almost everywhere in the world. By the 1900s, hunters had just about eliminated them in their greed to get the birds' spectacular white feathers. Most of the egrets surviving today live in Africa.

The Last of the Whooping Crane

The whooping crane, which got its name from the noise that it makes, has almost completely disappeared. It was common right up through the beginning of the 20th century. Hunting and the advance of towns and factories led to its downfall. Now, whooping cranes live in protected areas in Texas. Every year, they fly north to Alberta, Canada, where they nest and have their young.

A Handy Pelican Pouch

A pelican's mouth has a long beak, with a long, thin piece on the top and a large pouch of skin on the bottom. The pouch, which is quite big, can stretch to hold a lot of food. Since pelicans often hunt among schools of fish, they need to catch as many fish as possible. They simply stuff them into their storage pouches and go out and hunt more fish. Then, when they have enough, they sit down and eat.

The Life of a Parrot

Parrots mostly get around by climbing. The main use for their great strong beaks is to pull themselves along as they make their way up a tree trunk or branch. Parrots also like to live in groups rather than alone and they make their nests inside holes in trees.

◄ Talking Birds

Parrots can definitely be trained to talk, although the job is not easy. The most commonly used parrots are the blue-fronted parrot from the Amazon and the African gray parrot. Both parrots make good pets and can be taught to speak in just about any language.

A Bird That Can't Fly

The ostrich is the world's largest bird, but it cannot fly at all. A fully grown male ostrich stands about 8 feet (2.4 m) tall and can weigh as much as 286 pounds (130 kg). It is just too heavy to be taken through the air by its short wings. Ostriches are excellent runners, able to dash along at up to 40 miles per hour (65 kph). They are also good fighters, using their powerful legs to kick their enemies. As they run, they often leap a bit, making it look as if they are trying to fly.

Some Very Old Birds

Cockatoos live a surprisingly long time both in the wild and in the home as pets. In fact, they have been known to live for as long as 100 years.

The Remarkable Cat Family ◄

House cats are really members of the same animal family as fierce big cats. In fact, some of those fierce cats are not much bigger than a good-sized house cat. The bobcat (or lynx) of North America, for example, only grows to about 3 feet (1 m) in length.

Seeing the World Through a Cat's Eyes

Although cats have amazingly good nighttime vision, they cannot see in total darkness. Still, they can see in conditions that would be impossible for you or most four-legged animals. The reason for this is simple. In darkness, a cat's *pupils* (the part of the eye that lets in light) open wide, until they almost fill the eye. This allows any available light to enter, so that a cat can make out what's around it. In brighter light, a cat's pupil narrows.

Man's Best Friend

Bones found in ancient caves and other places show that people have kept dogs for at least 10,000 years—and probably longer. Those dogs weren't pampered pets, though. They were used for work, just like the dogs of American Indians and Eskimos. They were kept to hunt, to guard the family, and to haul things from place to place. Even though they were treated well, their first job was always to help out with whatever work had to be done.

Hamster Happenings

There are many different kinds of hamsters, and a number of them can live as pets or in the wild. The golden hamster—the one you see in pet stores all over—has only been found three times in nature. The first hamsters were not seen until 1830. Then, a hundred years later, a mother and 12 young hamsters were found in Syria. A pair of them were brought to England, where they lived quite happily. Just about all of the hamsters you see today are related to that pair of English hamsters.

A Pig That Isn't a Pig

Even though they share a name, there is nothing connecting barnyard pigs and guinea pigs. They do not even have any connection to the Guinea coast of Africa or the island of New Guinea in the Pacific. The guinea pig is a rodent (just like rats and mice) descended from a family called "cavies." Some guinea pigs still live in the wild in the Andes Mountains of South America.

The Mouse of the World ▶

A house mouse is the best-known mouse of all, probably because it is the one people see most often. It lives around people—in homes, offices, and even factories. It is at home in the city or country, in Europe, North America, or Africa. The house mouse originally came from Asia but quickly made its way to just about every place where there are people.

That's a Lot of Cattle

"Cattle" is the term used to describe all *bovines*, which is the scientific name for cows, bulls, steers, buffaloes, bison, yaks, and zebus. "Cow" is the name used for full-grown female cattle; "bull" is the term for full-grown male cattle; "heifers" are young female cattle; and "steers" are males that have been operated on so that they cannot breed.

From the Cow to You

A cow starts giving milk when her first calf is born. That cow will keep giving milk up until just a few weeks before her next calf is born, which is generally somewhere between 250 and 320 days. As long as a cow keeps having calves, it will keep giving milk—skipping only a couple of weeks each year.

More Milk Than You Can Drink

Cows give an amazing amount of milk. During the 250 to 320 days each year in which a cow gives milk, it can give over 4,200 quarts (4,000 liters) of milk. Some cows can more than double this figure, producing up to 9,500 quarts (9,000 liters) of milk each season.

Cows That Give Yellow Milk

Jerseys are the pretty, light-brown cows you see in pictures of all kinds. Although they originally came from the Island of Jersey off the coast of Great Britain, they are now found all over the world. Strangely enough, the milk of Jersey cows is often slightly yellow in color. This yellow color is caused by eating green plants. If Jerseys stop eating greens, the yellow color disappears.

Wonderful Arabians! ▲

Arabian horses are the oldest breed—they have been around for many thousands of years. They have very short backs, small heads, large eyes, and very sensitive nostrils. They usually stand about 15 hands high. Arabians are famous for their lively movements and their great speed. They are also considered the most intelligent of all horses.

The "Hands" of a Horse ▼

It's common to measure a horse in "hands," measurements that are probably based on the width of a person's hand. Each of these "hands" is 4 inches (10 cm). The measurement is taken between the ground and the point at which the horse's neck joins its back.

A Real Beast of Burden ▼

One of the best known and strongest horses that was bred especially for heavy jobs is the Shire horse. Standing over 17 hands high and weighing about 2,000 pounds (1 metric ton), it can pull a load of up to 10,000 pounds (5 metric tons). Belgian and Clydesdale horses are also bred for strength, but they find it hard to match the pulling power of the giant Shire.

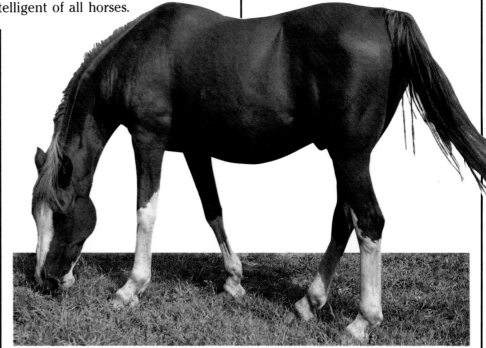

Counting a Horse's Teeth

It's easy to figure out a horse's age--just count its teeth. When a horse is between two and three years old, it sheds four middle teeth that are quickly replaced by adult teeth. Another four teeth, right alongside the others, are replaced at the end of the third year. After another year, four new adult teeth appear. After five years, the last baby teeth are shed and the horse has what is called a "full mouth." In most male horses, another four teeth appear. When a horse reaches the age of ten, a special "Galvayne" mark appears, which is a brown groove that runs down each corner front tooth. It remains until the horse reaches the age of 20.

Naming Horses By Color ▼

Horses come in all kinds of colors, although the names used to identify these colors are often confusing. A *bay*, for example, is a brown horse with black legs, mane, and tail. A *chestnut* is reddish-brown all over. *Palominos* are a beautiful gold color, usually with a light or white mane and tail. *Grays* are not really gray at all, but have black and white hairs on black skin. *White* horses are very rare, and most of the horses we call white are simply light-colored ones. True white horses are albinos, and they have red or pink eyes. Another well-known horse, the *roan*, has black, brown, or white hairs sprinkled with white. *Black* horses (the kind ridden by "the bad guys" in Westerns) have to be all black (including their noses, manes, tails, and legs) or else they are called "brown."

Palomino

Children's Favorite Ponies ▲

Shetland ponies are among the best known of all ponies, and they often show up in carnivals and shows, where children are given a chance to ride them. Shetlands are among the smallest of all ponies, usually growing no taller than about nine hands high. Because they are so small, people seem to take an immediate liking to them. Surprisingly, Shetlands are also among the strongest of all ponies. Years ago, they were used inside mines to haul heavy wagons of coal around the underground tunnels.

The Pony and the Horse ▼

There is really not much difference between a horse and a pony except their size, with anything smaller than 14 hands in height called a "pony" and anything larger a "horse." In fact, some horses that are technically ponies by birth are eventually called horses because they are more than 14 hands tall. At the same time, an Arabian is always called a horse, regardless of how tall it is—and it is quite often less than 14 hands tall. If all of this sounds terribly confusing, think of this: The horses used for playing polo are always called ponies—even though they are almost always more than 14 hands high.

Sheep of All Kinds

Even though we are used to seeing the plain white sheep from nursery rhymes like "Mary Had a Little Lamb" and "Little Bo Peep," there are actually hundreds of different kinds of sheep, with wool ranging from pure white to jet black. Some have short wool and others have long, shaggy wool. Even the horns (or lack of horns) differ among the many different kinds of sheep.

Drinking Goat's Milk

People have been drinking goat's milk for thousands of years. It is especially useful for babies and sick people, since goat's milk is much easier for people to digest than cow's milk. In some parts of the world, it is the only kind of animal milk used by people for drinking and for making cheese. Goat's milk is also popular because it causes fewer allergic reactions than cow's milk.

Taking Care of Sheep

Dogs have helped people take care of sheep for thousands of years. In fact, many dog breeds were created specifically to help with this job, since it calls for a dog that is lively, fast, and intelligent.

Unpopular Goats

Goats have been helpful to people for thousands of years and they still have a bad reputation. One reason for this is that the males, called "billy" goats, tend to have bad tempers and an equally unpleasant odor. In addition, goats chew grass and plants right off at the roots. Since they eat so much, they can quickly reduce a lovely field to a barren wasteland. As a result, other animals must move away and soil is washed away.

Useful Goats ▶

Goats provide people with more uses than just about any other animal. They provide milk, meat, leather, and even wool—all without needing a lot of care or feeding from the people who keep them. In some parts of the world, goats are even used as work animals, hauling sleds and carts wherever people need to carry things from place to place.

Getting Wool ▲

Shearing, the process of taking a sheep's wool off, usually takes place in the beginning of the summer when the sheep no longer needs its wool to keep warm. It doesn't hurt the sheep at all, as long as the shearer is careful not to cut or snip the sheep. The hardest part of shearing is cutting off the wool in one big piece, so the wool can be graded, classified, and processed all at once.

Dinosaurs

Stegosaurus may have used the large, triangular, horn-covered body plates along its tail and back to control or modify its body temperatures.

Tyrannosaurus had tiny front limbs and a huge skull with many sharp teeth that were very good for biting and tearing. Its teeth were six inches long and an inch wide!

The Age of the Dinosaurs

The Mesozoic era is divided into three periods: the Triassic (245-205 million years ago), the Jurassic (205-130 million years ago), and the Cretaceous (140-65 million years ago). Dinosaurs appeared at the end of the Triassic period and disappeared at the end of the Cretaceous.

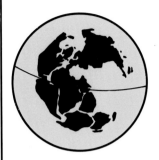  

Major Earth Changes

In the millions of years that dinosaurs were on the earth, the world underwent great changes. At first, all of the land was one big continent. Later, it broke up, causing mountains to form and seas to rise. Earth's climate changed, too. Swamps became deserts; flowers and trees appeared. As the earth changed, so did dinosaurs.

It's All in the Name

The word "dinosaur" comes from the Greek. *Dino* means "terrible" and *saur* means "lizard." It was probably coined as a name for these creatures because of their gigantic size.

Calling It by the Right Name

Dinosaurs are usually named after their distinguishing features or after the person who discovered their remains or where they were discovered. Interestingly enough, the scientist who named the *Apatosaurus* later named another dinosaur *Brontosaurus*. He later found out that *Brontosaurus* was just a larger *Apatosaurus*.

Dinosaur Discoverer

Gideon Algernon Mantell was a British paleontologist who discovered four of the five kinds (genera) of dinosaurs known during his time—*Iguanodon, Hylaeosaurus, Pelorosaurus,* and *Regnosaurus.*

Vertebrate Specialist ▼

Edward Drinker Cope discovered about a thousand species of extinct vertebrates (animals with backbones) in the United States. He is most noted for his knowledge on the vertebrates that flourished between the extinction of the dinosaurs (65,000,000 years ago) and the rise of man (2,500,000 years ago), part of which is known as the Tertiary Period of geologic time.

A Great Scholar ▲

Paleontologist Othniel Charles Marsh made extensive scientific explorations of the western United States and contributed greatly to knowledge of extinct North American vertebrates. In 1871, his group of scientists discovered the first pterodactyl (flying reptile) found in the U.S. He is credited with the discovery of more than a thousand fossil vertebrates and the description of at least 500 more. Marsh published major works on toothed birds, gigantic horned mammals, and North American dinosaurs.

Studying Fossils ▶

The study of fossils is important for at least three different reasons. First, the changes observed within an animal group are used to describe the evolution of that group. Fossils also provide geologists a quick way of assigning an age to the layer of rock in which they occur. Finally, fossil organisms may provide useful information about the climate and environment of the site where they were deposited and preserved.

Classifying Plants and Animals

Taxonomy is the science of classification of plants and animals. It compares what plants and animals are made of by methods of comparative anatomy and interprets differences and similarities through comparative genetics, biochemistry, physiology, embryology, behavior, ecology, and geography.

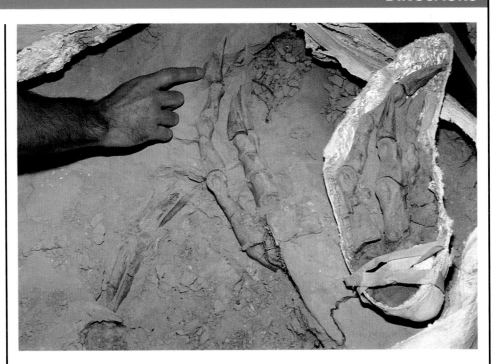

Apotosaurus fossils were used to reconstruct this skeleton

The Highest Grouping

Kingdom, divided into *Animalia, Plantae,* and others, is the highest grouping of taxonomy. After this comes the phylum, class, order, family, genus, and species.

Plants of the Dinosaur Age

In the latest part of the Triassic and in the Jurassic geological periods, the early dinosaurs lived in a world of conifers, ferns, and seed ferns. In the middle of the Cretaceous, new plants evolved. The familiar flowering plants and trees that we know appeared. Later dinosaurs fed on magnolia, laurel, dogwood, rose, oak, willow, birch, and others.

The Controversy Goes On

Years ago, scientists believed that all dinosaurs were cold-blooded. Recent studies have led some *paleontologists* (scientists who study fossils) to conclude that at least some dinosaurs were warm-blooded. Even though the controversy is still unresolved, scientists now agree that, contrary to the popular belief that dinosaurs were sluggish and slow-moving, many were fast and had high rates of metabolism.

All in the Family

Dinosaurs were reptiles and their closest living relative is the crocodile.

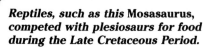

Reptiles, such as this Mosasaurus, competed with plesiosaurs for food during the Late Cretaceous Period.

Ruling the Seas

Two large groups of reptiles, the ichthyosaurs and the plesiosaurs, ruled the seas during the time of the dinosaurs. They were neither related to each other nor to dinosaurs.

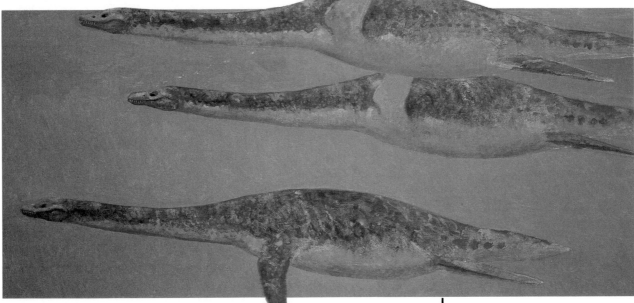

Marine plesiosaurs were meat-eating reptiles.

A Tough Survivor

Teleosts, or bony fish, were the most successful marine vertebrates of the Late Cretaceous Period. The shark, which was dominant during this time, has survived and changed little since the Mesozoic era.

Mothering Dinosaurs

Female dinosaurs probably laid eggs and sat on them or covered them with sand to keep them warm until they hatched.

Living Together

For many years, scientists believed that dinosaurs lived by themselves. New discoveries of bones and nests suggest that many dinosaurs lived in groups— like elephants and antelopes today.

Streamlined Bodies ▶

Ichthyosaurs from the Jurassic Period were very well known. Their bodies were streamlined and they had no distinct necks. Their heads blended smoothly into their bodies. These animals propelled themselves by means of well-developed, fishlike fins and by up and down movements of the body.

Fish Eaters

Ichthyosaurs were about 10 feet (3 m) long and were probably able to move through the water at high speeds. They probably fed on fish and other marine animals.

Animals of the Sea

It is unlikely that ichthyosaurs ventured upon the land. If stranded on shore, they must have been as helpless as modern beached whales and porpoises.

Made for the Water

Ichthyosaurs had very large eyes with their nostrils positioned far back on top of the skull. These made them very comfortable in the water and protected them from the water's pressure.

Long and Slender ▲

Nothosaurs were marine animals with long slender bodies, long necks and tails, and long limbs. They probably swam through the water whipping their long, slender necks in pursuit of fleeing fish. This early marine animal probably evolved from terrestrial reptiles.

Valuable to Scientists ▶

Ammonoids are very well-known marine invertebrates from the Mesozoic Era. Their straight or coiled, many-chambered forms are valuable to scientists who want to determine the age of things found from this time. They are relatives of the pearly nautilus and flourished in great diversity.

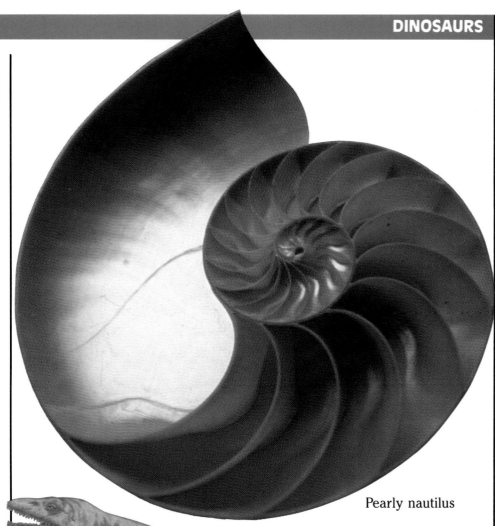

Pearly nautilus

A Long and Flexible Neck ▶

Plesiosaurus was about 15 feet (4.5 m) long, with a broad and flat body and relatively short tail. The neck was long and flexible. It had large teeth and nostrils far back near the eyes.

Feeding on Fish

Plesiosaurus probably ate by swinging its head from side to side through a school of fish. Apparently, it was able to use its large, paddlelike limbs to swim backward or forward or even to rotate itself.

Two Types of Reptiles

The early marine reptiles of the Jurassic and Triassic called plesiosaurs split into two main groups. Pliosaurs, the short-necked forms, had short necks and elongated heads. The elasmosaurs had relatively small heads and flexible snakelike necks.

Modern sturgeon

Longer and Longer

As plesiosaurs developed, they grew in size. *Kronosaurus,* an early pliosaur from Australia, was about 40 feet (12 m) long. The skull alone was 12 feet (3.7 m) long. *Elasmosaurus* had as many as 76 vertebrae in its neck and reached a length of about 43 feet (13 m). Fully half of it consisted of the head and neck.

A Primitive Fish ▲

The most primitive form of the bony fishes was the *Chondrosteiformes.* They are represented in modern times by sturgeon.

◄ Early Fish

The holost fishes replaced the chondrosts, but they declined in numbers and only a few forms, such as the Mississippi garpike, survived them.

Similar to Crocodiles

Phytosaurs were heavily armored semiaquatic reptiles that lived in the Late Triassic. They are not ancestors to modern crocodiles, although they probably resembled them and had similar habits. Their long and pointed jaws had numerous sharp teeth; phytosaurs probably preyed upon fish.

Finding Fossils

Phytosaur fossils occur in North America, Europe, and India, but their remains have not been found in the southern continents.

Opening Its Mouth Underwater

The nostrils of a phytosaur were high on its skull near its eyes. This allowed it to open its mouth underwater without drowning.

A Long Skull

Rutiodons were a type of phytosaur that was more than 10 feet (3 m) long; its skull alone was 3.5 feet (1 m) long.

A Very Good Mother

One duckbilled dinosaur named *Maiasaura*, whose name means "good mother dinosaur," cared for her young even after they hatched. Fossil remains of baby *Maiasaura* teeth suggest that they had been eating tough plants, which the mother must have brought to their nest. By taking care of her babies, this dinosaur ensured their survival.

Breaking an Egg ▼

Dinosaur eggs were not large. The largest ones were only 10-12 inches (25-30 cm) long and had thin shells. Eggs were small so that baby dinosaurs would be able to break their way out.

Evolving Reptiles

Archosaurs, or "ruling reptiles," were spectacular early reptiles. At first, they had crocodilelike forms and lived in the water. When they invaded the land, their strong hind legs and swimming tails allowed them to stand up on two feet. Dinosaurs developed from these reptiles.

From Reptiles to Birds ▲

Pterosaurs could not really fly because of their large, spreading wings. They glided instead, launching themselves from high places. Competition from birds may have hastened the extinction of the pterosaurs.

Mini Mammals

Mammals that lived during the age of dinosaurs were small, mouselike, and insignificant. After the disappearance of dinosaurs, they evolved and eventually took over the earth.

Dinosaur Types

There were two main types of dinosaurs that were categorized by the way that their hips were arranged. One group was called lizard-hipped; the other—bird-hipped. Lizard-hipped dinosaurs were either meat-eaters or plant-eaters. The meat-eaters were fierce and walked around on two legs. Some were very small. *Compsognathus*, for example, was no bigger than a chicken. Others were very large. *Deinonychus* was about the size of a man, but the resemblance ended there. It had a huge, sicklelike claw on its hind foot, which it used to attack other animals. *Tyrannosaurus* was the largest meat-eating dinosaur. It was 40 feet (12 m) long!

Reptiles that Fly

Some archosaurs developed into pterosaurs, which were flying reptiles that resembled birds but had broad leathery wings. Instead of feathers, they were covered with hair. Their wings were supported on an enormous fourth finger. *Quetzalcoatlus* had a wingspan of 39 feet (12 m).

The First Bird

The first known bird from the Jurassic Period (150 million years ago) was the *Archaeopteryx*. It resembled a small dinosaur with feathers. The many bird types that we have today developed from this creature.

Tyrannosaurus rex

Mostly Like Bats ▶

Pterosaurs are members of a group of flying reptiles that flourished in the Jurassic and Cretaceous Periods of the Mesozoic Era. Like bats rather than birds, pterosaurs formed a wing surface by means of a membrane of skin. Unlike in bats, however, the membrane was attached solely to the fourth elongated finger. From there it extended back along the flank to the knee; a second membrane lay between the neck and the "arm." The first three fingers were slender, clawed, and good for clutching.

Large Brains ▼

The brains of pterosaurs were large and apparently comparable to those of birds. Sight rather than smell seems to have been the dominant sense.

One Type of Pterosaur

Rhamphorhynchus had strong, sharply pointed teeth, relatively short bones supporting the fingers, and a long tail with a diamond-shaped rudder at its tip. Its wingspan was about 2 feet (0.6 m).

A Very Small Pterosaur

Pterodactylus was a small reptile, in some cases no larger than a sparrow. Features included a few small teeth, long finger bones, and a short tail.

The Largest Flying Animal

Descendants of the *Pterodactylus* continued on into the Cretaceous Period and were much larger. Parts of three very large specimens were discovered in Big Bend National Park, Texas, in 1975. The wingspan of the largest specimen was about 51 feet (15.5 m), making it by far the largest flying animal of which there is knowledge.

From Reptiles to Mammals ▲

Therapsids were reptiles of the Permian and Triassic Periods that developed into mammals. Among meat-eating therapsids, gorgonopsians and therocephalians were characteristic of the Permian, and cynodonts and bauriamorphs were later representatives.

A Small Dinosaur ▲

During the Late Jurassic there was a small dinosaur in Europe called a *Compsognathus.* It was only as large as a modern chicken. It was lightly built and able to move very fast on its two strong hind limbs. Its forelimbs were suitable for grasping.

Very Salty Water

Some scientists believe that the oceans during the Late Permian were extremely salty. Very little marine fauna were present at the time.

A Very Fierce Creature

Tyrannosaurus, whose name means "tyrant lizard," had tiny front limbs and a huge skull with many sharp teeth that were very good for biting and tearing. Its teeth were six inches long and an inch wide. Their edges were ragged like a steak knife. This creature was powerful enough to attack any of its contemporary dinosaurs!

Walking Along

Unlike meat-eating dinosaurs that walked on two legs, plant-eating dinosaurs generally walked on four legs.

Some Very Big Dinosaurs

Plateosaurus was one of the first plant-eating lizard-hipped dinosaurs. It had a very long neck and could walk on either two or four feet. This creature could eat both meat and plants. Some of the dinosaurs that this creature developed into were truly amazing. *Diplodocus*, for example, was 87 feet (27 m) long with a long neck and long tail. The *Brachiosaurus* and its relatives were even bigger. Some actually were 100 feet (30 m) long and weighed 165 tons. *Brachiosaurus* is the largest known dinosaur.

Plateosaurus

The Longest Land Animal ▲

Diplodocus of the Late Jurassic in North America was the longest land animal that ever lived. The longest one found was 87.5 feet (26.7 m). Its skull was unusually small, elongated, very light, and sat atop a very long neck. Its brain was extremely small. The tail was very long and probably extremely flexible. It is possible that its tail was a defensive weapon that could be lashed out at predators with great force; it is also possible that it was used to move through water.

Eating Soft Vegetation

The pencillike and dull-edged teeth of *Diplodocus,* as well as their location, indicate that this animal probably fed on soft vegetation.

Not a Second Brain

Because *Diplodocus* had such a long body, transmission of nervous impulses from its tiny brain to the hindquarters was a very slow process. As a result, a spinal node—often mistakenly called a second brain—was developed to compensate for the time lag.

Spending Time ▶ in Water

Diplodocus probably spent a great deal of time in the water with its head sticking out. It may have moved around freely on dry land; its limbs were stout and the feet broad, much like those of the modern elephant.

A Very Large Animal

Apatosaurus, found in the Late Jurassic Period, was one of the largest land animals of all time. It weighed as much as 30 tons and was as much as 70 feet (21 m) long, including its long neck and tail. It had four massive and pillarlike legs.

Change of Opinion

The size, shape, and features of the *Apatosaurus* head were disputed for more than a century. At first, the head was thought to be a massive, snub-nosed skull with spoonlike teeth. In 1978, scientists concluded that the animal had a slender, elongated skull with long, sharp teeth.

Maximum Size

It is probable that *Apatosaurus* represents the maximum size and bulk that a land animal can attain before becoming aquatic (a sea animal).

All for Defense

It is likely that the long and powerful tail of *Apatosaurus* was its main defense and that it sought refuge from pursuers by retreating to the water.

Walking on Two Legs

Allosaurus walked on two legs and had very strong hind legs. Its forelimbs, or arms, were much smaller than its hind limbs and were probably used for grasping. They had three fingers ending in sharp claws. The skull of the *Allosaurus* was very large in relation to its compact body and was lightened by the presence of several large openings.

Eating Other Dinosaurs ▶

It is probable that *Allosaurus* preyed upon the medium-sized dinosaurs, especially the duck-billed forms. It may have also been a scavenger, feeding upon carcasses of dead or dying animals. *Allosaurus* may have hunted in groups.

An Enormous Tail ▲

Allosaurus was a meat-eating dinosaur that weighed 2 tons and grew to 34 feet (10.4 m) in length, half of which consisted of a well-developed tail that probably functioned as a counterbalance for the body.

Big Plant ▶ Eaters

Sauropods, or plant-eating dinosaurs, generally had massive bodies, strong limbs to support their massive weight, long tails and necks, and a small head. The larger sauropods spent most of their time feeding on vegetation.

▼

Adept at Eating Plants

The *Iguanodon* was the first dinosaur to be discovered in the early 19th century. It was a bird-hipped dinosaur that had birdlike feet. As all bird-hipped dinosaurs, this creature only ate plants. It had no teeth at the front of its jaw—only a bony beak. Its cheek teeth, however, were bony and rigid. This creature probably pulled plants into its mouth with its tongue, and nipped them off with its beak.

It's All ◀ in the Head

Duckbilled dinosaurs belonged to the plant-eating group. They all had long heads that ended in front with broad, flat bills. Some had different sizes of crests made of bone; others were flat-headed. Duckbilled dinosaurs ate plants, twigs, and pine needles. As their teeth wore down, they grew new ones.

Frills and Horns ▶

Triceratops, a large plant-eating dinosaur of the Late Cretaceous, had a massive body (25 feet (8 m)) long, very long skull, large bony frills around the neck, and three long, pointed horns—one on the nose and two longer ones above the eyes.

A Sizable Skull

The horns above the eyes of *Triceratops* were more than 3 feet (1 m) long, and the skull alone was sometimes more than 6 feet (2 m) long.

Fit for Eating Plants

The mouth of *Triceratops* was beaklike in the front and probably effective for nipping off vegetation. The cheek teeth could effectively chew plant material. The skeleton was massive, the limbs were very stout, and the feet ended in stubby toes probably covered by small hooves.

A Heavy Dinosaur ▲

It has been estimated that *Triceratops* must have weighed as much as eight or nine tons when fully grown. These creatures traveled in groups or small herds.

Now That's a Lot of Teeth ▶

Duckbilled dinosaurs, or hadrosaurs, had ducklike snouts and very large numbers of teeth. Some of these creatures had as many as 2,000 teeth that they used for grinding hard vegetables.

Making Noise ▲

Corythosaurus was a duckbilled dinosaur that appeared at the end of the Cretaceous Period. Its nasal tubes ran from the nostril on the snout up into the crest and then down again into the mouth. This dinosaur may have used this complicated breathing system to make loud sounds and honks.

One of the Last to Go ▼

Triceratops was the largest horned dinosaur. It looked a bit like a rhinoceros with its heavy head shields and defensive horns mounted on its face. This creature was one of the last dinosaurs to disappear.

Armored Dinosaurs ▲

Other types of bird-hipped dinosaurs had armor. Stegosaurs—*Stegosaurus* is the best known—had rows of plates and spikes down their backs. Ankylosaurs were squat creatures with plates covering their backs, their heads, and their tails. *Scolosaurus* was a famous ankylosaur. They were all peaceful plant-eaters that moved slowly.

Large Animal with a Small Head ▶

Stegosaurus was an armored dinosaur of the Late Jurassic Period. It reached a length of about 20 feet (6.5 m). Its skull and brain were very small for such a large animal.
Stegosaurus had forelimbs that were much shorter than its hind limbs, giving its back a very arched appearance. Its feet were short and broad.

Controlling Body Temperature ▼

Stegosaurus had a series of large, triangular, horn-covered bony plates along its tail and back. Originally, scientists thought that these plates served a defensive purpose. In the 1980s, they began to think that these plates may have helped *Stegosaurus* control or modify its body temperature. By positioning itself so that the plates faced the sun, *Stegosaurus* could have warmed itself. Similarly, by standing so that the plates were not struck by direct sunlight, the dinosaur could have avoided overheating.

Spiky Tail

There were pairs of long, pointed spikes on the tail of *Stegosaurus*. These were probably used as a lethal weapon. *Stegosaurus* was a plant eater, probably feeding on soft vegetation.

◄ Catching its Prey

Ornitholestes was about 6 feet (2 m) long and had a very flexible neck. Its forelimbs were very well developed and ended in fingers longer and slimmer than are common in dinosaurs. This indicates that *Ornitholestes* could catch quick-moving and elusive prey.

The Bird Robber

It has been suggested that *Ornitholestes* may have preyed upon the early birds, hence the name, which means "bird robber." It is equally probable that it ate small, speedy lizards and even early mammals.

A Complete ► Skeleton Found

A small, lightly built dinosaur found as fossils in Late Jurassic deposits of North America was *Ornitholestes*. It is relatively well known, since a complete skeleton was found in Wyoming.

Walking on Two Legs

Pachycephalosaurus was a dinosaur of the Cretaceous Period. It grew to be about 30 feet (9 m) long, walked on two legs, and had strong hind limbs and much less developed forelimbs.

A Domelike Skull

The unusual and distinctive feature of *Pachycephalosaurus* was the high, domelike skull formed by a thick mass of solid bone growth over the tiny brain. Abundant bony knobs in front and at the sides of the skull further added to its unusual appearance.

Bone-headed Dinosaurs

Pachycephalosaurus and closely related forms are known as the bone-headed dinosaurs.

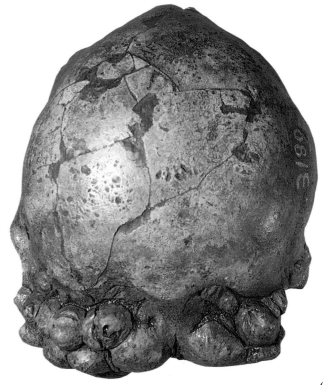

Bony Plates and a Club

The back of the low, flat body of the *Ankylosaurus* was covered with bony plates that were pointed at the flanks of the animal. At the end was a thick knob of bone that could have been used as a club.

Different Kinds of Armor

Some relatives of *Ankylosaurus* had different kinds of armor. Some varieties had long, pointed bony spikes at the end of their tails. Others had spikes of bone in the shoulder region.

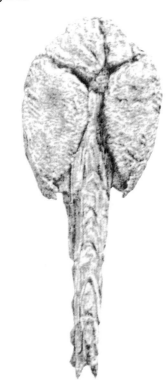

Wearing Armor

Ankylosaurus was an armored dinosaur of the Late Cretaceous Period of North America. It was about 15 feet (5 m) long, with hind limbs larger than the forelimbs.

An Amazing Neck

The small, light skull of *Struthiomimus* was perched atop a long, slender, and very flexible neck. The forelimbs were long and slender. The three-fingered hand had sharp claws adapted for grasping.

Egg-eater

The jaws of *Struthiomimus* were toothless and probably covered with a rather birdlike horny beak. Some scientists believe that this dinosaur fed upon the eggs of other dinosaurs.

Like an Ostrich ▶

Struthiomimus was an ostrichlike dinosaur of the Cretaceous Period in North America. It was about 8 feet (2.5 m) tall, walked on two legs, and was adept at rapid movements on well-developed and strong hind limbs with three-toed, very birdlike feet.

Primitive Members

Protoceratops were dinosaurs of the Late Cretaceous Period. They were found in the Gobi Desert in Mongolia. They were one of the most primitive members of the last major group of dinosaurs to evolve.

Bony Frills on the Skull

Protoceratops was a relatively large animal. Adults were about 7 feet (2 m) long and weighed about 400 pounds (180 kg). The skull was very long. Bones in the skull had grown backward into a perforated frill that probably served as a surface for the attachment of chewing muscles and for shielding the vulnerable neck region from attack by predators.

Part Aquatic

The jaws of *Protoceratops* were beaklike and contained some teeth. A wrinkled area on top of the snout of the fossil may mark the position of a hornlike structure. The tail was well developed, suggesting that *Protoceratops* was at least part aquatic.

▶

All Kinds of Remains

The remains of more than 80 individual *Protoceratops* have been found in all stages of growth. The eggs, about 6 inches (15 cm) long and oval in shape, appear to have been laid in circular clusters.

◄ A Well-known Bird

Hesperornis is an extinct genus of birds found as fossils in Cretaceous deposits. It is the best-known bird of the Cretaceous Period. It combines primitive and advanced characteristics.

A Very Active Bird ▲

The legs of *Hesperornis* were powerfully developed and clearly adapted for rapid diving and swimming through the water. The neck was long and slender and the head smallish; both were probably capable of side-to-side movements. *Hesperornis* was clearly an actively swimming bird that probably chased and caught fish.

Early Beak

Teeth were present in the back of the lower jaw of *Hesperornis*. It has been suggested that the horny beak that has come to be characteristic of birds was in the process of formation in the front part of the jaw.

65

A Dinosaur Site

Dinosaur National Park in northwestern Colorado and northeastern Utah was set aside in 1915 to preserve rich fossil beds that include dinosaur remains. It covers an area of 211,061 acres (85,416 hectares).

Finding Dinosaur Remains

Dinosaur skeletons are often found as an assortment of bones left on top of the ground, when the rock they were fossilized in wore away.

Gathering Information

Reconstructing a dinosaur skeleton not only tells a scientist what the animal looked like. It also indicates how an animal moved and, from the chemical composition, what it ate.

Disappearing Animals

Dinosaurs are not the only type of animal that is extinct. Scientists estimate that 90 percent of all the animal species that have ever lived on earth are extinct.

Shrinking in Size

For a long time, the only land animals were reptiles. Among these were the dinosaurs. Strangely, most dinosaurs were very large in size, although their brains were quite small. After dinosaurs died out, reptiles developed into much smaller creatures.

Recreating a Dinosaur

When dinosaur fossils are found, uncovered bones are painted with varnish to harden them. Then, they are covered in a layer of plaster of Paris for protection. The entire rock the remains were found in is shipped to a museum in one piece, where the bones (or skeletons) are carefully chipped away from the rock. Again, the fossils are hardened with varnish and cemented together. Models are made for the missing pieces. Finally, after careful study, all of the pieces are fitted together to make a full-scale skeleton. Dinosaur skeletons can be seen in many major museums.

The Disappearance of Dinosaurs

At the end of the Cretaceous Period (about 65 million years ago), all of the dinosaurs seem to have died out. With them, many other animals—including the swimming and flying reptiles of the time—also disappeared. This left the world to be populated by mammals.

◄ Changing the Climate

Some scientists believe that dinosaurs became extinct as a result of an asteroid or meteor with a 6-mile (10-km) diameter hitting the earth. If this happened, disturbance in the earth's climate may have occurred, killing off all living things.

A Continuing Debate ►

Many scientists believe that the extinction of dinosaurs was gradual and was, perhaps, due to changes in climate and geography. No one knows for sure and the debate continues.

Human Body

The pupil of the eye has no color at all. It looks black because it opens directly onto the inside of the eye.

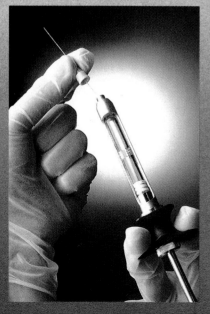

Humans and other mammals have bones in four shapes: long, short cancellous, flat, and irregular. The human skull is made up of flat bones.

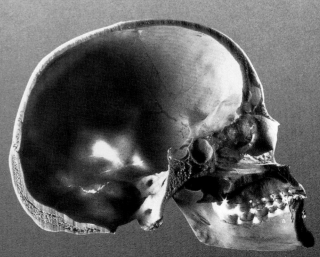

A Special Kind of Muscle ▼

Hearts are made of a special kind of muscle that is found in no other part of the human body. This muscle has the power to relax and contract in a rhythm (the "lub-dub-lub-dub" sound you hear when you listen to your heartbeat). This expanding and contracting action pumps blood through the body's blood vessels.

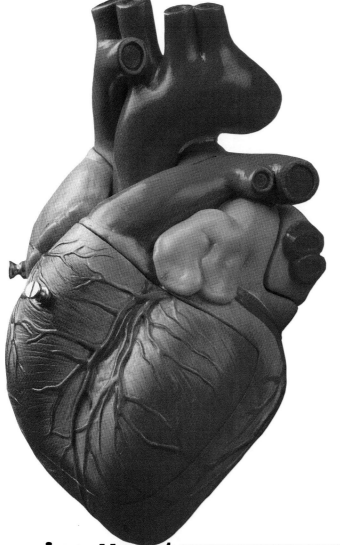

The Pumping Heart

The right side of your heart pumps blood through your lungs. That blood takes in oxygen, sending carbon dioxide back into the lungs to be breathed out. The oxygen is linked up with chemicals in the blood. This oxygen-rich blood then goes back to the left side of the heart, which pumps it out to the body.

The Heart of the Matter

Although some people are known as big-hearted, the size of a human heart depends on how large a person is, not on how nice or generous he or she is. The average adult heart weighs about 11 ounces (300 grams) and is about the size of a clenched fist.

Only a Heartbeat Away

When you are at rest, your heart beats about 70 times a minute—fast enough to send your entire blood supply through your body every minute. Here's how it works. Your body has about 8 to 10 pints (5 liters) of blood in it, and each beat of your heart sends about 2.5 ounces (50 ml) of blood out into your bloodstream. At a rate of 70 beats a minute, that works out to about 8 to 16 pints (5 to 8 liters) of blood moving through your body every minute. When you exercise, your heart beats faster—sometimes three times as fast as normal—to get more oxygen and nutrients to your hard-working muscles. When you sleep, your heart beats slower since your muscles need less oxygen.

Getting Energized

Blood is one of the busiest—and most important—parts of the body. First, it takes up the waste products that your body's tissues make as they work. Kidneys and other organs filter these waste products from the blood and turn them into urine that can be passed right out of the body. The blood also picks up the products of digestion—all the nutrients in your food—and takes them to the liver and other organs where they are turned into energy that helps you grow and work. Some of that energy is even stored away so that it is ready to be used when you are not eating.

Life-giving Oxygen

The cells in your body need oxygen to convert food into usable energy through chemical reactions. Without oxygen, the cells can't produce the energy, and they quickly die.

Heart Attacks are Serious

The official name for a heart attack is *myocardial infarction*. A small blood clot blocks one of the arteries that supply blood and oxygen to the heart muscle, causing part of the heart muscle to become damaged and die. The person having the heart attack may die without quick medical attention.

Your Racing Heart ▲

Since the times of ancient Egyptians, people have believed that your heart is tied to your feelings. One reason for this is that your heart does react to what you do and how you feel. When you exercise or get excited, your heart works harder and beats faster. It also beats faster when you are frightened or angry. Illness makes your heart beat faster, too, so it can get fresh, oxygen-filled blood to your body. And, when you are rested and calm, your heart slows down.

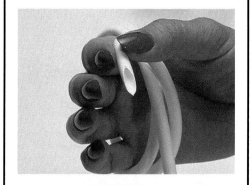

▲
Replacing Arteries

Recently, doctors have learned how to replace unhealthy arteries with healthy ones taken from other parts of the body—or even with ones made of plastic. This gives new hope for a better life to people whose arteries have become too narrow to give them enough oxygen-rich blood.

Getting Energized

Blood is one of the busiest—and
most important—parts of the body.
First, it takes up the waste
products that your body's tissues
make as they work. Kidneys and
other organs filter these waste
products from the blood and turn
them into urine that can be passed
right out of the body. The blood
also picks up the products of
digestion—all the nutrients in your
food—and takes them to the liver
and other organs where they are
turned into energy that helps you
grow and work. Some of that
energy is even stored away so that
it is ready to be used when you
are not eating.

Life-giving Oxygen

The cells in your body need
oxygen to convert food into
usable energy through
chemical reactions. Without
oxygen, the cells can't
produce the energy, and
they quickly die.

Heart Attacks are Serious

The official name for a heart
attack is *myocardial infarction.* A
small blood clot blocks one of the
arteries that supply blood and
oxygen to the heart muscle,
causing part of the heart muscle to
become damaged and die. The
person having the heart attack
may die without quick medical
attention.

Your Racing Heart ▲

Since the times of ancient Egyptians, people have believed that your
heart is tied to your feelings. One reason for this is that your heart does
react to what you do and how you feel. When you exercise or get
excited, your heart works harder and beats faster. It also beats faster
when you are frightened or angry. Illness makes your heart beat faster,
too, so it can get fresh, oxygen-filled blood to your body. And, when you
are rested and calm, your heart slows down.

▲ Replacing Arteries

Recently, doctors have
learned how to replace
unhealthy arteries with
healthy ones taken from
other parts of the body—or
even with ones made of
plastic. This gives new hope
for a better life to people
whose arteries have become
too narrow to give them
enough oxygen-rich blood.

70

Blood-carrying Tubes ◀

Arteries and *veins* are both tubes that carry blood around your body. Arteries have very thick walls because they have to be strong enough to stand up to the pressures created by the heart as it pumps blood through them. They usually lie deep inside the tissues of your body, although in a few places they are near the surface of your skin—at your wrists, the side of your forehead, your neck, and even on the top and sides of your feet. Because the blood in the arteries is so filled with oxygen, arteries look bright red, the color of oxygen-rich blood. Veins, on the other hand, have much thinner walls because the blood inside them has lost much of the surging pressure it had when it first left the heart. They look blue because the blood in them is much darker after it sent oxygen out to the body. Veins bring blood safely back to the heart, which pumps it through the lungs to pick up more oxygen.

You Are What You Eat ▶

Bad food—food that has too much saturated fat, for example—can cause different kinds of problems. It can lead to "hardening of the arteries," in which arteries become clogged and gradually grow narrower, so that blood cannot pass through them properly. Eating too much bad food can also lead to obesity (being overweight) and high blood pressure, which can put great strain on a person's heart and cause disease and sometimes even death. This is why doctors urge people to avoid the kinds of fat in meat and fried foods and instead eat fruits and vegetables.

Massaging the Heart

When a heart stops working, it can sometimes be coaxed into working again. Doctors and paramedics massage the heart, for example, to try to get it to start its normal pumping action. They can also use electric shocks to make the heart muscle expand and contract—often, the heart begins working on its own again.

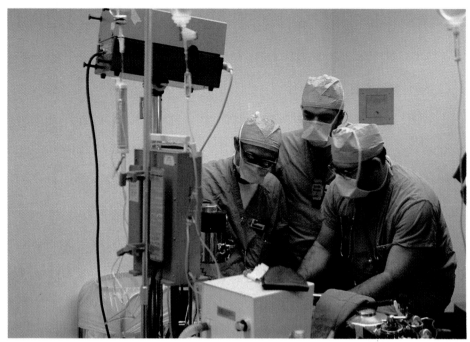

A Heart Transplant

During heart transplant surgery, a healthy heart is taken from a "donor," a person who has just died from something other than heart disease. The diseased heart is removed from the transplant patient and replaced with this new, healthy heart. The transplant is difficult, since the new heart has to match the new owner's blood, chemistry, and tissues. If it does not, the person's body may "reject" the new heart, and the person may die.

Regulating Your Heart Beat

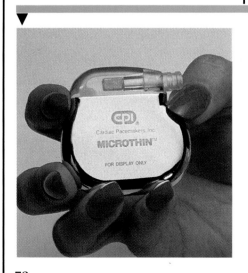

A *pacemaker* is a special device that helps control the speed at which a heart beats. Some people's hearts beat too slowly. To correct this, doctors insert a tiny wire into the wall of the heart. Small electric shocks—70 per minute—are given to the heart to keep the person's heart beating at exactly the right speed.

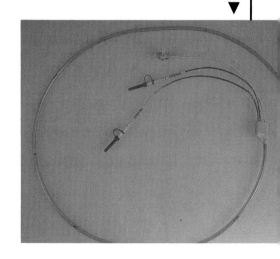

Our Body's Covering

Skin is a covering over the outside surface of humans that protects us from weather, injury, and germs. It is actually made up of three separate layers. The outermost layer, the one we see when we look at ourselves or another person, is called the "epidermis." It is made up of several kinds of cells. The middle layer is called the "dermis." It is much thicker than the outer layer, and it is made up of cells and fibers that are loosely woven together. Blood vessels, sweat glands, nerve endings, and the roots of our hair are all in the dermis. The inner layer is called the "subcutis." It is made up of fat that helps to cushion the organs in the body.

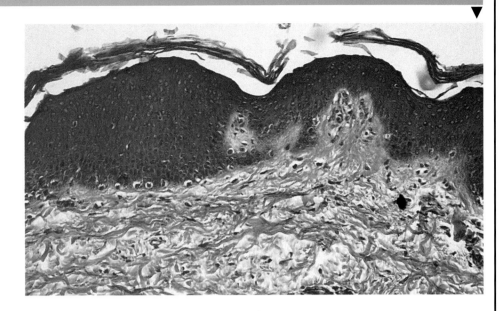

Giving Your Skin Color

Pigments, which give color to skin the same way they can give color to paint or crayons, are found in the epidermis. Actually, they are found in an inner layer of the epidermis called the "Malpighian layer," named after Marcello Malpighi, an Italian scientist who discovered it in the 1600s. Pigment makes people pale pink, red, yellow, brown, or black and causes freckles and suntans.

Leaving a Scar

When skin is cut or damaged in any way, the skin around it grows together to cover the injured area. Manually closing the gap made by the cut will make it easier for the new skin to grow, which is why bandages and stitches are used to "close" a cut. Sometimes, when this repairing process is not complete, a line is left without new skin. This is called a "scar."

Through Thick and Thin

Skin is thickest over the soles of our feet, a place that is exposed to pressure, friction, temperature changes, and sharp objects. It is thinnest on the eyelids, where it does the delicate work of protecting our eyes.

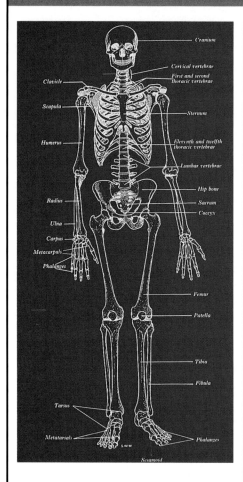

Hard as a Bone

Bone is a hard, grayish-white substance. Two-thirds is inorganic (mineral) matter, made up primarily of calcium in phosphate of lime, which gives it hardness. The remaining third is organic (animal) matter to give the bone toughness and a certain amount of flexibility that helps it not to break. About one-third of the weight of a bone is water.

Different Kinds of Bones ▼

Bone tissue is described as being compact (dense and smooth) or cancellous (resembling sponge inside). Humans and other mammals have four different shapes of bones: long bones, which are found in the limbs and are compact; short cancellous bones, such as those in the wrists and ankles; flat bones, which make up the skull; and irregular bones, such as those of the spine.

Inside a Bone

Some bones are hollow and are filled with a substance called marrow. The marrow is yellow and fatty in the long bones of adults. In other bones, the marrow is red and is filled with the red and white blood cells. There are also tiny passages or canals in compact bone. These carry blood, lymph (a watery fluid), and nerves through the bone, since bone is a living, highly active tissue.

A Very Tough ▲ Skeleton ■

There are a total of 206 bones that make up the human skeleton. Together they form a supporting and protective framework for the body that is nearly as tough as cast iron yet less than half the weight.

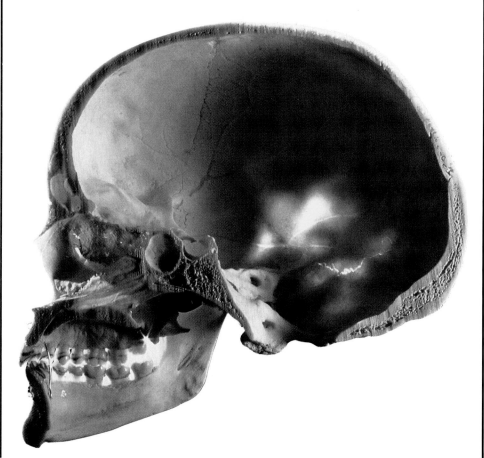

Using Your Joints▶

A joint is formed at the point where two separate bones meet. It is at these points that movement can take place. There are basically two types of joints. "Hinge" joints are found in the fingers, toes, knees, and elbows. They are simple joints that work like hinges. "Ball and socket" joints, found in the shoulders and hips, have large bones fitting into a socket. This type of joint offers a very wide range of movement.

Healing a Broken Bone

A fractured bone must be set. This is done by placing the broken ends together so as to get the bone into its normal position. A sling or splint is then applied to let the bone knit. During this process, tiny cells known as *osteoblasts* produce a substance that makes the bones hard and firm again. These cells also help in natural growth. Other cells called *osteoclasts* tear down old bone tissue. This double process of building up and tearing down goes on in the bones all the time.

Uses for Animal Bones

Animal bones are often treated chemically to prepare them for the making of different products. Among the uses for animal bones are fertilizer (artificial manure), gelatin, glue, and bone ash.

Holding Bones in Place

Ligaments are the strong bands of fiberlike tissues that hold two bones close together at a joint. They prevent a joint from moving too far and damaging the tissue inside. The strongest ligaments in the body are at the hip joint.

◀Broken Bones

A broken bone is called a fracture. Fractures can be of several different kinds, the two main types being simple and compound. In a compound fracture, the tissues of the body are torn and the bone is exposed to the open air. This is a very serious injury, since blood is lost and there is danger of infection. A simple fracture is one where the bone is broken but there is no wound.

Getting Rid of Dead Skin

The epidermis is actually made up of several layers of cells. New skin cells are created in the innermost layer and gradually work their way to the surface. As they reach the outer layers, they die. These dead cells are constantly being rubbed away every time your skin brushes against your clothing, your hands, or even the sheets you sleep on at night.

Using Your Brain

All animals have brains. Snails, worms, and other simple creatures have only a thickened nerve for a brain. More sophisticated animals need more complicated brains in order to control and carry out all of their different functions. Because we do more than any other kind of animal, the human brain is the most complicated. But it is made of the same materials and controls the same functions as the brains of many other animals.

Working Up a Good Sweat

Sweat helps control our body's temperature. In our skin are coiled tubes called "sweat glands." Each of these opens onto the outer surface of the skin through a tiny hole called a "pore." The sweat that comes through our pores is made up of water and our body's waste products. As the water evaporates, it draws heat away and keeps our body's temperature in a safe range.

An insect has a very simple brain.

The Control Center

The brain is the source of what we know about the world. It is the center of our intelligence, our memory, our personality, and our awareness of the world around us. It is the brain that tells us what our eyes are seeing and what our ears are hearing. The brain controls our breathing, our digestion, and all the other activities that go on inside our bodies. It is the brain that solves math problems and remembers the punch line to a funny joke. The brain also controls what we do with our bodies—from walking and sleeping to talking and sneezing.

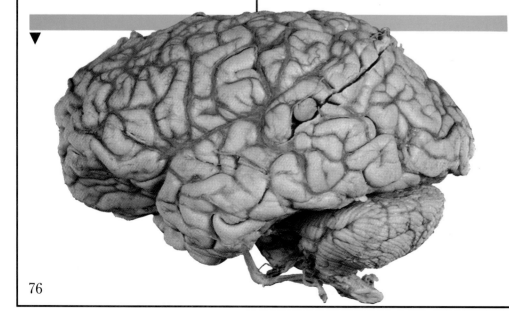

All Sorts of Brain Cells

The human brain is made of millions of tiny nerve cells called "neurons." Some are long and carry information to the different parts of our bodies through the spinal cord. Others are shorter and connect the different parts of the brain together.

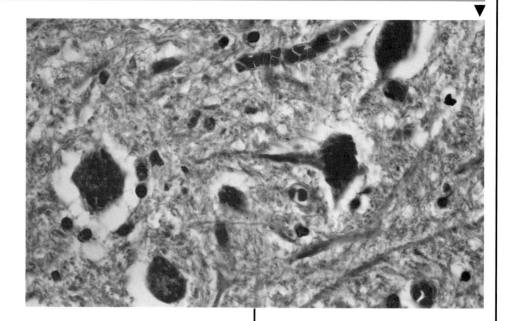

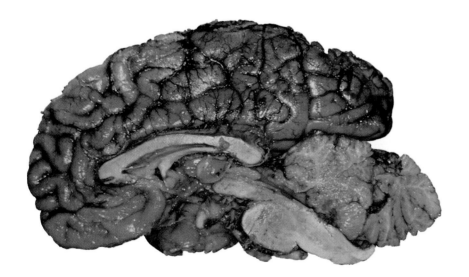

The Largest Part of the Brain

The part of the brain that deals with our thoughts, emotions, and personality is the *cerebrum*, which is the largest part of our brain. The cerebrum is so large that it must be wrinkled and creased in order to fit inside our skull. (If you took the cerebrum out of the skull and spread it out flat, it would be the size of a pillowcase.)

Listening to Your Brain

The cerebrum is the part of the brain that deals with feelings, thoughts, and awarenesses, letting us know, for example, that something feels hot and what hot means. Then, the cerebrum sends out instructions telling the body—or even another part of the brain—what to do about this information. Those instructions can be anything from telling our finger to get away from a hot match to informing another part of the brain to make our mouth and tongue say certain words.

A Place for Everything

The cerebrum is carefully organized, so that control of each of our senses goes on in a particular part of the brain. The cells that control vision, for example, are located in the back part of the brain. The cells that control speaking are closer to the front of the brain. Each of these areas is linked to others so that the cerebrum can get complete information on what is happening throughout our body.

A Very Structured Brain

You might not believe it, but the areas of the cerebrum that control faster and more delicate movements are larger in size than those that control other movements. Since our hands often need to make fine, rapid movements, there is a large part of the cerebrum set aside for maneuvering our hands. Since the ankle and foot seldom make fine movements, there is only a small area set aside for controlling them.

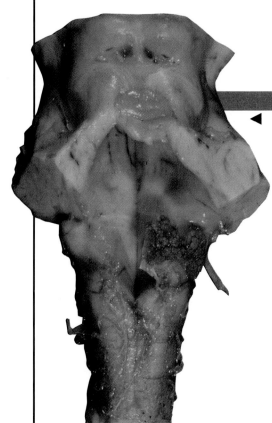

The Brain Connector

The *brain stem* connects the brain to the spinal cord and the rest of the body. It contains nerve fibers that control the body's internal organs—the lungs, liver, stomach, kidneys, and so on. It also controls the speed at which our heart beats and at which we breathe.

Having a Headache

Strangely enough, in spite of all the nerve cells inside the brain, the brain has no sensory nerves of its own. It cannot feel either pleasure or pain. What we call a "headache" actually comes from the membranes and tissues around the brain or from the muscles of the scalp, neck, or face.

Letting the Light in

The circle of color and the dark spot in the very middle of the eye are the *iris* and the *pupil.* The pupil lets light into the eye. The iris controls the amount of light coming in by changing the size of the pupil—just like the shutter that opens and closes inside a camera. In bright light, the tiny muscles inside the iris can close the pupil to the size of a tiny pinhole. In darkness, the iris opens the pupil up so that more light can get in.

A Round and Firm Eye

Vitreous humor is a jellylike substance inside the eye that helps keep the eye round and firm. Without it, the eye would get out of shape, collapse, and become totally useless.

An Eye Like a Camera

Like a camera, your eye has an opening that can adjust from one size to another. This opening is the *pupil,* the dark spot in the center of your eye. The eye also has a sensitive "film" on which the image of objects outside the eye are detected. The "film" is the *retina,* which is made up of cells that turn light rays into electrical signals that go to the brain to tell you what you are seeing.

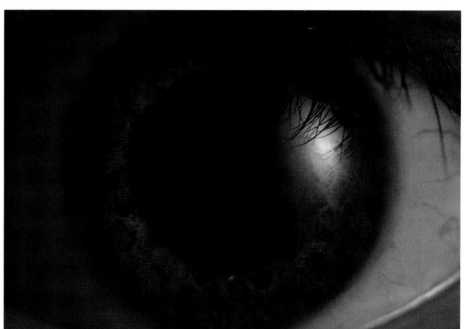

Straight into the Eye

The pupil has no color at all. It looks black because it opens directly onto the inside of the eye. When you see a black pupil, you are looking straight through to what is in the eye itself.

Seeing the World Around Us

Light entering the eye makes its way to the retina—the "film" at the back of the eye's camera. Once the light has been turned into electrical signals and sent to the brain, the brain takes over. It sorts out the signals and relates them to familiar objects, colors, shapes, and other features. It is actually the brain that lets us see.

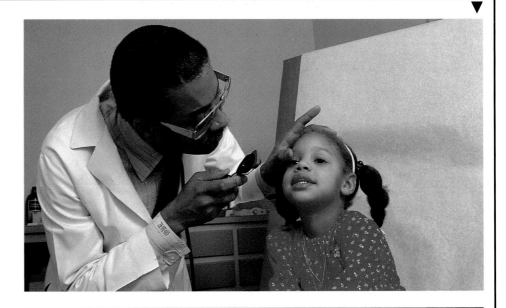

In Living Color

The *rods* and *cones* are the two kinds of cells inside the retina. (Remember, the retina is the "film" at the back of the eye that receives the image of what is outside.) The rods detect light—and they see only in black and white. The cones see colors. However, they are not as sensitive, and they work well only in bright light. As a result, we tend to see only in different shades of gray when someone turns off the lights.

Blinking the Dust Away

Blinking is a *reflex*—something that happens automatically without our control. It helps to keep our eyes clean. Each time you blink, you clear away dust, dirt, and anything else that might have gotten onto the surface of your eye. It also helps to keep unwanted objects out of the eye.

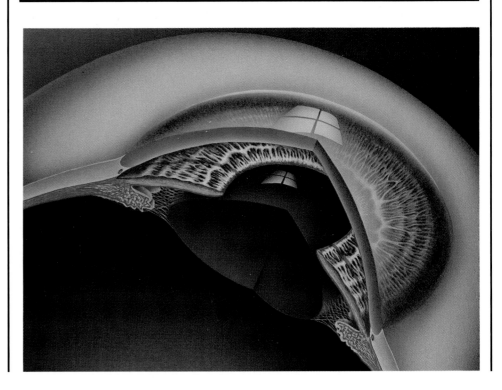

Cleansing Tears

Tears are not just a sign of being sad or upset. They are an important part of seeing because tears help wash away dust, germs, or dirt that get into your eyes. The tear glands at the upper, outer part of your eye socket release small amounts of this salty liquid. After tears have collected this dust and dirt, they make their way to your *tear ducts*, which are little tubes on the inner side of your eye socket near your nose. The tears go through the tear ducts into two sacs, which drain into your nasal cavities. They take the dirt, dust, and germs with them as they go. When your eyes are tearing heavily, tears may also drip down your face.

Animal Eyes

Animals with backbones tend to have eyes much the same as ours. Some of them can see even better than we do—hawks, eagles, and other birds of prey, for example.

Compound Eyes of Insects

Insects have a completely different kind of eye than people do. Their eye is called a "compound" eye. It contains many tiny lenses clustered together, much like a honeycomb. Worker bees, for example, have up to 5,000 of these tiny lenses in each eye. Each lens detects a small part of the scene. The insect's brain puts together all of these thousands of tiny pictures to see what is going on.

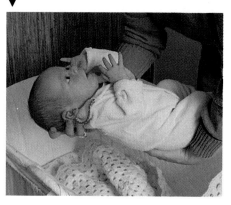

Through Baby's Eyes

A newborn baby can see, but cannot clearly see things that are far away. He or she can detect changes in brightness, contrast, and movement. The newborn will stare intently at his or her mother's face when she brings it close to his or hers. After about two weeks, the infant will look at large objects with interest. By about eight to ten weeks of age, the newborn will use his or her eyes to follow an object that is passed in front of his or her face.

Curing a Wandering Eye

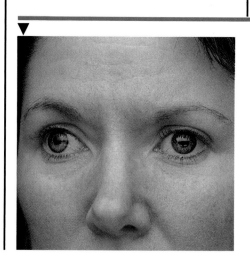

In order to see properly, both of your eyes must work together. They must both be able to focus on the same object at the same time. Then, they can relay their signals to the brain, which translates the two signals (one from each eye) into a single, three-dimensional image. Sometimes, the eyes of babies or young adults do not point in the same direction. This condition is called *strabismus.* One eye may be turned inward (called "cross eye") or it may point upward (called "wall-eye"). This problem can often be corrected by a doctor through the use of an eye patch, eye drops, or special muscle exercises. Surgery to adjust the length of the muscles that move the eye may also be used. If the condition is not corrected early, the brain may begin to ignore the signals coming from the wandering eye, and permanent vision damage may result. This condition is called *amblyopia* or "lazy eye."

Nose Jobs

Besides helping us smell, the nose is one of the links between the outside air and the blood that takes oxygen to all the different parts of your body. Your nostrils take in the air, filter out dirt and grit, and pass it inside. Inside the nose, mucous membranes covered with tiny hairs sweep the dust and germs toward the nostrils to be sneezed out or toward the back of the nose to be swallowed, where stomach acid will eliminate them. Blood vessels inside the nose warm the air so that, before it goes on to your lungs, it has been warmed, filtered, and even moistened.

What a Nice Smell

Odors are detected by two small areas at the top of your nose called the "olfactory epithelium." These areas, which are outgrowths of the brain, are filled with nerve cells. As smells are breathed in from the air, their small particles are dissolved in the mucous lining. A reaction is caused in certain cells, depending on what odor is present. Our nose helps us to identify thousands of different smells.

The Sound of Your Voice

Your nose also influences your voice. When your nose is clogged, the sound of your voice changes. The size and shape of a person's nose can also affect his or her voice.

A Keen Sense of Hearing

Even though the human ear is a first-rate device for hearing, certain animals have better hearing. Dogs and wild animals, for example, can hear much softer, fainter sounds than we can, while bats can hear high-pitched sounds that people cannot hear at all.

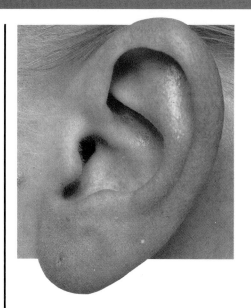

Anatomy of an Ear

Human ears actually have three parts. The outer ear (the part that sticks out a bit from the side of your head), or "auricle," is a flap of skin and gristle that protects the rest of the ear and funnels sound into the ear. It contains a short tube whose inner end is closed by a tiny membrane called the "eardrum." Just beyond this is the middle ear, which is a small space that holds three small bones. Behind this is another tube, called the "Eustachian tube," which runs to the back of the nose and helps to keep the proper air pressure within the middle ear. The middle ear is connected to the inner ear by the oval window, which is covered by the base of one of the inner ear bones.

Sorting Out the Noise

The brain plays an important part in hearing. Once the sound waves are turned into electrical signals and are sent to the brain, the brain identifies whether the sounds are high-pitched or low-pitched and whether they are loud or soft. If several sounds are heard at the same time, the brain sorts them out so you can concentrate on one of them at a time. Then, it identifies the sound—recognizing what it is, exactly who is speaking, what song is being sung, or whatever. It is a complicated job, but one that takes our brain just a fraction of a second to carry out.

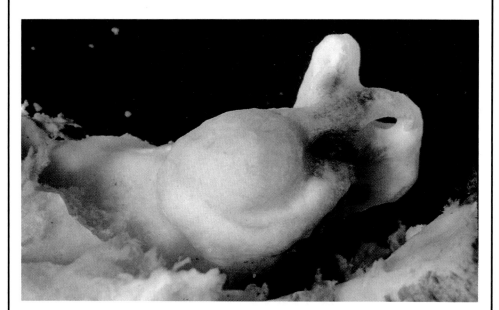

Functions of the Inner Ear

The most important part of the inner ear for hearing is the *cochlea*, which is shaped like the shell of a snail. Inside it are fluid and tiny hairs. When vibrations reach the inner ear, they are caught by this fluid and passed on to the hairs, which are stimulated to produce nerve signals. These signals are then carried by the auditory nerve to the brain.

Very Little Ear Bones

The hammer, the anvil, and the stirrup are the three small bones in the middle ear that magnify the vibrations that are made as sound waves strike the eardrum. These vibrations are then passed on to the inner ear, where they are translated into nerve signals and sent to the brain.

Responding to the World

In human beings, the nervous system is controlled by the brain and the spinal cord, which together make up the central nervous system. The central nervous system receives information from and sends out instructions to the body through a network of small nerves called the peripheral nervous system. With these two systems—the central and peripheral—the body knows what is going on around it and can respond to any changes. This is the same type of nervous system that other mammals have. In contrast, human beings have a brain whose function is to deal with thinking, memory, emotions, and all the other things that make up the human personality and intelligence.

Fast Nerve Impulses

Each individual peripheral nerve is a bundle of thousands of very small nerve cells called *neurones*. Each neurone has a central nerve fiber (axon) surrounded by an insulating nerve sheath (myelin), and every neurone has its own cell body that controls the chemical reactions of the cell. Information is carried as a small electrical current along the axon. The myelin sheath prevents the nerve impulse from leaking out and speeds up the impulse to over 164 feet (50 m) a second.

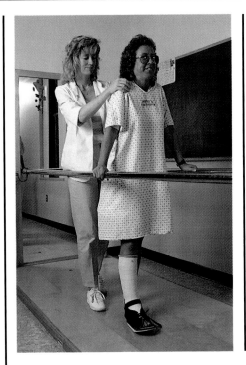

Unusual Body Cells

As body cells, neurones are unusual. Once damaged, they are rarely able to mend themselves. However, by using other, undamaged nerve pathways, the affected person can often make a good recovery.

An Automatic Nervous System▾

The nervous system also controls the workings of all the internal body organs. For example, the brain affects the speed of the heartbeat and the workings of the intestines. We are not aware that this control is happening. It is automatic and is performed by a separate network of nerves called the automatic nervous system.

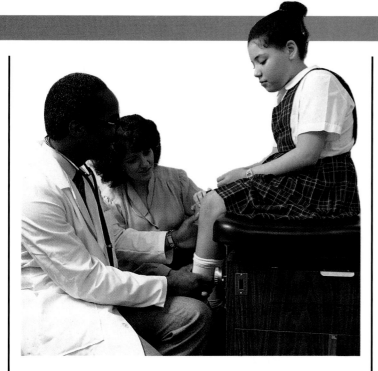

A Very Common Reflex ▲

An example of a reflex is a muscle stretch reflex. If you sit relaxed with one leg crossed over the other and sharply tap the knee just below the kneecap, the leg will jerk as the thigh muscles contract. In this reflex, the sensory nerves in the thigh muscles detect a slight stretch of the muscle when you tap the knee. This is converted into a nerve impulse that travels to the spinal cord, which tells the muscle of the thigh to contract to overcome the stretch. This particular reflex is not under the control of the brain and is called a spinal reflex.

Running the Automatic Nervous System

The hypothalamus at the base of the brain runs the automatic nervous system. It sends impulses to control the vital body functions of the heart, lungs, kidneys, intestines, and bladder. The hypothalamus also controls the production of chemical substances called hormones, which circulate around the body in the bloodstream. They control the many biochemical processes and also the way in which we grow and develop.

Walking Across the Room

In addition to the activities that go on without our knowing, the brain allows us to carry out actions whenever we want. This is called voluntary activity. For example, if you decide to walk across the room, your brain will organize the muscles needed to perform these movements.

Difficult to Understand ▲

The most difficult feature of the nervous system to understand is the control of our emotions and personality. These are called higher nervous functions. They enable us to overcome our instincts and reflexes—for example, to sacrifice our own safety.

85

A Real Balancing Act

One of the most important jobs of the ear has nothing to do with hearing—the ear helps us to keep our balance. Inside the inner ear are three canals, all shaped like half-circles. These canals are filled with fluid, and, together with sight, they help the brain to detect the body's movement and the position of the head, giving us a sense of balance. Infections and disorders in these canals can cause dizziness and difficulty in walking.

Smelling the Taste

A great deal of what you taste is actually a matter of smell. To test this, try eating something when you have a cold or when you are holding your nose. (Remember when you did this whenever you had to eat something you didn't like?) You'll find that what you eat seems almost tasteless, simply because you cannot smell it.

The Sense of Taste

Taste buds are little taste detectors in the mouth. Most of them are on the tongue, but a few are scattered around the inside of the mouth and the back of the throat.

Learning About Food

All children seem to be fussy eaters. They are learning what food they like and dislike and are trying to convince grownups to give them only the foods they like best.

Four Basic Tastes

Believe it or not, all tastes—from apple pie to your favorite burger and sauce—come from four basic tastes. These are salty, sour, sweet, and bitter. All the different flavors you get from what you eat and drink are just mixes of two or more of these main tastes.

Seeing Your Breath

Our bodies get rid of the air inside of us because much of it has been turned into carbon dioxide, which can be poisonous. So, we breathe the carbon dioxide back into the air outside. The air we exhale also contains quite a bit of water vapor from the moist lining in our lungs. On cold days, this vapor condenses into little drops of water as we exhale. When it comes in contact with the cold outside air, it forms the steam that comes from your mouth on a winter day.

Breathing for Life

When blood returns to the heart from its trip around your body, the heart pumps the blood through blood vessels in your lungs. The lungs are the main organs for breathing. Air comes into the lungs from the nose and throat. Oxygen from that air then passes through the thin lining inside of the lungs into the bloodstream. Carbon dioxide, which was picked up from tissues throughout the body, passes from the blood into the lungs. We then breathe the carbon dioxide out into the outside world.

Breathing Often

The air we breathe only contains about 20 percent oxygen. In order to get the oxygen we need, we have to breathe often.

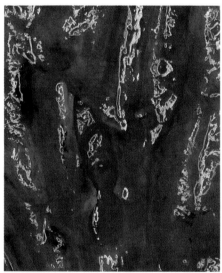

Lung tissue

Light and Airy

Lungs are light and spongy because they contain so much air. In fact, each of your two lungs weighs only about a pound ($1/2$ kg). They are also very elastic, stretching each time you breathe in and springing back to their normal shape when you breathe out.

Breathing Through a Mask

Many problems can be caused by breathing in harmful substances. There are many "dust diseases," for example, that affect miners, farmers, stone masons, and other people who work in dusty areas. Asbestos is another substance that can harm your lungs, as is tobacco. Many people who work in dangerous environments now wear masks, so that the dust and harmful poisons can be filtered out before reaching their lungs.

Lots of Air Bubbles

The body's main breathing tube is the windpipe, which runs through your throat. When it reaches the upper part of your chest, it divides. One main airway goes into each of your two lungs. Inside your lungs, these airways divide again and again, becoming smaller and smaller. They finally end in tiny air bubbles shaped like bunches of grapes. There are about 300 million of these tiny air bubbles in each of your lungs. Each time you breathe, air passes through the wind pipe, down the airway, and into these air bubbles. It is from these air bubbles that oxygen passes into your bloodstream.

Different-shaped Stomachs

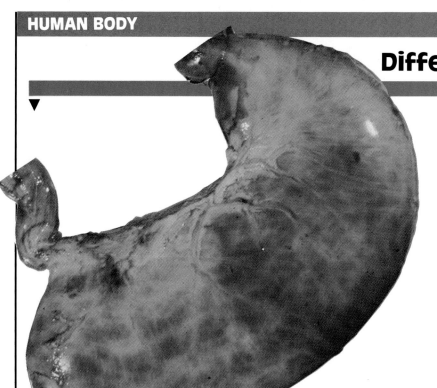

The stomach is between the gullet, the tube that food passes through on its way to the stomach, and the small intestine. Some stomachs are shaped like a half-moon; others look like an *S* or a *J*. There is no known reason why all stomachs do not look the same.

The Process of Digestion

As food passes into the upper part of the stomach, gastric juices break it up so that it can be absorbed in the small intestine. The food then moves to the middle of the stomach, where more digestion takes place. To mash and pulverize food, the stomach has three layers of muscles along its inside walls. Finally, the partly digested food goes to a narrow area, which acts as a kind of valve to control the rate at which the food passes into the small intestine.

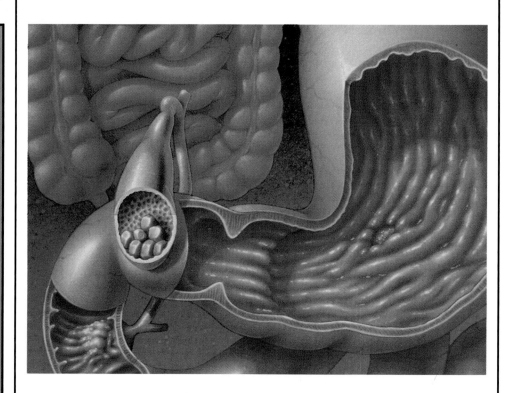

Putting Food in Your Stomach

Because your stomach churns food around and mixes it with enzymes and other gastric juices, it quickly turns your food—anything from pretzels and potato chips to steak or yogurt—into a thick, soupy liquid. Scientists and doctors call this liquid "chyme." When chyme is watery enough, it passes on to the small intestine, where it can be absorbed into your body.

No Digestion Needed ◄

Water, pure honey, and fruit sugars are absorbed by the body almost immediately. They pass through the stomach and into the small intestine with hardly any action on the part of the stomach.

That Burning Sensation

Heartburn is a burning sensation in the stomach that is caused when acidic, half-digested food backs up into the esophagus. This is most common when a person lies down or bends down after eating a big meal. Antacids and other medicines may relieve this uncomfortable feeling.

Working on Your Food

Your stomach is lined with millions of tiny glands that pour gastric juice on the food that enters your stomach. Your stomach mixes the food together so that these gastric juices get a good chance to "work" on the food. The juices themselves contain a lot of different things, including hydrochloric acid and enzymes. These enzymes help digest all the different kinds of food, from proteins to carbohydrates.

Digestion Time

How long it takes for digestion to take place varies, depending on what you ate and how much you ate. It takes longer to digest some foods than others—milk and lamb chops, for example, are much harder to digest than a glass of orange juice. Likewise, a big meal means more work—and a longer time—than a small snack.

An Upset Stomach

"Indigestion" is a word we use to cover a lot of different feelings and discomforts. It can be caused by an infection of bacteria or viruses or by eating foods—like beans, cucumbers, and other items—that introduce gas into the intestines. The discomfort usually passes within a few hours.

Ulcers Aren't Fun

An ulcer is a raw spot on the lining of a part of the digestive system—the stomach, the duodenum, or even both. Scientists are not sure exactly what causes ulcers.

The Growth of Hair

The hair on our heads grows about 2/5 inch a month (1 cm) or 5 inches (13 cm) a year. However, it hardly ever grows more than about 20 inches (51 cm) long because each hair lives for only three or four years. It then falls out and a new one starts growing at almost the same point to take its place.

Shorter Body Hairs▲

Our eyelashes and eyebrows and the little hairs on our skin grow more slowly than the hairs on our heads. They also have a much shorter life. For these two reasons they never grow very long.

Straight and Curly Hair

If you cut different hairs across and look at them through a microscope, you will see that some are rounder than others. The rounder a hair, the straighter it will be, and the flatter a hair, the more it will curl.

Different Amounts of Hair

▼

Among human beings, some Chinese have very little hair and almost no beards. The people called the Ainus of Japan are hairy almost all over.

No Hair at All

Babies are born with a covering of fine down, which is replaced with the usual growth of hair as the child grows older. This hairy coat is barely noticeable, since it consists of very fine hair that is light in color. However, a human being's skin is hairy almost everywhere except on the palms of the hands, soles of the feet, and the lips.

Growing Teeth

Most babies are born without teeth. First teeth appear at about six months. By the age of about two and a half, all of the 20 deciduous (milk, or first) teeth have appeared.

A Second Set of Teeth ▲

The permanent, or second, set of teeth forms in the gum below the first teeth and pushes them out as they grow up. There are 32 of these, 16 in each jaw. The eight at the front are cutting teeth called *incisors;* the next four are pointed teeth called *canines;* eight, the *premolars,* take the place of the earlier molars of the first teeth, and the back twelve, called *molars,* are grinding teeth.

Wise Third Molars

The permanent teeth appear between the ages of 6 and 14, except for the four "wisdom teeth" whose proper name is third molars. These do not appear until the ages of about 20 to 25, when people are supposed to have reached the years of wisdom. In some people, they never grow.

Tooth Decay ▲

The most common cause of toothache is caries, or decay. If teeth and gums are not properly cleaned, tiny pieces of food are left sticking to them. The sugar in food, bacteria, and the acids made by the bacteria cause the enamel to decay.

Muscle Action ◄

Muscles are the body's "movers," which control most of your actual actions. Without them, you would not be able to walk, eat, talk, or even breathe.

Cardiac muscle is only found in the heart.

Muscular Types

There are three different types of muscles in your body. The first is *involuntary*, or smooth, muscle. The fibers of these muscles are made up of long, spindle-shaped cells that are pointed at each end. They are found in blood vessels and hollow organs, and they carry out the automatic functions of the body. The second type of muscles are the *voluntary* muscles. These are made up of bundles of long fibers, with each fiber connected to a nerve ending. Whenever a motor nerve receives a signal from the brain, it passes it on to the muscle fiber, which then contracts. When all of the fibers shorten at the same time, the muscle shortens. The third kind of muscle is the *cardiac* muscle, found only in the heart. Like the other two types of muscles, cardiac muscle has the ability to contract. But, cardiac muscle does not require a signal from the nervous system in order to contract. The heart has a built-in pacemaker that triggers the contractions that we call heartbeats.

Resting Tired Muscles ▼

When our body turns sugar into energy, it also produces lactic acid, which collects in the muscle that is being used and makes it feel tired. When the muscle is involved in a quick discharge of movement, the body may not be able to move the lactic acid quickly enough. The buildup may make the muscle so tired that it can do no more work until the lactic acid is removed. To get rid of the buildup of lactic acid, the body needs oxygen. This is one reason why you breathe heavier—and feel a need to rest—after running to catch a bus.

A runner covers his legs with a "space blanket" to keep warm after a race in order to avoid muscle cramping.

Let's Exercise

Muscles need exercise in order to remain elastic—bendable, movable, and strong. Without exercise, they begin to decrease in size. They may also become less efficient at the work they are designed to do. That's why it is so important for people—especially children—to exercise regularly.

Giving Your Body a Rest

When you are asleep, you are unconscious—unaware of anything that is going on. You are also resting more completely than at any other time. During the time when you sleep, certain chemicals in your body get a chance to build up again, just as muscles and other parts get a chance to rest and rebuild their strength.

Deep Sleep, Light Sleep

Scientists know that there are two different kinds of sleep. REM sleep (REM stands for "rapid eye movement") is the period of sleep during which your eyes flicker rapidly and you dream. NREM (meaning non-REM) is divided into four progressively deeper stages of sleep. Although you may sleepwalk during NREM sleep, you generally do not dream. These two kinds of sleep alternate the whole time you are asleep. NREM sleep accounts for about 80 percent of your sleep time, while REM sleep accounts for about 20 percent.

The Common Cold

The common cold is a viral illness of the upper respiratory system—the nose and throat. The usual symptoms are sneezing, stuffed or runny nose, watery eyes, aching, and scratchy throat. Earache, headache, and a fever are also possible.

Taking Aspirin

For high fever in adults, aspirin may be used. Parents, however, should consult a doctor *before* giving a child aspirin, because aspirin has been linked to a life-threatening childhood disease called Reye's syndrome.

A Cure for the Common Cold

There isn't any way to cure a cold. Your body simply builds up *antibodies*, special forces that act against the viral infection, and the cold just goes away. Rest and drinking plenty of fluids help your body fight back.

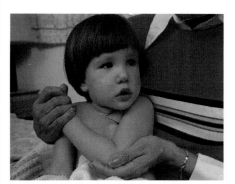

A child with a cold is having his temperature taken in the armpit.

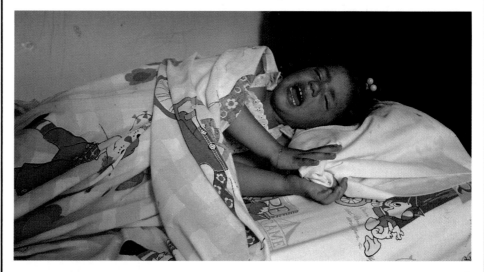

In Bed with the Flu

Influenza, better known as the flu, is a more serious viral infection, usually of the nose, throat, and lungs. Flu symptoms may include high fever, chills, cough, headache, sore throat, muscular aches, and weakness. Stuffy nose, diarrhea, and vomiting are also possible. In mild cases, most symptoms disappear in about five days. Sometimes, however, the body's weakened condition can lead to other infections, including pneumonia. Rest and drinking plenty of fluids are essential as the body fights the infection.

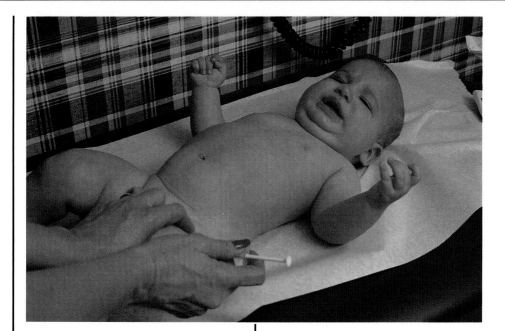

Vaccines to Combat the Flu ◄

A flu vaccine works by causing the body to produce antibodies to fight against a specific influenza virus. The biggest problem is that flu viruses keep changing. As soon as a vaccine is developed that works against one type of flu virus, the virus changes a little and the vaccine no longer works. Even so, certain groups of people who have a higher risk of complications, such as the elderly, may be advised to get a flu shot.

Passing It Along ▲

One reason that measles and German measles spread so quickly is that they are caught by being exposed to someone else's sneezes or coughs. Another reason is that parents often think that the disease is over once the fever is gone (but before the red spots or rash appear), and they send their children back to school. Unfortunately, the children still have the disease at this point, and they end up passing it on to many other children at their school.

Miserable Measles

Measles, also called *rubeola*, is one of the most widespread diseases of all. It is caused by a virus and can be spread from person to person by sneezes and coughs. It begins in the nose and throat like a cold; a high temperature follows. Three to five days later, red spots appear on the skin of the face, ears, and neck. They spread all over the body and last for about four days. Once you've had measles, you will not catch it again. Measles can be prevented through vaccination in childhood.

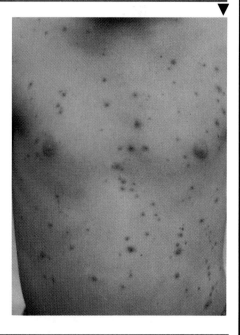

Catching German Measles

German measles, usually called *rubella,* is a mild viral infection. Symptoms include fever, swollen glands, joint pain, and a pink or red rash on the face and body. German measles are not dangerous to most people except pregnant women. If a pregnant woman catches the infection, her baby may be born with birth defects, for example, deafness. Vaccination in childhood is encouraged mainly to keep children from catching German measles and spreading it to pregnant women.

Pretty Much Under Control

Tuberculosis, or TB, is a disease caused by a tiny, rod-shaped germ that is spread in the air when a TB victim coughs. It can also be spread by a germ that lives in the milk of cows that have the disease. Tuberculosis can be very dangerous—years ago, patients who had it simply wasted away and died. Today, tuberculosis is rare in the United States.

Combatting a Killer

In the United States today, advances have been made in the detection and treatment of tuberculosis. Simple skin tests can be given to people who are suspected of having the disease or who are at risk of having it. Those who are at risk can be given a vaccine called BCG. In this country and in many others, cows are tested regularly to prevent dangerous, TB-infected milk from reaching the public. Milk is treated with a special process called "pasteurization" to kill the deadly germs before it is sold.

Sick with the Mumps

Mumps, like measles, is caused by a virus, and there is very little you can do to get rid of it. The illness begins with a fever, neck pain, headache, and weakness. A day or two later, the glands in the neck begin to swell and it becomes hard to open the mouth or swallow. After four or five days, the temperature and swelling go down. All you can do for mumps is to stay in bed and eat whatever you can swallow. Mumps is not usually a serious condition, although the risk of complications appears to be somewhat higher in adults who catch it.

A Very Nasty Virus

Poliomyelitis, or polio for short, is another disease caused by a virus. It usually affects children and young adults, and it is generally caught by either being in contact with someone who has polio or by being in an area with poor health standards. The disease begins with a fever, a sore throat, and vomiting. In most cases, the disease is fairly mild. It can, however, attack the nervous system and spine, leaving the patient partially or even fully paralyzed. Polio can be prevented through a series of vaccinations. Vaccination has made polio rare in the United States today.

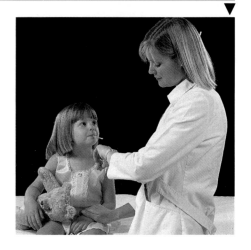

A Disease Carried by Mosquitoes

Malaria is one of the most common diseases in tropical areas. It brings on high, violent fevers in which a person feels unbearably cold and then, terribly hot. It is spread by mosquitoes, which deposit the germ directly into a person's blood when he or she is bitten. The best way to prevent malaria is to get rid of mosquitoes by draining swamps and mosquito breeding grounds and by using insecticides. People who travel in areas where malaria is common can also take certain drugs to help prevent the disease.

The Second-leading Cause of Death ▼

Cancer is the name we give to a whole group of diseases in which strange lumps occur and spread into other parts of the body. No one knows exactly what causes cancer, but it seems to be linked to abnormal growth patterns in cells. Removal of the lumps, radiation, and treatment with chemicals are used to treat cancer once it is found. Cancer is the second-leading cause of death in Western countries.

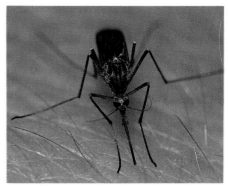

A bite from an infected mosquito can result in malaria.

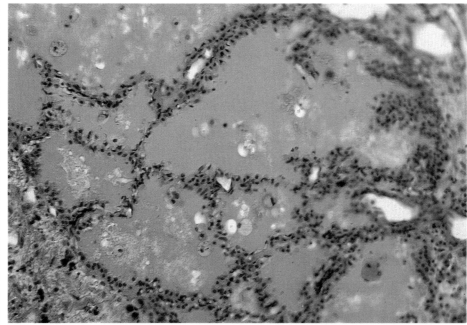

Cancer cells

Nature

Gold is a heavy metal that is often found embedded in "veins." It must be separated from the rock by breaking it into tiny pieces so that it can be processed.

Many volcanoes are located on ridges in the middle of the ocean or along the edges of the world's oceans.

Keeping Track of Weather

Weather is the state of our atmosphere. These conditions may change from day to day or even from hour to hour, and they include clouds, rain, wind, cold, heat, or even sunshine or snow.

Temperature fluctuations gauge

What's the Weather Like?

Knowing what the weather will be does more than help us decide what clothes to wear or whether or not to bring an umbrella with us. Farmers need to know the weather in order to plan when they will plant seeds in the ground and when they will harvest their crops. Power plants can get ready to supply heat in case it gets unusually cold. People can get buildings ready or can get themselves to safety if they know a huge storm is coming. And ship captains and pilots can steer away from storms or other problems if they know about them ahead of time.

Climates vs. Weather

Climate is the average effect of weather—what it is like over a long period of time. Even though it might be rainy today, for example, an area's climate might be called dry because it only has about fifteen rainy days each year.

99

Cloudy Days, Sunny Days

Some parts of the world have more clouds than others. The air over deserts, for example, is so dry that clouds do not form very often. Areas around oceans and seas have a lot of moisture in the air. As a result, there are a lot more clouds in these locations.

Dew drops form on the morning grass.

Up in the Clouds

Clouds are made of millions of drops of water or ice, all floating together in the air. Clouds form when air is cooled and the water in it begins to condense into droplets. If this happens on the ground, dew—the drops of water you see on the grass in the morning—forms. If it happens up in the atmosphere, clouds form as the air rises higher and higher into the sky.

Different Kinds of Clouds

Scientists have found ten types of clouds that they have named. The three that we see most often are: *cirrus* clouds (the feathery clouds that float very high up in the sky); *cumulus* clouds (the puffy clouds that are flat at the bottom and rounded on top); and *stratus* clouds (layered clouds that seem to hang like a gray blanket over the earth).

It Sure Looks Like Rain

Rain is caused by water vapor (visible moisture) in the air. Air always contains a certain amount of moisture. If that air cools, it *condenses,* or forms into water. At first, droplets are very small. They slowly get bigger until they are too heavy to stay up in the air. Then, these drops fall to earth as rain.

Caught in the Rain

"Cloudburst" is a name that we give to a sudden, hard rainstorm. You probably have seen this kind of rain—it seems to suddenly just pour down from the heavens.

Different Sizes of Raindrops

The average raindrop is about $1/100$ of an inch ($1/2$ mm) around. In the heavy showers of the tropics, however, they can be much, much larger—up to $1/50$ to $1/12$ of an inch (1 to 3 mm) across.

Rain or No Rain?

The rainiest place in the world is probably in Assam, in northern India. An average of 425 inches (10,820 mm) of rain falls there each year. The driest place is the Atacama Desert in northern Chile. No rain has fallen there for hundreds of years.

Keeping the Ground Warm with Snow ▼

Strangely enough, a layer of snow can help keep the ground warm enough to stop it from freezing. There is a great amount of air in the midst of all those crystals of ice that make up a snowflake. Since air is one of the best non-conductors of heat and cold, a covering of snow actually acts like a blanket on the ground. It keeps in the warmth that built up in the ground over the summer and fall. It also keeps out much of the cold that comes from the air above. Although some of the top layers of soil may freeze, the rest of the ground will usually be much warmer.

White Flakes of Snow

Snow is caused by the same conditions as rain. The difference is simply a matter of how cold it is in the air when the water vapor condenses. When it is cold enough, the vapor changes directly into ice crystals. At fairly low temperatures, the crystals stay separate and float in the air as glittering specks. Once the temperature goes below the freezing point (32°F or 0°C), the ice crystals join together into white flakes we call snow.

Beautiful Snowflakes

The size and shape of a snowflake depend on the temperature outside and on the amount of water in the flake itself. This tends to make each snowflake unique. It is also true that all snowflakes are basically *hexagons*, shapes with six sides.

Blowing Blizzards ▶

Years ago, the term "blizzard" was used only for the extremely cold snowstorms that blew across the Great Plains of North America. Now, we use the term a lot more loosely. To most of us, a blizzard is simply an extremely big snowstorm that brings with it high winds and blowing snow.

Hail from the Sky ▲

Hail is made up of little balls of ice up to 4 inches (10 cm) big. Hailstones are formed in thunderclouds. When a strong draft of air carries water droplets to the top of a thundercloud, they freeze and turn into tiny balls of ice. These small balls of ice then fall to the lower part of the cloud where more water droplets cling to them and freeze around them. If these frozen balls of ice meet more updrafts of air, they can be carried up and down several times. Eventually, they collect enough layers that they fall out of a cloud and reach the earth as hail.

Damaging Hailstones

Most of the time, hailstones are so small that they cannot harm people. But, they often damage farmers' crops, beating down wheat, cotton, or corn and damaging trees. When hailstones are quite large—as big as a tennis ball—they can be very dangerous. Reports have been heard of chickens, dogs, and even cows being injured or killed by hailstones.

The Force of Tornadoes

Tornadoes have been known to pick up just about anything in their swirling, twisting winds. Trees, automobiles, and even heavily loaded freight trains have all been lifted up by these fierce storms.

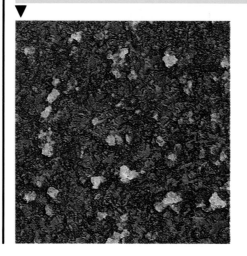

A Sheet of Sleet

Sleet is smaller-sized hail. It is made up of tiny globes of ice, usually no more than $1/5$ inch (5 mm) in diameter. It forms when raindrops or partially melted snowflakes freeze.

Snow Clouds ◄

Although precipitation (rain, sleet, hail, and snow) can form in many different kinds of clouds, snow, hail, and sleet seem to come most often from cumulus clouds—those puffy clouds with round tops and flat bottoms.

North vs. South

North of the equator, in the Northern Hemisphere, cyclone winds turn counterclockwise. In the Southern Hemisphere, however, they turn in exactly the opposite way—clockwise.

Cyclones leave devastation in their paths.

Spiraling Storms

Both cyclones and tornadoes are storms made up of spiraling, twisting winds. Tornadoes, though, are usually more violent. Cyclones can form at any time, and they often bring with them snow, rain, or hail. Tornadoes usually (although not always) start when thunderstorms are forming, and they do not always bring precipitation with them.

Where Most Cyclones Occur ▬

Cyclones have been known to form everywhere on earth except around the equator. However, they are more common in the middle latitudes of both hemispheres—along the American Middle West, for example, and through the middle of South America and Australia.

Twisting Tornadoes ▬▬▬ ▲

Tornadoes move across land at up to 40 miles (64 km) per hour, but their winds move at far greater speeds. A typical tornado has winds moving at up to 300 miles (480 km) per hour. The winds at the center of some tornadoes have been measured to be twisting around at almost 500 miles (800 km) an hour.

Tornadoes of the Seas

For centuries, sailors have made reports about twisting storms called "waterspouts." Most waterspouts are tornadoes that have moved over a lake or ocean and draw water up into the air. A slower and less severe type of waterspout is caused by a warm air pocket drawing the tip of a rain cloud down to a body of water.

Tropical Storms Called Hurricanes

Hurricanes are violent tropical storms that start up in areas of unstable wind conditions and a large area of water with warm temperatures (80°F; 27°C). Because of the way the earth turns, the winds end up traveling in a spiral. (Like cyclones and tornadoes, hurricanes in the Northern Hemisphere have winds traveling counter-clockwise; in the Southern Hemisphere, they travel clockwise. A hurricane is like a giant wheel lying on its side, with winds up to 100 miles per hour (160 kph) spinning around a calm center.

The Salt of the Ocean

The ocean is salty because rivers have been carrying pieces of soil and rock into the oceans of the world for millions of years. Some of these pieces sink to the bottom of the ocean and become part of the sediment at the bottom of the sea. Some particles end up being dissolved in the ocean. Salt is the most common natural substance dissolved in this way.

Freezing Salty Water

As water becomes more and more salty, it takes colder and colder temperatures to freeze it. As a result, the average temperature in the ocean is usually too high to ever really freeze the water. Even when the surface does freeze, as it does at the North Pole, the depths beneath it do not. At the North Pole, for example, there is only about 50 feet (15 m) of ice.

More and More Salt

Our oceans are actually getting saltier every year because water evaporates more quickly than is added by rain, while dissolved salt stays there forever.

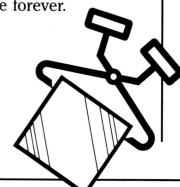

Watching the Waves

Waves form when wind blows over the water from the same direction for several hours. The longer the wind blows in that direction, the bigger and longer-lasting the waves will be. These waves even continue after the wind dies down, although they get weaker and weaker. That's one of the reasons why the water is so calm in some areas—it is far from the "prevailing winds" (the direction from which wind usually comes).

A Warm-water Current

The Gulf Stream is an ocean current that runs from the Gulf of Mexico all the way to the Arctic Ocean. Helped by the wind, it brings warm water into the Atlantic and carries it northward.

From Warm to Cold

There are several currents in the Atlantic. In fact, the Gulf Stream flows very close to one of the other currents, the Labrador Current. Near Newfoundland, on Canada's eastern coast the warm Gulf Stream and icy cold Labrador Currents are actually just a few yards apart. The waters of the two currents never mingle together—temperatures may vary tremendously between the two areas just a few yards apart.

High Tide, Low Tide

Tides are movements of the oceans' water that are caused by the moon's and sun's gravity. For part of a day, each section of a seacoast has a high tide when the water rises high up on the beach and a low tide when the water falls back. Since the moon and the earth rotate around each other, the water on the side of the earth away from the moon is constantly being thrown outward, creating a bulge of water on that side of the earth. On the side of the earth facing the moon, there is another bulge since the pull of the moon is strongest here. The earth spins on its axis once every 24 hours—any place on earth passes through a region of high water twice a day.

Powerful Ocean Currents

Some currents are caused by winds, which blow across the ocean in the same direction all year long. As these winds blow, they move the surface of the sea with them, carrying along particles of water. Some currents, like the Gulf Stream in the North Atlantic, are surface currents. Others run deep below the surface of the sea. These currents are caused by the earth's rotation, moving the water at an angle of about 90° to the direction of the prevailing wind.

Making Coral

Coral comes from the skeletons of dead sea animals, or polyps, which contain a hard skeleton of calcium carbonate. The skeletons join and link together to form fans, reefs, and even whole islands. Meanwhile, other living polyps move in among the skeletons where they eventually die, keeping the reef or island growing layer by layer.

Cold-water Coral

Most of us think of coral as something found only in the warm waters of the Pacific or the Caribbean. It is true that coral does much better in water above 70°F (21°C). However, it does grow in other places—even in the North Atlantic and the icy fjords of Norway.

Different Names for Different Shapes

Coral polyps often live together in colonies. They assume a distinctive shape, after which their coral is named. "Brain coral," "stag horn coral," and "mushroom coral" are just a few of the many different kinds of coral that can be found in the sea.

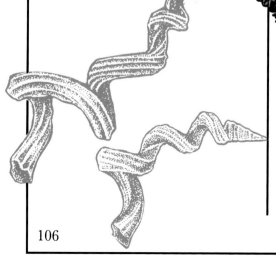

Coral Jewelry

For thousands of years, the red coral found in the Mediterranean has been treated as a precious stone. Ancient Romans even believed that it could keep diseases away from children. Today, we use red coral for jewelry, a function that regular reef coral can't provide.

Great Barrier Reef

Building a Reef ▲

A reef is the result of millions of years of polyp skeletons piled layer upon layer. The coral rock in a reef is fairly soft, so many sea creatures find shelter in its twists, turns, and folds. The Great Barrier Reef off the northeastern coast of Australia is one of the largest and best-known reefs in the world.

Brightly colored reef fish make their homes on coral.

All Reefs are not Alike ▼

There are three basic kinds of reefs. *Fringing* reefs surround islands and continents, without leaving room for water between the land and the sea. *Barrier* reefs are like fringing reefs except that they are much farther away from the land. There is often a channel wide and deep enough to allow ocean-going ships to pass between the reef and the land. The third kind of reef is an *atoll,* which is shaped like a ring or horseshoe.

Fascinating Reef Creatures ◄

Reefs are full of unusual creatures. Among the best known are brightly colored reef fish. These fish find an excellent home in reefs because the coral gives them places to hide from larger fish. Many kinds of shellfish also make their homes in reefs, including starfish, shrimp, and crabs. One of these shellfish, the crown-of-thorns starfish, actually feeds on coral polyps, and is responsible for destroying huge sections of Australia's Great Barrier Reef. Another reef-dweller is the great moray eel, a deadly creature that uses needlelike teeth to tear apart almost anything.

Volcanic Reefs ▲

Atolls, unlike other reefs, are usually found in the open ocean. They begin as ordinary coral reefs that surround, or fringe, an island formed by a volcano. As these island volcanos sink very slowly into the sea, the coral grows upward very quickly in order to get to the light of the sun. In time, the volcano disappears completely and all that is left is a ring surrounding an empty center.

Record-breaking Eruption

The biggest volcanic explosion in the recent past took place on Rakata, an island in Indonesia. In 1883, there were several earthquakes and small eruptions. A series of huge explosions followed, destroying most of Krakatoa, a volcano on the island, and the island itself. The noise of the blast could be heard 3,000 miles (5,000 km) away. Over 36,000 people were drowned by the waves set off by the eruption of this volcano.

Lakes of Water ▲

A lake is a large sheet of water surrounded by land. The water is in a basin, or hollow, in the surface of the earth. A rim around the basin keeps the water from flowing out.

Dying Lakes

From the moment they are formed, lakes start to "die." The streams and rivers that flow from a lake, for example, grow deeper and deeper as they cut into the soil and rock they run through. As a result, more and more water fills them—and runs out of the lake. Streams flowing into a lake also bring in mud and pebbles that gradually fill in the lake itself. More recently, pollution of the air and water has added another factor—algae, weeds, and acid rain are clogging our lakes.

Islands Formed from Volcanoes

Many volcanoes are located on ridges in the middle of the ocean or along the edges of the world's oceans. The Hawaiian Islands, for example, are volcanic islands located on a ridge in the Pacific; Iceland is another volcanic island located in the North Atlantic. Elsewhere, the Aleutian Islands are formed from a chain of volcanoes, while the Andes Mountains of South America began as volcanoes along the coast.

How Lakes are Made

Lakes are formed in many different ways. Many lakes were formed during the Ice Age, when glaciers carved great hollows in the earth's surface. As the glaciers moved rocks and blocked ancient rivers, dams were created that turned the areas behind them into lakes. Most of the world's biggest lakes were formed by movements in the earth's crust. Earthquakes, cracks, and collapses all formed lakes in their own ways. Volcanoes have also formed many lakes, as the hollow at the center of a dead volcano slowly fills with water.

A Lake by any Other Name . . .

There are many interesting lakes in the world. One of them, the Dead Sea, is not even called a lake at all. Another sea that is really a lake is the Caspian Sea in Central Asia. The deepest lake in the world is Lake Baikal, which is almost 5,000 feet (1,525 m) deep.

River Water Travelers ▲

Rivers do not just carry water; they also carry soil and rock. The muddy color of many rivers comes from the particles of clay that are carried along by the flowing water. All of these particles of dirt and rock, along with the water that carries them, slowly wear away the river bed. As a result, even more rock and soil are carried by the river. Although it takes a long time, this can create very deep cuts in the earth. In fact, the Grand Canyon was formed in this way.

The Story of Salty Rivers

Some rivers are actually salty because of the action of tides, which draws the sea's saltwater up into the river. They also get salty in dry, hot weather when the fresh water of a river evaporates and leaves salt behind.

Disappearing Water

Water disappears in three main ways. Some of it *evaporates*, meaning that as it gets warmed by the sun, it turns to vapor and is carried off by the wind. Some gathers together to form streams. The rest sinks into the soil and then reappears through springs and flows into streams, rivers, and lakes.

Little Streams, Bigger Rivers ▲

Rivers are formed when streams join to form larger streams, these larger streams join together to form still larger streams, and so on. Rivers then carry water along until they deposit them in other rivers, the ocean, or the sea.

Cavernous Caves

Caves are deep hollow spaces that are found in the rocky sides of hills or cliffs. Very large caves are sometimes called caverns.

How a Cave is Made

Caves near seaside cliffs are often made by waves bashing against the rocks. Other caves are formed as hard rocks rub against softer rocks. Most caves away from the shore, however, are formed by underground streams and rivers that slowly wear away layers of soft rock.

Interior Wonders

Stalactites and stalagmites are formed by mineral deposits in a cave. *Stalactites* hang down from the ceiling of a cave; *stalagmites* grow up from the cave's floor. They grow slowly, as calcite from rocks outside the cave passes into the cave. As water comes into the cave, it is deposited very slowly, particle by particle, until the long form of stalactites or stalagmites is formed. This takes a long time—sometimes hundreds of years—but the results are wonderful to see.

A Very Big Cave

Mammoth Cave, in Kentucky, is one of the largest and most spectacular caves in the world. The land above it takes up an area almost 9 miles (15 km) wide, and it contains more than 155 miles (250 km) of tunnels and hallways.

The Story of Cavemen

There really were cavemen thousands of years ago. Scientists have found hundreds of caves in which people lived. Not all prehistoric people were cave dwellers, but many of them did take shelter in the deep, warm caves of Europe and Asia.

Cave Inhabitants

Deep inside Mammoth Cave are some of the world's most unusual creatures. Eyeless, blind fish swim in the cave's streams and rivers. Blind grasshoppers, beetles, rats, and huge numbers of large bats also live in the cave.

Moving Glaciers

A glacier is a mass of ice moving along the surface of the earth. Some glaciers move only an inch or two each year, while others may move as much as several hundred yards (or meters) in a single year.

Glaciers Around the World

Glaciers are found just about anywhere there is a lot of snow. You can find them at the North and South Poles, in high mountain areas, and in the frozen Arctic regions. It's also why you find glaciers along the equator in Africa—they are so high up in the mountains that it is freezing all year round.

From Glaciers to Icebergs

Glaciers begin to melt whenever they reach the *snow line,* the point above which snow stays in summer. However, some glaciers are so big that they reach all the way past the snow line to the sea. In cold regions, like the Arctic and Greenland, glaciers often reach the sea, where huge blocks of ice often break and drift off as icebergs.

Glacier Power

Glaciers changed the face of the earth by moving slowly along the surface carrying along rocks, dirt, and even giant boulders. All of these scrape the ground beneath and around the glacier, slowly cutting away the surface to form valleys, hollows, and other shapes. Glaciers often just drop off some of this material, making hills and other land formations.

Grouping Mountains

Most mountains are found in groups called "chains," "ranges," or "massifs." The highest mountains of all are found in two long lines, one circling the Pacific Ocean and the other stretching from Spain to the East Indies. Most of these were formed by the action of rivers and glaciers on large portions of the earth that have been pushed up by action in the earth's interior.

Mountain Measurements

According to most scientists, a mass of rock must be at least 1,640 feet (500 m) high in order to be considered a mountain. Anything smaller than that is just a hill.

Mountain Greats

The highest mountains in the world are the Himalayas, in northern India and Tibet, and the Andes, in South America. Each of these great mountain ranges encircles a high flat plateau over 13,000 feet (4,000 m) in the air.

Rocky Mountains

Frost, running water, and glaciers give mountains their rocky appearance. These elements cut and scrape away at the surface, creating peaks, gorges, cuts, and valleys. Without this, mountains would be just round- or flat-topped masses of soil.

Down in the Valley

Valleys are natural troughs or hollows in the surface of the earth. At the bottom of a valley is its floor, a flat surface that slopes off in one direction or another. The sides, called slopes, are then angled up.

Not a Real Valley ▲

Death Valley, like the Great Valley of California, was not formed in the ways valleys usually are and is not a valley at all. It was formed when a long, narrow section of the earth's crust sank below the surrounding area.

Making a Valley ▲

Most valleys were formed by streams, rivers, and floodwaters running over them. The running water carries rocks and soil along with it, slowly cutting into the surface of the earth until the trench of the valley is formed. Other valleys have been created by the movement of glaciers as they scraped their way along the earth.

The Grandest Canyon of All ▼

A canyon is nothing more than a valley with extremely steep sides. One of the most famous canyons is the Grand Canyon, in Arizona. It is over a mile (1.6 km) deep in many spots and ranges from 2 to 18 miles (3 to 29 km) across.

It's Worth Its Weight in Gold ▲

Gold is valuable because it is a very stable substance in terms of its chemistry and is not affected very much by weather, air, or even water. Gold lasts a very long time and doesn't change much over the years. Gold is also very scarce. If you lumped together all of the gold produced and used in history so far, you would end up with a block the size of a large house. With only a little bit of gold in the world, it's no wonder that people pay a high price for it.

From Pebbles to Rocks ▶

Rock is a solid material that makes up the earth's crust— the layer of earth just beneath the soil. Rocks are made of one or more minerals, which are natural chemical substances. There are many kinds of rocks, and they come in all shapes and sizes, from tiny pebbles to giant volcanic rocks, like the Devil's Tower, in Wyoming.

There is Nothing Like Gold ▶

Gold is a heavy metal that is often found embedded in rock in "veins." It must be separated from the rock by breaking it into tiny pieces so that it can be processed. Once this process is completed, the gold can be purified, refined, and made into anything from plates to jewelry.

Almost as Good as Gold

There is far more silver in the world, so it has never been as valuable as gold. It is also very soft. Silver is so soft that it could never stand the wear and tear of being used as a knife or fork or coin without having other metals added to it to make it sturdy and strong.

Nothing Sparkles Like a Diamond ▲

Both coal and diamonds are formed from carbon. Diamonds, however, are the result of great pressure, which has turned them into pure carbon of amazing clearness and hardness. Diamonds are the hardest known substance on earth, and they are able to cut through any other rock or substance.

A Real Jewel ▼

Jewels are nothing more than rocks that people have decided are particularly beautiful. Because they are rock, they tend to last a long time, which makes them even more valuable.

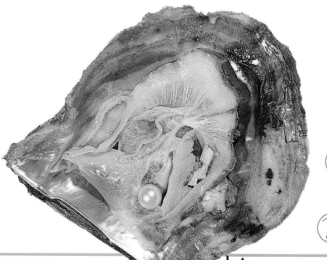

▲ Pearls of Nature

Pearls are not jewels. They are formed around an irritation in an oyster, such as a grain of sand. This grain of sand or dirt inside the oyster's shell slowly becomes covered with a pearl sac. Then nacre, or mother of pearl, is gradually layered onto it. In time, a pearl forms.

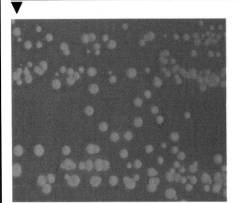

A bacterial culture

Dangerous Bacteria

Typhoid fever, tuberculosis, pneumonia, and even leprosy are all caused by bacteria.

Fruits and Vegetables ▶

A vegetable is just about any plant that you can eat, and the term includes everything from corn to carrots. Fruit is the ovary of a plant—part of its reproductive system that contains seeds. Despite this scientific distinction, we often use the terms incorrectly. Peas, for example, are actually fruit, as are beans and tomatoes.

Life in Miniature

Bacteria are living things so tiny that they can only be seen with the help of a powerful microscope. They were discovered in the 1600s, when lenses and microscopes were first being developed. Since then, scientists have worked hard to understand these strange living things that are neither plant nor animal but are found everywhere—in the soil, the air, the food we eat, and even the depths of the ocean.

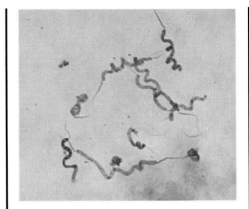

Bacteria News ▲

Bacteria come in all shapes and sizes—although most are colorless. Many are shaped like rods, balls, or corkscrews. Some link together in a chain; others look like a bunch of grapes. There are also bacteria that have tiny hairs on them, which they wave around in order to move from place to place.

Using Bacteria

There are bacteria that are not harmful at all. Bacteria, for example, cause the decay, or rotting, of dead plants and animals. This breaks down the plant or animal parts into simple substances that, in turn, are used to create new living things. Bacteria also help us make useful items—from leather and cloth to cheese and tea. They are also used to create vaccines, drugs, and other chemicals.

Eat Your Vegetables! ▲

Vegetables are among the most healthy things you can eat. They contain a wealth of minerals (especially iron and calcium) and vitamins (especially Vitamin A and Vitamin C). Vegetables are also rich in carbohydrates, fats, and proteins. They also provide roughage, the bulk that helps digestive juices work.

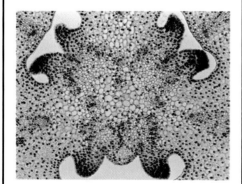

Cell Life ▲

Plants are made up of cells, which are the tiny units from which all life is made. Most plants contain hundreds or even millions of cells, each of which has its own particular job or function to do for the plant to stay alive.

Carrots and Your Eyes

Carrots are rich in *carotene,* a substance that gives them their orange color. Carotene is also rich in Vitamin A, which helps your skin, teeth, and bones. People who do not have enough Vitamin A in their bodies often have "night blindness"—they cannot see in dim light or in the dark. Eating Vitamin-A rich carrots is one way to add carotene to your system and improve your night vision.

◄ Living Things of All Sizes

Plants are one of the two great groups of living things. (The other group, of course, is animals.) They come in all sizes, ranging from one cell all the way up to the largest living things on earth, the giant redwoods (also called sequoias) of California.

The Smallest Living Things

Viruses are the smallest and simplest living things that we have yet discovered. They are so small that if you put one or two million of them side by side they would measure less than half an inch (1 cm).

Plants We Use

Plants are useful to people in many ways. They provide us with the oxygen we breathe. Without them, there probably would not be any life on earth. They provide us with food and clothing and can even be turned into homes. Medicines are also made from many plants.

Plant Production

Scientists experiment with plants in order to have them grow in certain kinds of soil or weather, have more vitamins or minerals, or be better able to stay fresh in your refrigerator. Scientists, for example, have worked to produce new kinds of wheat that have larger grains, more grains, and more food value. These new kinds of wheat even have stronger stems so the plants won't blow down so easily in the wind or rain.

These logs may have ended up as the paper this book is printed on.

Problem Plants

Not all plants are useful. Some plants, like dandelions, ruin people's lawns. Pollen from certain plants causes many people problems with allergies. Other plants attack crops and cost farmers millions of dollars each year. Overgrown plants, like algae and other water-growing plants, can choke out our lakes, rivers, and streams.

The Oldest Living Plant

The bristlecone pine tree in California is probably the oldest living plant on earth. It is between 4,000 and 5,000 years old.

◄ Making New Flowers

A flower—which can be anything from an acorn to a lovely orchid blossom—is the part of a plant that makes the seeds that will someday become a new plant.

The Breath of Life

Photosynthesis is the process by which plants turn the energy of the sun into chemical energy. Plants carry out photosynthesis in order to make their food. This process has an important side effect: As it makes its needed chemical energy, the plant also produces oxygen, which it gives off through its leaves for people and animals to breathe. After people and animals breathe and take in the oxygen they need, they breathe out carbon dioxide gas—which is what plants need to take in to carry out photosynthesis. This exchange between plants and animals helps keep all living things alive on our planet.

Practical Flowers

Flowers are useful—they are not only pretty. For one thing, many of them are used in medicines. Others are used to make perfumes, skin conditioners, and even shampoos. They are especially useful because they help plants reproduce.

Crossbreeding Plants

New kinds of plants are created through "crossbreeding." By finding a wild plant with a certain characteristic that they want to add to another plant, scientists carefully exchange pollen so that the plants will reproduce. Over time—and after generation after generation of plants—scientists can create new plants with the qualities they want.

Bees to Honey ▲

Bees love nectar, a sweet liquid found in many flowers, which they use to make honey. When a bee sees a flower, it will almost always stop to check and see if there is any nectar inside. This process helps both the bee and the plant. When a bee crawls inside a flower, pollen dust falls on it. When it flies off, a bee carries the dust with it until it falls off inside another plant. Spreading pollen this way helps plants reproduce.

The Largest Plants on Earth ◄

Sequoias (also called redwoods) are the world's biggest trees, in part because they are so large in diameter. "General Sherman," the largest sequoia, stands 272 feet (83 m) tall and has a diameter of more than 30 feet (9 m). Mountain ash and Douglas fir trees actually grow taller, even though they are smaller around. The tallest of these trees have reached 330 feet (100 m) in height.

A Few Treeless Spots

Trees of one kind or another will grow just about anywhere. The only parts of the world without them are the Arctic, the Antarctic, and a few desert areas.

Hearty Eaters

Most meat-eating plants can manage to survive without the insects or small animals they catch, even though they are much healthier if their diet includes them. Strangely enough, these plants do not suffer if they "overeat." One poisonous plant, the pitcher plant, has been known to eat as many as 73 cockroaches in two weeks.

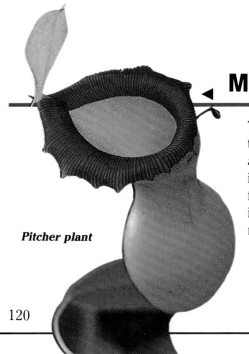

Pitcher plant

Meat-eating Plants ◄

There are over 500 different plants that eat meat of one kind or another. Most of them catch insects or tiny animals for their food. Bacteria and chemicals inside the plant help it to get the nutrients out of its victim.

Two Ways to Shed Leaves

Unlike *deciduous* trees, which shed their leaves every winter, evergreens keep their leaves (or needles) all year long. They lose their leaves little by little all the time. This allows them to grow new, fresh leaves whenever they need them and still stay green all year long.

Saving the Forests

Forests are important because trees, like other green plants, carry out photosynthesis. The oxygen they make is an important part of our world. It is so important, in fact, that if our forests were destroyed, we probably would not be able to survive. For this reason, so many people are concerned that our forests are being cut down all over the world.

Enticing Plants

Pitcher plants are tropical plants that are shaped like a large jug or "pitcher." When insects come close, they get interested in the plant's bright colors and by the sweet-smelling liquid inside the jug. They hurry to the edge of the pitcher to see what is inside—and fall down into the liquid and drown. Once the victim is inside, the plant uses its special chemicals to absorb the insect. Some insects, including some types of flies and mosquitoes, can live inside the pitcher plant's trap with no trouble.

Plants to Drive You Crazy

Locoweed (whose name comes from *loco,* the Spanish word for "crazy") grows in the Midwest and Southwest, and it really is dangerous to horses and cattle. When an animal eats locoweed while grazing, it loses control of its movements and runs around wildly.

The Most Famous Meat-eater

The Venus flytrap, which grows only in North and South Carolina, is the most famous meat-eating plant of all. When it is "hungry," its leaves divide into halves that are hinged together like sections of a book. In the middle of each leaf are three hairs, which are sensitive to the slightest touch. When a fly or other insect sets down on one of these leaves, the two halves snap shut, trapping the insect inside. Ten days later, the insect is gone; it has been "eaten" by the plant.

The stems and leaves of potato plants are poisonous.

Plants to Avoid

There are more than 700 kinds of poisonous plants growing in the United States and Canada alone. Many of them look or smell so nasty that people keep away from them without even thinking. Many plants that we see all the time, or even eat certain parts of, are actually poisonous. Did you know, for example, that the leaves of potato plants and apricot and cherry pits are poisonous? Many poisonous plants harm people and animals if they are eaten. Others cause skin problems or harm the eyes or ears. Some cause problems only to people who are allergic to them.

From Poison to Medicine

People have found that some poisonous plants can be turned into medicines. The foxglove plant, for example, can be quite poisonous, but it can also be turned into the medicine digitalis, which is given to people with heart trouble. In the same way, controlled doses of aconite (sometimes called "monkshood"), morphine, quinine, and even strychnine can be used as medicines.

A Deadly Poison

DDT, introduced in the 1930s, was a well-known pesticide that was used worldwide. It was especially useful in getting rid of mosquitoes, which spread many diseases in tropical and swampy areas. However, it was found that DDT poisoned birds and fish as well as rivers and lakes. Insects also gradually became immune to the effects of DDT, so that it became less and less useful. In the 1970s, it was taken off the market in most countries.

Identifying Plants

The only way to tell if a plant is poisonous is to identify it. You have to look at the plant (or at least pictures of it) and learn what it is and what it does. Do not eat any plant that you do not know about until you check it out.

Traveling Weeds

Weeds get from place to place by the wind or by people or animals. They can even attach themselves to other plants that people actually want. When those plants are put into the earth, the weeds are planted right along with them.

Good Riddance

Weeds are wild plants that grow where they are not wanted. They are extremely tough and hardy, making them almost impossible to get rid of. The most common weeds in the United States are thistles, ragweed, and crabgrass. They cause problems for other plants because they draw food and energy away from them. Weeds also crowd out other plants and spread disease.

Beware of the Weeds!

Certain weeds are really dangerous. In Australia, for example, two different kinds of wild tulips were brought in from South Africa. They have taken over thousands of acres of pastureland, crowding out all the other plants and grasses that could be grown instead. They are also poisonous, so animals (especially cattle) must be kept away from these wild tulips at all times.

Dangerous Pests and Pesticides

For many years, people used pesticides, or chemicals that destroy pests, to help them get rid of unwanted insects that destroyed crops, made recreation areas unpleasant, and caused damage to homes and other buildings. Scientists soon discovered that these chemical pesticides were causing a great deal of damage to our environment—perhaps more harm than they were worth. They entered fruits and vegetables, spreading poisons to birds, animals, fish, and even people. Today, scientists and concerned people are trying to find other ways to get rid of pests.

Getting Rid of Weeds

There are several ways to get rid of weeds. Sometimes, they can be pulled out of the ground. They can also be "starved" by fertilizing the plants you want to grow. As these plants grow and take up more space, they crowd out the weeds. In the past, weed killers were used, but these can also damage good plants as well. Even more importantly, they can cause lasting harm to the soil, allowing terrible poisons to build up in the ground. These poisons can then enter the water supply and reach people and animals. They can also harm other plants— ones that eventually are eaten by people and animals.

Getting Rid of Pests Naturally

"Biological controls" are new, safer ways to control pests such as insects, mice, and rats. Often, one kind of creature is used to get rid of another. Dragonflies, for example, love to eat mosquitoes and gnats. Many governments, therefore, have gone to great lengths to breed and purchase dragonflies so that they can be let loose in areas where people want to get rid of mosquitoes. In the same way, hawks, owls, and other birds of prey can be used to keep down populations of mice and other rodents. Scientists are only beginning to learn about biological controls, but they believe that these controls will help us deal with our environment in a safer, better way in the future.

Pollution Perils ◄

Pollution is anything that poisons the air, water, or land around us. Although there has always been pollution of one kind or another, it clearly is worse—and more dangerous—than ever before. Smoke from factories and cars is one of the main causes of air pollution. Many of the chemicals in this smoke can cause serious health problems. In many cities, these chemicals form *smog,* which is short for "smoke and fog." Smog is a great threat to people who already have problems with their lungs and breathing. It also poisons trees and other plants.

Spreading Acids ▼

Fuels like coal, oil, and gasoline give off acidic fumes when they are burned. Every time the furnace heats your home or you drive in a car, you are sending acids like sulfur dioxide and nitrous dioxide into the atmosphere. These fumes rise up into the air, where they mix with water vapor and form drops of sulfuric acid and nitric acid. These drops fall when it rains, spreading acids all over the planet.

Keeping a Lid on Pollution ▲

Pollution must be controlled, and to do it most of us will have to make changes in how we live. Filters can be used to stop dangerous chemicals from going up into the atmosphere from factories and homes. Cars can be built that burn less fuel and do not cause smog and other problems. Plastic and throw-away containers may have to eliminated in order to prevent the soil from being poisoned. These and other measures will probably have to be taken before the air, water, and soil around us is clean and safe.

◀

Altering Our Climate

The "greenhouse effect" comes from the buildup of carbon dioxide in a layer around the earth as we burn coal, gasoline, and oil. As more and more of these fuels are burned, more and more carbon dioxide is added, trapping the heat of the sun beneath the layer close to the surface of the earth. This "greenhouse effect" (the layer of carbon dioxide is like the glass of a greenhouse, keeping in warm air and stopping cool air from being added) slowly makes the temperature on our planet warmer and warmer. Some scientists believe that the "greenhouse effect" will cause temperatures to rise several degrees in the next 50 years or less. If this happens, weather will change dramatically: Areas where we now grow wheat or corn might suffer from great droughts and the ice at the North and South Poles would begin to melt, causing the sea to rise almost 16 feet (5 m). This could flood many cities and low-lying lands.

Ban that ▶ Aerosol Can!

The ozone layer is a region high in our atmosphere in which there is a large amount of the chemical, ozone. Because it is able to absorb ultraviolet light, this layer helps protect the earth from possibly dangerous radiation. It also helps keep the temperature on our planet fairly comfortable most of the time. Unfortunately, air pollution has begun to damage this ozone layer. One of the main offenders is the sprays used in aerosol cans—the cans we use for everything from window cleaner to hair spray. Even though many of these products have been taken off the market, there is still much to do before the ozone layer is safe.

Harmful Acid Rain ▼

Acid rain is harmful to the water in our soil, ponds, and lakes. As trees become more acidic, they become brown and turn sickly, animals cannot find homes or food and disappear, and minerals in the soil wash away. Ponds and lakes become so acidic that nothing— not even the smallest fish or algae plant—can survive in them.

A Lot of Water

Humans have made tremendous demands on the earth's facilities. For example, if all of the fresh water that was diverted from nature for people's use in one year was collected, it would fill a lake the size of Europe with a depth reaching halfway to the earth's core.

From Forest to Desert

The spread of agriculture has had devastating effects, particularly in the poorer parts of the world. Woodlands and scrub are usually invaded by browsing animals such as goats, wood is cut and burned for fuel, and forests are cleared haphazardly for crops. Too often the woodlands and scrub are removed without precautions of terracing and draining channels; the exposed soil is eroded by wind and rain. Erosion now affects two-thirds of the world's nations. In quite a few areas, land has changed from forest to desert within a single generation.

◄ Growing Deserts

In 1985, a government report in Australia warned that two-thirds of the country's tree cover had been destroyed and that more than half of the agricultural land was in need of treatment for erosion. In the Third World, the desert is expanding unchecked. Around the area of the Sahara in Africa, new desert is being created at a rate of 420 acres (170 hectares) an hour.

Lost Species

Scientists believe that at least one unique life form disappears from our planet every day. Many biologists now accept the fact that, unless drastic measures are taken, the earth will have lost between a quarter and a third of all its species of plants and animals by the year 2500.

Threatened Wildernesses

The Arctic and Antarctic are the last two wildernesses of the world that are in danger. These regions are threatened by the lure of wealth. The Antarctic has vast amounts of fish and krill, which is a small shrimplike organism that may someday be exploited as a source of protein. The Arctic, from Alaska through northern Canada and across Siberia, has some of the world's largest deposits of iron, coal, lead, copper, zinc, gold, wolfram, uranium, diamonds, and phosphates, as well as huge untapped reserves of oil and natural gas.

Coexisting with Nature

Conservation of nature is the protection of animals and plants in their natural homes. It includes preserving the great variety of species that live on the earth. It also involves the sensible use of all of the earth's resources: its water, soils, minerals, trees, birds, animals, and fish, so that none of them become exhausted and disappear.

Breeding in Captivity

When an animal has become very rare, captive breeding has proved useful to conservationists. The Arabian oryx, the Hawaiian goose, the Puerto Rican parrot, and several other species have been brought back from the verge of extinction by being captured in the wild and bred in zoos. One of the most recent captive breeding programs involves the California condor, which has a wingspan of over 9 feet (3 m). So far, 15 young condors have been hatched in incubators.

▲

Beautiful National Parks

All over the world, nature reserves and national parks have been developed to protect wildlife and to foster public enjoyment of nature. Yellowstone National Park was the first such park founded in the United States in 1872. The second was the Banff National Park established in Canada in 1885.

Saving the Tropical Forests ▶

In 1985, the World Bank and the World Resources Institute announced their Action Plan for Tropical Forests. The plan includes extensive replanting, aid for poor farmers, and a comprehensive network of large protected areas. Its cost is one billion dollars per year until the end of the 20th century.

Science

Saturn has seven flat rings surrounding the planet's middle. They are made up of tiny particles, including grains of dust and pieces of ice, and large bolders that sometimes are as big as the moon.

White light from the sun has the whole rainbow of colors in it. That rainbow, which is called the "spectrum," contains red, orange, yellow, green, blue, indigo, and violet.

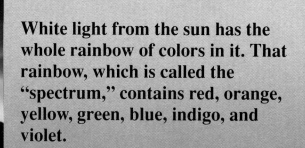

It's Elemental

Everything in our universe, from people to the air itself, is made up of chemical elements. Mixing the different elements in various ways makes up what we see and feel all around us. ▼

Down to Basics

The basic building block of our universe is an element. It is a substance that cannot be split up into other substances by heat or other actions; each chemical element is made up of one basic kind of atom. Over the years, scientists have discovered (and even made) many elements. As of today, scientists believe that there are 107 of these basic substances in the world.

Elements Old and New

Some elements have been known for thousands of years, and they are called by their age-old names. Other elements have only been found recently. Some have been named for famous people—Einsteinium, for example, was named for the great scientist, Albert Einstein. Others were named for places, like Europium, which was discovered in 1901, and Americium, discovered in 1944. Some elements were even named for what they look like. Chlorine, for example, is green in color, and its name comes from the Greek word for "green."

$$E = Mc^2$$

An Element Found Everywhere

Hydrogen is the most abundant element in the universe and the ninth most abundant element (by mass) in the earth's crust and atmosphere. It is present in water, in acids, in all plants and animals, and in most of our food. Hydrogen is invisible and has no taste or smell.

A Very Useful Element

Aluminum is the most common metallic element in the earth's crust. It makes up nearly 8 percent of it. It is used in more ways by people than any other metal. Ground up into a fine powder, it is mixed with oils and used as a paint. When a small amount of aluminum is added to steel, gas holes are eliminated and the material is more solid. It is also used in motion picture film, aluminum foil wrapping, tubes for shaving cream and toothpaste, and other products.

A Noble Gas

Helium was first discovered by the English scientist Joseph Norman Lockyer in 1868 by studying the spectrum of the flame surrounding the sun. It is the second-lightest element and has neither color nor smell. Helium stays in the gaseous state at lower temperatures than any other gas. It only changes into a liquid at −452°F (−268.6°C). Helium is one of the noble, or rare, gases. It is inert, and does not react with other substances. As a result, it is often used to pressurize the very thin walled fuel tanks in spacecraft, which would otherwise collapse under their own weight. Helium is also used to fill lighter-than-air baloons.

A Liquid Metal

Mercury, otherwise known as quicksilver, is a silvery white metal. It is unusual in that, unlike other metals, it is a liquid at ordinary temperatures. It does not become solid until cooled to its freezing point of −38°F (−39°C). Since mercury expands a good deal when it is heated, it is useful for most thermometers.

Conducting Heat

Most metals are good conductors of heat because the atoms are closely packed in the crystal, and the vibrations involved in the conduction of heat are readily passed on through the structure. If you held an iron rod with one end in a fire, the other end would soon become hot. On the other hand, an iron rod with a wooden handle can be held in the same manner for a long time without getting hot because wood is a poor conductor of electricity.

Working a Metal into Shape

Metals are worked into the shape needed by rolling or hammering them while hot. When the metal has already been rolled into fairly thin sheets (such as for motor vehicle bodies or aluminum saucepans), further heating is unnecessary and shaping is done in a press while cold.

Making a Metal Strong

The strength and hardness of metals can be controlled by alloying and heat treatment. A metal is usually at its softest and weakest when pure and can be strengthened by alloying (mixing) with another metal. For example, pure copper and pure tin are soft and weak, but if the two are melted together they make bronze, a hard, strong alloy.

A Thin Coat of Metal

To prevent rust on steel articles, as well as for improving appearance, thin coatings of metal are made by dipping an object in molten metal. Galvanized steel and fencing wire are coated by being dipped in molten zinc, and "tin cans" are still sometimes made by dipping cans made of very thin steel into molten tin.

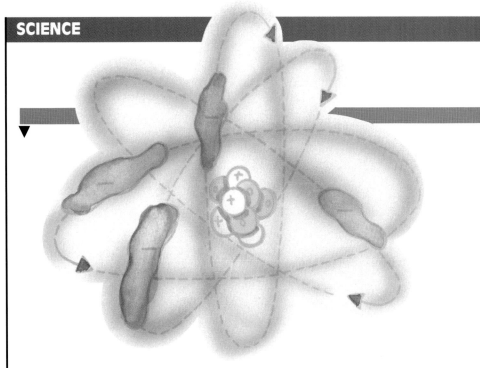

At the Heart of the Atom

The nucleus contains most of an atom's mass. It is made up of two kinds of particles called "protons" and "neutrons." Protons have a single positive charge—the kind of charge that marks the positive end of a battery, which is marked with a (+) sign. Neutrons have no electrical charge. Scientists have come to believe that both protons and neutrons are made up of smaller particles called "quarks." Each proton and neutron is made up of three quarks.

Unleashing Nuclear Power

In the 1940s, scientists tried to unleash the energy stored inside the atom. Their plan was simple: If high-speed particles could be shot into the nucleus of an atom, the nucleus would split into two smaller atoms releasing a great amount of energy.

Atomic Energy in Use

There are many uses for the energy that is generated by splitting the atom, or atomic energy. It was used in atomic bombs. It is also used in atomic power plants that produce electricity, for ships and submarines, and even for tiny pacemakers that help people who have heart conditions.

Splitting the Atom

Although it took the work of hundreds of scientists to actually split the atom, the basic idea came from one of the most famous scientists of all time, Albert Einstein. His "Special Theory of Relativity," which he published in 1905, gave him—and others—the idea that energy would be released if atoms were split.

The First Atomic Bomb

When the first atomic bomb was dropped, it sped toward earth just like any other bomb. About 1,850 feet (564 m) off the ground, an explosion was set off inside. Uranium atoms were split, which shot speeding particles of uranium into the mass of uranium inside the bomb, creating a tremendous amount of energy.

Nuclear Devastation

The bomb dropped on the Japanese city of Nagasaki had the force of 21,000 tons of TNT explosive. The blast was so deadly that almost 39,000 people were killed.

Modern Nuclear Reactors ▲

In a modern nuclear reactor, uranium is sealed in containers called "rods" that are grouped together. These containers are arranged so that a coolant can flow into the reactor if it gets too hot. Control rods of other materials (such as boron) are used to absorb neutrons and keep the nuclear reaction from turning into an atomic explosion. There is also a thick shield of concrete or steel to contain the radioactivity.

The Dangers of ▲
Atomic Fallout

An atomic explosion draws dust and dirt into the giant mushroom-shaped cloud that rises over the place where the bomb went off. As this happens, this dirt and dust are covered with radioactive particles, which are carried up into the atmosphere to drift around with the wind. Eventually, they fall back to the earth—far from where the bomb exploded. These deadly radioactive particles are called "fallout."

In 1986, there was an atomic power accident in what was then the Soviet Union, at Chernobyl, near the large city of Kiev. One day in April, there was an explosion inside the nuclear reactor. A huge cloud of radioactive particles escaped from the reactor, which swept westward and northward, covering much of Europe. Only 31 people were killed in the Soviet Union, but 200,000 were taken from their homes for their own safety. Even worse, millions of people and other creatures were exposed to the possibly deadly radiation that made its way as far away as Scandinavia.

A Nuclear Accident

In 1979, there was an accident at the Three Mile Island nuclear plant near Harrisburg, Pennsylvania. The core of the plant's reactor suffered a partial meltdown—it was partially destroyed by overheating—releasing radioactive gases into the air. The event led to many changes in the way nuclear power plants are run and to more criticism of atomic power.

The Study of Substances

Chemistry is the study of substances. People study chemistry for two reasons: To discover what the substances on earth are like, and to try to make new substances that can be useful for mankind.

The Branches of Chemistry

Scientists have divided chemistry into several different branches. Organic chemistry studies carbon-containing substances. Physical chemistry studies chemistry that is linked to physics, the science that deals with matter and energy. Analytical chemistry studies what objects are made of. Structural chemistry studies how atoms are arranged in a substance. Biochemistry studies the compounds and chemical reactions found in living organisms.

Chemicals All Around

The chemical industry uses chemicals—and the discoveries of people who study chemistry—to create products for people to use. The chemical industry began in the 1800s when people wanted new, different-colored dyes for their clothes. Scientists experimented until they found new ways to produce colors that could be used safely and efficiently in the clothing industry. Today, the chemical industry is everywhere we look—from our clothing and our food to the furniture in our homes and the cars we drive.

Discovering Gravity

Newton, who is generally considered to be the founder of modern physics, made several very important scientific discoveries. According to a legend that probably is not true, Newton saw an apple drop straight down from a tree branch and decided that the earth attracted the apple. This led him to discover the law of gravity.

All Kinds of Energy

Physics, the oldest of all sciences, is the study of matter and energy. It studies the different states of matter—solid, liquid, gas, and plasma—and their makeup. It also studies light, heat, sound, electricity, and radio waves.

Water changes from liquid to vapor (or gas) when it is heated to boiling in a teapot.

135

All Living Things

Biology is the study of all living things—from bacteria so small that you cannot see them without a powerful microscope to trees like the giant redwoods of California, which grow up to more than 300 feet (90 m) high.

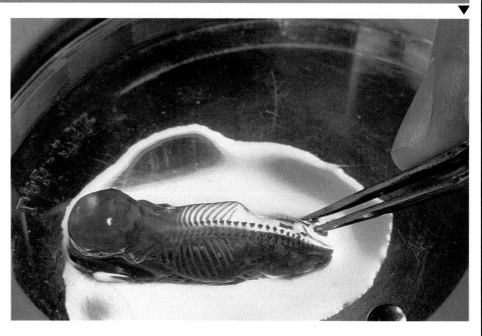

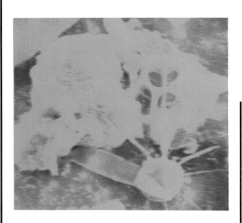

Plants and Animals ▲

Biologists, like all scientists, tend to specialize in one subject or another. Basically, biology is divided into two main branches. Botany is the study of plants, and zoology is the study of animals.

Studying the Stars

Astronomy is the study of the planets and stars. Astronomers not only study what the planets, stars, and galaxies of the universe are like, they also try to answer questions like "How are stars born, and why do they die?" and "How did the universe come about?"

Living by the Stars

Thousands of years ago, people used the stars to figure out the time of year and the time of day in order to know when to plant and harvest their crops. People who could "read" the stars were treated with great respect, often becoming religious and political leaders in the community.

Measuring the Galaxy

An American astronomer named Henrietta Leavitt (1868-1921) was one of the first scientists to think of a way to measure our galaxy. She identified certain stars, called Cepheid variables, which could be used for distance finding. She was able to calculate that Andromeda, another galaxy close to ours, is a little over 2 million light years away.

Babylonian Calendars

As far as we can tell, even cave people studied the stars to learn about weather and seasons. The first serious students of the stars were the ancient Babylonians. They began keeping accurate records of what happened in the sky over 5,000 years ago, and they were able to use their discoveries to create accurate calendars.

A Star Called the Sun

Our sun is exactly the same kind of object as the other stars in the nighttime sky. The only difference between the sun and any of the other stars you see is that it is closer to earth than they are.

Studying Sunspots

Scientists did not get interested in how the sun looked until the first telescopes showed sunspots that could be seen on the surface of the sun from time to time. Galileo, the great scientist of the 1600s, began keeping records of these sunspots in 1610. Scientists have studied them—and the sun—ever since.

Looking at the Sun ▼

The light and energy of the sun come from nuclear reactions deep inside the sun itself. Because huge amounts of heat and light are produced, looking at them can damage your eyes permanently. You should also never look at the sun through a telescope without some kind of protection for your eyes.

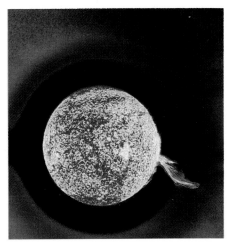

Glowing Arcs of Light ▶

Far to the north—and far to the south—the nighttime sky is sometimes filled with brightly colored lights. These lights flicker across the sky in glowing arcs, in spreading fans of light, or even in bright flashes like giant searchlights. These lights—or *aurora*, as they are called by scientists—are caused by great explosions, or "flares," on the surface of the sun. When a flare takes place, millions of small, electrically charged particles are shot into space. When they reach earth, they bump into the atoms of the air. These tiny collisions produce the light of the aurora.

The Sun's Cool Spots

Sunspots are large markings that appear from time to time on the surface of the sun. They look dark to us because they are thousands of degrees cooler than the parts of the sun around them. The sizes and numbers of these spots change over time, but no one knows why this happens. Sunspots seem to reach a peak every 11 years or so; then their number and size decrease for six years before starting to increase again.

Catching the Lights ▲

In the northern half of the globe, you can best see the Northern Lights around Hudson Bay in Canada, in northern Scotland, and in Norway and Sweden. The Southern Lights are best seen from Antarctica, which is why few people have ever seen them.

◀ A Very Big Sun

The sun is almost 864,900 miles (1,390,000 km) in diameter, which is around ten times bigger than Jupiter, the biggest planet, and about 109 times bigger than Earth. Even though the volume of the sun is almost 1,300,000 times as great as the volume of the earth, the amount of material inside the sun—its mass, as scientists call it— is only about 333,000 times as great as the earth's. This means that the matter inside the sun is really only $\frac{1}{4}$ as dense as the matter inside the earth.

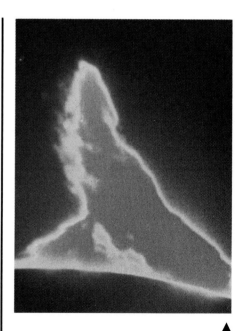

That's Very Hot!

The surface of the sun usually runs about 10,800°F (6,000°C). Scientists believe that the center of the sun is a little more than 25,000,000°F (or 14,000,000°C).

Inside the Sun ▲

The sun is a ball of hot gas, with no solid or liquid center at all. It is mostly made up of hydrogen gas, along with helium and small amounts of a few other elements. There are no solids because the sun is so hot that even iron is present as a gas.

The Color of the Sun

Particles in our atmosphere change how the sun looks to us on any given day. It may look white, or yellow, or even red. Scientists have more exact ways to study and label stars and suns. They put stars on a scale that ranges from bluish-white to red. On this scale, our sun is yellow.

A Halo Around the Sun

The corona is the part of the sun's atmosphere that is farthest away from the sun itself. It actually looks like a glowing white halo around the sun. It is made up of electrically charged particles that are only $1/7$ as hot as the center of the sun itself.

Stars of All Sizes

Scientists classify stars by size and density, from giant stars down to tiny neutron stars that are only 12 miles (20 km) in diameter. On this scale, our sun is called a "dwarf."

Our Ever-burning Sun

Scientists believe that the sun has been sending out heat and light for about five billion years. They expect it to go on for another five billion years or so before it finally burns itself up.

◄ Seeing the Moon

The moon has no light of its own; it shines only because it reflects the sun's light. As the moon turns on its axis and travels around the earth, each side of the moon has two weeks of darkness and two weeks of light. When the moon comes between the earth and the sun, the side that is always turned toward the earth is in darkness and is invisible to us. We call this the "new moon."

A Lunar Eclipse ▼

Sometimes the moon is on the opposite side of the earth to the sun. When this occurs, it may move into the earth's shadow, forming a lunar eclipse.

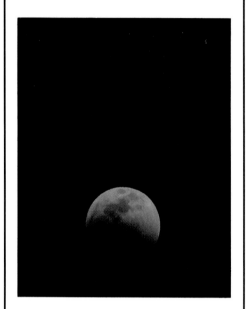

A Solar Eclipse ▲

A solar eclipse occurs when the moon passes between the sun and the earth and blocks out the sun's light.

The Dark Side of the Moon

One of the curiosities about our moon is that one side of it—the side we call the "dark side of the moon"—is always facing away from us, even though it receives more sunlight than the side we face. This is especially strange, since the moon turns around and around in space, just the way the earth does. The moon turns around once in almost exactly the same length of time as it takes for it to move around the earth. As a result, it always shows us the same side.

Craters on the Moon ▲

The moon's craters are giant holes or dents. Some are quite small, but they average about 4,900 feet (1,500 m) across. Most of them were made by meteors striking the moon from space. Others have rings around them, perhaps because they were volcanoes at one time.

Our Spotted Moon ◀

The dark spots on the moon—called *maria* or "seas"—have few craters. Scientists believe that these seas are made of lava from volcanoes. The lava probably filled in the craters in that area and left a dark "stain" on the moon's surface.

A Mistaken Planet

In 1972, scientists announced that there was another planet, called Planet X, beyond Pluto. Within a short time, however, it was clear that no such planet actually existed.

Real Moon Rocks

The "moon rocks" brought back by American astronauts gave scientists a real first-hand look at what the moon was actually made of. They learned that the moon was chemically different than the earth. This discovery convinced scientists that the moon was not a part of the earth that broke away.

Our Sun's Planets

There are nine major planets in our solar system. Each of them moves around our sun in its own orbit. In order of their distance from the sun they are: Mercury, Venus, Earth, Mars, Jupiter, Saturn, Uranus, Neptune, and Pluto.

Fiery Mercury ▲

Because Mercury is so close to the sun, it takes far less time to complete its trip around the sun. As a result, its year is only 88 days—about as long as one of the seasons we have on Earth. Mercury turns very slowly, so that each of its days lasts almost 180 of our Earth days. Mercury's position near the sun also gives it extremely high temperatures. Because Mercury is so small, its gravity is so weak that it cannot even hold the gases of its atmosphere close to the planet.

The Morning Star

Venus's path around the sun is inside Earth's path, so the planet appears to us as a morning or evening star, rising just before or setting just after the sun. In some places, Venus "rises" as much as three hours before dawn and "sets" three hours after sunset. Because it is so bright, people often think of it as a star rather than a planet.

Beautiful to Look At ▲

People of ancient times named Venus after the Roman goddess of love, because they thought the planet looked so beautiful. The surface of the planet is anything but beautiful. In fact, it has one of the most hostile environments in our solar system. Its atmosphere is 96 percent carbon dioxide, and its top layer is made up entirely of dangerous sulfuric acid. Chemical reactions in the atmosphere create lightning and other electrical disturbances all the time. And, the temperature on the surface is around 860°F (560°C)—hotter than most fires.

Our Sister Planet ◄

Mars is so much like Earth that it is often called our "sister planet." It is close to Earth in size and distance from the sun. It also has a temperature closer to ours than other planets. Mars even has an atmosphere of sorts. The Martian day is about the same length as ours, although a year on Mars is almost twice as long as one of Earth's years.

The Red Planet ▲

Mars often appears red in color because of the orange sands that cover its surface. It looks red even to people looking at it without telescopes. This color led people to name the planet after Mars, the Roman god of war who was associated with the red color of blood.

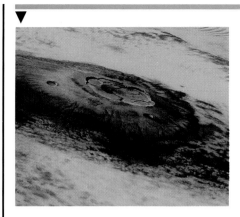

The Last Planet Discovered

Pluto, the ninth planet from the sun, was discovered in 1930 by an American scientist working in Flagstaff, Arizona. As they had done with the discovery of Neptune, scientists used mathematical calculations to predict where it would be.

Moons Big and Small

Saturn has 21 separate moons. They range in size from little moons barely 50 miles (80 km) in diameter up to the largest one, Titan, which is 3,170 miles (5,100 km) in diameter. Titan is so big that it even has its own atmosphere. It would not be nice to breathe this air, since it is made up of nitrogen and the deadly poison, cyanide.

Is There Life on Mars?

In the 1800s, Italian astronomer Giovanni Schiaparelli discovered dark markings on Mars. He called these markings *canali*, which was erroneously translated as "canals" instead of "channels." As a result, people thought that since the planet seemed to have water, it might very well have life of some kind. Later astronomers even thought the bands of color were plants. These observations led people to think that, of all the other places in our solar system, the most likely place for life was Mars.

Jupiter's Unpleasant Climate

Like many other planets, Jupiter has a hostile environment. It is mostly liquid hydrogen, with a solid core deep within the planet. Its huge atmosphere is made of hydrogen with clouds of ammonia. The outer layer of that atmosphere is just about all that we can see of Jupiter from the outside. It also has unpleasant temperatures. The outer atmosphere may be as cold as $-202°F$ ($-130°C$). Near the planet's center, the temperature probably reaches $45,000°F$ ($25,000°C$).

The Rings of Saturn

Saturn, the sixth planet from the sun, has a system of rings around it. Until recently, people thought that Saturn was the only planet with rings. Now, scientists know that both Jupiter and Uranus have rings as well, although they are not as large and spectacular as the rings of Saturn. Saturn has seven flat rings surrounding the planet's middle. They are made up of tiny particles, including both grains of dust and pieces of ice that sometimes are as big as small moons.

Experiments on Mars

On July 20 and September 3, 1976, two American space expeditions landed on Mars. These unmanned space ships, called *Viking Landers,* carried out many experiments on the planet's surface. They found no sign of life on the planet, although some experiments gave signs that there might be micro-organisms of some kind in the planet's soil. These and other space program flights convinced scientists that Mars's famous "canals" were an optical illusion caused by shadows of craters and mountains on the planet's surface.

The Largest Planet ▲

Jupiter is the largest of the planets in our solar system. It was named after Jupiter, the most powerful and greatest of the Roman gods. Jupiter is over 11 times bigger than Earth in diameter and 300 times bigger in mass. In fact, it is bigger than all the other planets put together.

A Man on the Moon

Apollo 11 was the first spacecraft to land humans on the moon. On July 20, 1969, the lunar module Eagle, carrying Neil Armstrong and Edwin Aldrin, landed in the area known as the Sea of Tranquility. Armstrong became the first man to set foot on the moon with the words, "That's one small step for a man, one giant leap for mankind." Together with Aldrin, Armstrong spent about two hours outside the spacecraft, taking photographs, setting up scientific experiments, and collecting rock samples.

Satellite Firsts

The first unmanned satellite was Sputnik 1. It was launched by the Soviet Union on October 4, 1957. It was soon followed by Sputnik 2 in November of 1957. The second satellite carried the dog Laika, which was the first living creature to orbit Earth. The first American satellite, Explorer I, was launched in January 1958.

Spending Time in Space

Skylab was a 99-ton (90-tonne) orbital laboratory, observatory, and workshop. Beginning in May of 1973, three crews of astronauts spent long periods of time in Skylab. The first crew stayed 28 days, the second, 59 days, and the third, 84 days. All the astronauts returned from these long spaceflights fit and well.

Studying the Moon ▲

Five more manned moon landings followed Apollo 11. In all, the Apollo astronauts brought back 848 pounds (385 kg) of lunar soil and rocks and an enormous quantity of information that is still being studied by scientists.

A Very Long Journey

In 1972, the United States launched Pioneer 10 on a 620-million-mile (1-billion-kilometer) voyage to Jupiter. After its encounter with the planet, Pioneer headed out of the Solar System, which it left in June 1983, when it was nearly 3 billion miles (5 billion kilometers) from the sun. Just in case it eventually encounters intelligent beings from other worlds, it carries a plaque showing human beings and their planet Earth.

Another Type of Space Exploration ▲

A new era in space exploration began on April 12, 1981, when the American space shuttle first went into orbit. It was the first reusable spacecraft that was able to fly back from space and land like an aircraft. Mainly used to launch satellites, the shuttle flights also carried specially designed payloads. One was Spacelab, a reusable space laboratory built by the European Space Agency.

Artificial Satellites

There are many different kinds of artificial satellites. *Communications satellites* are used for broadcasting, telephone, and radio. *Weather satellites* are helpful in weather forecasting. *Earth survey satellites* detect mineral deposits, diseased crops, and sources of pollution, and aid in the making of maps. *Military satellites* are used for reconnaissance and intelligence gathering. *Astronomical satellites,* which are observatories in space, orbit above the blanketing layer of the earth's atmosphere.

Revolutionizing Long-distance Travel

HOTOL (Horizontal Take-off and Landing) is intended to be a cross between an airplane and an orbital spacecraft. Its designers hope that it will revolutionize long-distance flights around the world. For example, a journey from London, England, to Sydney, Australia, could take as little as 40 minutes.

When Sparks Fly

If an object is highly charged with electricity, tiny particles of electricity may jump off of it. These electrons, as they are called, actually form a spark. That spark is nothing more than the glowing path made by millions of electrons as they jump through the air.

Letting Electricity Flow

In the world of electricity, a conductor is a medium that electricity flows through quite easily. Water is an excellent conductor of electricity—which is why you are always told not to swim during a thunderstorm. Most metals are also good conductors of electricity.

Flashes of Lightning

Lightning is really nothing more than electricity. Scientists believe that lightning is produced when tiny particles of ice and drops of water inside a cloud are tossed around and knocked against each other by the wind. When they rub against one another, they produce an electrical spark, sending lightning down from the cloud.

Curbing the Flow of Electricity ◄

An insulator is a medium that does not conduct electricity well. Rubber, glass, plastic, and dry air resist the flow of electricity and can be used to insulate objects from electrical flow.

Magnet Mystery

In 1820, Danish scientist Hans Oersted discovered that a magnetic compass needle would swing in a different direction when an electric current was brought near it. This led to the invention of the electromagnet (electrical wire wound around a piece of iron), which can be turned on and off.

A scrap yard crane is an electromagnet that can lift a heavy load.

Inside a Battery

Batteries are simple devices. They consist of two or more "cells" (a flashlight battery usually has two to three). The simplest cells are made up of plates of two different kinds of metal, which are kept in salty or acid liquid. When the two plates are connected by a wire, electrical current flows between them.

Letting Electricity Pass

An electrical circuit is a path going from one place to another that allows electricity to pass through it. The "path" is usually made of metal wire, since it conducts electricity very well.

Switching On and Off

An electrical switch is simply a device that interrupts the flow of electricity. It usually does this by creating a gap in the wiring of the circuit. This keeps the electricity from flowing all the way through the circuit until the switch is closed again.

Keeping a Check on Electricity

When electricity is used, there is always the chance that too much electrical power will pass through the wires of the electrical circuit. If this happens, the wires can become too hot and start a fire. To protect against this danger, fuses are placed in the electrical circuit. A *fuse* is nothing more than a short length of a wire that melts very easily. This way, if the wires on the electrical circuit start to get too hot, the metal in the fuse will melt and break the circuit before the main wires get too hot and start a fire. In many homes, fuses have been replaced by circuit breakers—simple switches that automatically turn off when the power passing through a circuit gets too great.

Bringing Electricity to Your Home

Electricity is first made in huge power plants. It flows through a switchgear, which controls its flow and can cut it off if there are any problems along the miles of wires ahead. From here, it goes to a transformer, which increases the pressure so that it can be sent over long distances. High voltage lines then carry the electricity to an area near to where it will be used. The power goes on to a substation, where other transformers reduce the electrical pressure (or "voltage" as it is called), so that it can be safely used. Finally, it is delivered over other wires to your home, business, store, and every other place that uses it.

Back and Forth

Alternating current (AC) flows back and forth in two different directions. The electrical current switches directions so quickly that there is not even the slightest flicker in a light connected to it. Alternating current is used in most of North America because it is easy to send over long distances and because little electricity is wasted as it travels.

Power Plant Particulars ◄

There are two main kinds of power plants. *Thermal plants* use steam turbines to drive generators to make electricity. The steam to drive these turbines comes from burning fuel like oil or coal or even from a nuclear reactor. *Hydroelectric plants* use falling water from a waterfall or dam to drive the turbines. The difficulty with hydroelectric plants is finding a suitable location—they must be built where the water flow is suitable and where they would be close to the towns or factories that need the power.

Hoover Dam in Colorado produces hydroelectric energy.

Measuring Electricity

We measure electric pressure—the amount of electricity flowing through a circuit—in volts. In the United States, most circuits in our homes are set up to run with 110 volts; heavy-duty circuits for washing machines, dryers, and dishwashers are set to have 220 volts. In Great Britain, homes use between 200 and 250 volts.

Generating Electricity

A *generator* is a simple device for making electricity. The very first one was made in 1831 by Michael Faraday, an English scientist. Faraday moved a magnet close to a coil of wire, discovering that this action made electrical current flow through the wire. Ever since, generators, or *dynamos,* as they are sometimes called, have been used to make electricity for everything from homes to ships.

149

Let It Shine

Light helps us see in two different ways. First, many objects, such as the sun, stars, flames of a fire, and even light bulbs, send out light of their own. More often, we see things because they reflect the light that is shining on them from some other source of light—a lamp, the sun, and so on.

Light's Radiation

Light is actually a kind of radiation. It is different from other radiation in the way that it can be seen by the human eye. Scientists generally identify light as electromagnetic radiation with a wavelength between that of cosmic rays and radio waves.

Partial Light

A translucent object allows only some of the light to pass through. You generally see only shadows or just a general brightness rather than the actual shapes, colors, and surfaces of objects outside.

Absorbing the Light

An opaque substance absorbs or reflects all of the light falling on it. This means that it is impossible to see through an opaque object.

Spectrum Reflections

The color of an object depends on which part of the spectrum it reflects. Most objects reflect some colors and absorb others. Something green looks that color because it reflects most of the light in the green part of the spectrum.

Just Passing Through ▶

An object is transparent when all of the light falling on it is able to pass through it entirely.

Bouncing Off a Surface ◄

Reflection is light bouncing off a surface. The word *reflection* comes from a Latin word that means "bending back." Light that strikes an object bends back in exactly the same way that a wave bounces back from the side of a bathtub or from a rocky cliff.

Changing Directions

In 1621, a Dutch scientist named Willebrord Snell discovered that the direction of light changes when it passes from one transparent substance to another. When light passes from air to glass, it bends or "refracts." It also refracts when it passes from air to water. This happens because the speed of light is different as it goes through each substance. It is fastest going through air.

A Spectrum of Light ▲

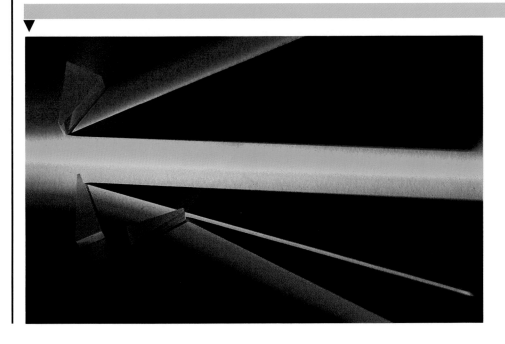

Back in the 1600s, Sir Isaac Newton discovered that white light actually has the whole rainbow of colors in it. That rainbow, which is called the "spectrum," has red, orange, yellow, green, blue, indigo, and violet light in it. When white light (the kind that comes to us from the sun or from a regular light bulb) passes through a prism—a specially shaped piece of glass—it breaks down into these seven colors. A similar phenomenon occurs when light passes through water—which is why you see a rainbow after it rains on a sunny day.

Traveling in Waves ▲

One of the main effects of light is *polarization*. It is best explained by thinking of light as traveling in waves, like ripples, along a rope. If you shake the rope quickly—up and down, side to side, or at an angle—the ripples will travel down the length of the rope. But, if you try to shake a rope that passes between upright sticks, you would only be able to shake it up and down—not side to side. When you coat a piece of glass or plastic with a chemical called herapathite (or a chemical like it), you make the light that passes through the glass or plastic move only in certain directions. This helps make the light less bright, which is why polarized plates are used in making sunglasses and scientific instruments.

Speed of Light

Light travels at a speed of 186,000 miles (300,000 km) per second when it travels in outer space or in an area without air to slow it down. (Light, as you know, travels at different speeds, depending on what it is traveling through. It would be slower through water, glass, or other substances.)

Well-traveled Light ▲

The light that comes to us from the sun (about 93,150,000 miles, or 150,000,000 km, away from us) takes about eight minutes to get here. In a single year, light travels 5,880,870,000,000 miles (9,470,000,000,000 km).

Powerful Lasers ◀

Lasers can send an intense beam over long distances because they are different from regular light in one important way. Ordinary light contains waves vibrating in several different directions. Lasers are *coherent*—all of their waves are vibrating in the same direction at the same time. This makes them powerful and intense—able to do everything from burn their way through metal to "read" the messages coded onto the surface of a CD disc.

To Make a Picture

Photography film is coated with crystals of silver bromide. Energy from light is absorbed by these crystals. As this happens, they are changed so that when the film is developed, the crystals that have been struck by light will react differently from those that have not been struck by light. This accounts for the different colors and shapes that you see in the finished picture.

Traveling by Waves

The term *radiation* comes to us from the Latin word *radius* meaning "beam" or "ray." In science, radiation is the term used for anything that travels by waves—light, heat, X rays, or even cosmic rays.

Very Short Waves

X rays are electromagnetic waves that have wavelengths between $1/10$ of a nanometer and 100 nanometers. (A *nanometer* is 1-billionth of a meter, about 0.000000039 of an inch.)

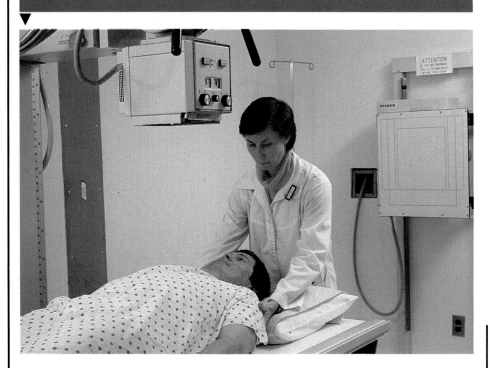

Valuable X Rays

X rays pass through many kinds of materials that reflect light. When an object is exposed to X rays, we can often see right inside. When a broken arm is placed between a source of X rays and a piece of photographic film, the X rays pass right through a person's clothing and skin to show us a picture of a dark shadow that is actually the person's bone. As you probably know, X rays are very valuable in medicine.

This doctor is studying an X ray to determine the extent of an injury.

Sunlight and Ultraviolet Light

Ultraviolet rays have a longer wavelength, beginning where X rays leave off and extending up to almost 400 nanometers. Sunlight contains ultraviolet rays, which is beneficial to us since these rays help our bodies produce Vitamin D.

From Violet to Red

Visible light is made up of radiation with wavelengths that are a little longer than those of ultraviolet rays. It runs from about 400 nanometers, which is the color violet, up to about 740 nanometers, the color red.

Radiation Spectrum

Gamma Rays	High Frequency ↑
X Rays	
Ultraviolet	
Visible Light	
Infrared	
Microwaves	↓
Radio Waves	Low Frequency

154

Colors of Decreasing Wavelengths ▼

The colors that we see through a spectrum or in a rainbow are simply light waves arranged in order of decreasing wavelength: Red, orange, yellow, green, blue, and violet.

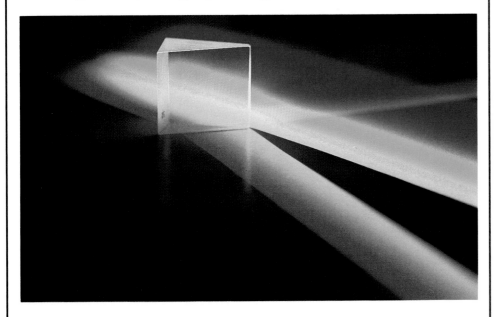

This rainbow in Hawaii is a beautiful sight.

▼

Feeling the Sun's Heat

Infrared rays are longer than those of visible light, running from about 740 nanometers up to 100,000 nanometers. Short infrared waves can travel through mists and clouds that normally stop visible light. Longer infrared waves are felt as heat, which is why the sun's light feels hot to us.

The Long and Short of It ◄

Radar, microwaves, radios, and televisions all use electromagnetic waves to send signals or perform tasks. The waves used in microwave ovens, for example, are about 4.7 inches (12 cm) in length. The ones used for television broadcasting are a little over two yards (two meters) in length. Radio broadcast waves are the longest of all. They are about 2/3 of a mile (1 km) in length.

Beware of Sunburn

Sunburn occurs when too much ultraviolet light comes in contact with the skin. This can lead to more than just redness and discomfort, since scientists now believe that long exposure to ultraviolet light can cause skin cancer.

Radio Waves

When Guglielmo Marconi showed the world his first wireless "radio" in 1896, it made use of electromagnetic waves to send sound from place to place. Marconi's device was simple. It had a coil connected to a battery, which caused high voltage across two metal spheres. Because of the presence of electricity in the spheres, a stream of sparks jumped across the gap between them whenever Marconi tapped an electrical switch. This stream of sparks sent vibrations, or oscillations, up an antenna—and out into the atmosphere.

Dangerous Waves

The beta rays that come from radioactive materials are extremely dangerous. They can cause burning as well as skin cancer. Gamma rays (the shortest waves of all) and X rays can cause even more damage. In small doses, they are often used to kill dangerous cells, like cancer cells, within the body. Long contact with them, however, can kill healthy cells and cause permanent damage to the body.

Radio Wave Discoveries

Radio waves have helped uncover many unusual things. One of these is a *pulsar*, a tiny, heavily condensed neutron star. Another is the remains of *supernovas*, huge explosions in which giant stars blew themselves up. They have also helped scientists discover galaxies almost 500 million light years away. They even helped scientists discover *quasars*, objects that appear something like stars but are much farther away and have vast amounts of energy.

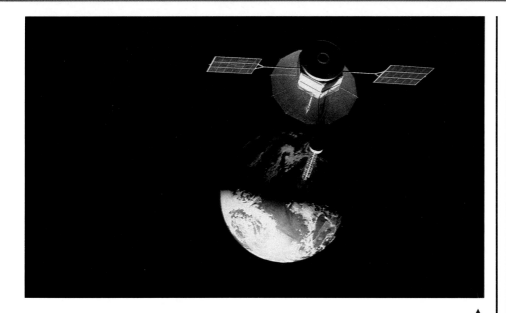

Receiving Radio Waves

Radio waves get weaker and weaker as they cover great distances. A radio or TV program that is being broadcast over a long distance needs to be received and rebroadcast at several stops along the way in order to be received well. Scientists have solved this problem by using communications satellites above the surface of the earth. Signals are sent up to these satellites, which then beam down to exactly where they are to go—without lots of stops, towers, or radio equipment along the way.

Reflecting Radio Waves

In 1902, Arthur E. Kennelly and Oliver Heaviside discovered that there was a layer of *ionization* or electrified particles, high above the earth's surface. This layer acts as a mirror to reflect radio waves back to the earth instead of having them go off into space. Because of this layer of ionization, radio waves can be sent from North America to Europe.

Carbon-14 Dating

All living things contain particles of the element carbon in the form of carbon-12. However, there is always a tiny amount of radioactive carbon, called carbon-14, present in all living things. As time goes on, this carbon-14 breaks down. It takes a long time to do this—about 10,000 years or so—but, once a plant or animal dies, carbon-14 breaks down steadily enough for scientists to measure exactly how much of it has disappeared over time. In this way, scientists can figure out how old something is. Carbon-14 dating has helped scientists discover the age of everything from cave paintings to fossils.

Radio Telescopes ▶

Until recently, most astronomers worked with giant optical telescopes. Now, they use radio telescopes to send out radio waves in order to detect radio waves coming to us from the sun, the planets, the stars, or other bodies in space. Since these radio telescopes are more sensitive and more accurate than old-fashioned telescopes—and can identify objects farther away—scientists have found objects in space that they did not know existed.

157

How Things Work

Helium gas or hot-air is used to make a balloon and its passenger compartment lighter than the air around it, causing the balloon to rise up into the sky.

Today, our telephone system uses satellites to connect one phone to another in a process that takes just seconds to complete.

Staying in the Air

Airplanes stay in the air because their wings provide lift to hold them up. Airplane wings are flat on the bottom with an asymmetrical curve on top. Air moving over the upper surface of the wing has to travel faster and farther than air moving under the wing. This causes low pressure above the wing that sucks the wing upward and keeps the plane in the air.

Taking Off

The most difficult part of aircraft flight is actually getting the plane into the air. In order to lift itself up into the air, a plane must be moving forward very fast. This speed gets the air moving over the wings in such a way that it can lift the plane upward. Today's jumbo jets are so large that they must often use a runway 10,000 feet (3000 m) long in order to get enough lift to go up into the air. The power for getting down the runway and moving through the air comes from the plane's engines.

For the Adventuresome

Gliders stay in the air by going fast enough for the wings to give them the lift needed to stay in the air. The pilot simply keeps the glider pointed slightly downward so that the air under the wings pushes the glider upward as it heads back to the ground. Gliders are easy to keep in the air because they are light in weight and have very long wings. Their weight and wings help them catch upcurrents of air, or "thermals."

Glider

Getting Gliders To Fly

The biggest problem in flying a glider is getting it into the air. Many gliders are towed into the air behind airplanes. Others are launched from behind fast-moving cars. Some gliders have even been shot into the air by giant rubber cords—like a slingshot shooting a rock or stick.

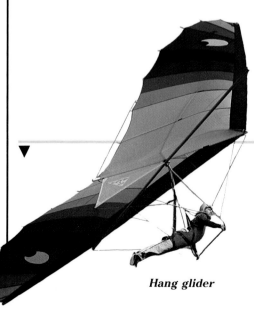

Hang glider

That's a Big Kite!

A modern hang glider is really very much like a kite. The airfoil, or wing, is made of cloth that has been stretched over a lightweight metal frame. The pilot hangs underneath in a special harness. In most cases, the pilot gets the hang glider into the air by running down a hillside. Once the glider is in the air, currents of warm air lift it and keep it soaring along. The pilot can steer the hang glider by moving the control bar. This moves the position of the airfoil and allows the hang glider to change directions.

Whirlybird Maneuvers ▶

Helicopters use their whirling rotors to lift themselves from the ground. They can go up or down depending on how the rotors are angled. If the rotors are angled sharply up, for example, the helicopter will go up. By tilting the rotors one way or the other, a pilot can also make a helicopter go right or left.

Let's Go Fly a Kite ▲

All kites work in pretty much the same way. The body of the kite gives it enough lift to stay in the air. To get a kite up, start by unwinding a few feet of the flying cord. Then run into the wind until the kite lifts up into the air. Once the kite is in the air, stand with your back to the wind. Let out more cord whenever the wind carries the kite farther up into the air. Pull in the cord whenever the kite falls back toward the ground.

Balloons Afloat ▲

A helium balloon floats because it weighs less than the air it moves through, since helium is an extremely lightweight gas. It is lighter than the air around us. Therefore, when the balloon has been filled with helium, it can rise up and float through the air.

Riding in a Hot-air Balloon ▼

Giant, colorful, hot-air balloons are filled with hot air or helium gas. This makes the balloon and its passenger compartment lighter than the air around it, so the balloon rises up into the sky. In fact, a filled balloon wants to rise so much that it must be held down by heavy sandbags kept inside the passenger compartment. Ropes are also used to tie balloons to the ground until everyone is ready for liftoff. The pilots can make the balloons go higher by throwing sandbags out of the compartment. When they want to land, the pilots simply let air out of the balloon.

Boats Afloat

Boats float for the same reason that branches, leaves, or even light pieces of metal do not sink in the water. They float because they weigh less than the water that is pushed out of the way as they go along the surface. Boats are man-made objects that are light enough to do the same thing. This is why the first boats were dugout canoes—logs that were hollowed out to take away weight and to make room for people to sit. Later, reeds and lightweight wood were used. Today, steel and fiberglass are most often used, since these are both light in weight and strong enough to hold people and goods safely.

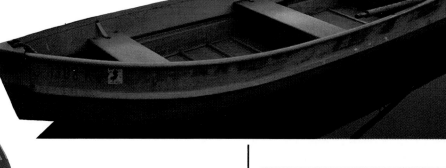

Catching the Wind

Sailing with triangular sails became popular when people realized that they could shift the sail from side to side in order to keep it filled with wind. This way, they could sail from place to place even if the wind was not blowing exactly in that direction.

Propeller Wonders▲

Propellers have blades coming out of a central hub. Each of these blades forms a spiral from the hub. When the propeller turns, air or water is pushed around and around and "thrust," as movement forward or backward is called, is produced. This pushes the boat or airplane. Turning the blades in the opposite direction can make a boat move backward. Airplanes, as you've probably noticed, do not really back up too often.

Steering a Sailboat

A boat's sails must be kept pointing either toward or away from the wind so that they stay filled with wind. The boat is actually steered with a piece of wood or metal called a "rudder." The rudder sticks out behind the boat and controls how the water moves past it. By moving the rudder to the left, for example, the boat will move to the right, and vice versa.

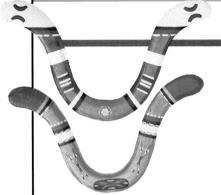

Amazing Boomerangs

You probably will be surprised to learn that not all boomerangs come back to you. Some boomerangs are straight, not curved, and they are used as deadly hunting weapons. "Return" boomerangs are curved and have one flat side and one that is rounded.

Switching Gears

Gears are different-sized wheels that control how many times you must pedal in order to turn a bicycle's back wheel. If the bike's chain wheel (the wheel that the chain is on) were the same size as the wheel it was attached to at the back of the bike, the rear wheel would turn around once each time your pedals went around. If that chain wheel were twice as big, the rear wheel would go around twice each time your pedals turned. By having the bicycle chain work wheels of different sizes, you can make it easier to pedal when you are going up a hill and give yourself more pedaling power when you are cruising along a flat road or rushing down a hill.

It's as Easy as Riding a Bike

Today's bicycles are made of a metal— usually steel or aluminum—frame between two wheels of the same size. When the rider pushes down on the bike's pedals, the crank (the long piece of metal that the pedals are mounted to) turns the chain wheel and chain. The chain is connected to the rear wheel so that the rear wheel turns as you pedal. This pushes the bike forward. The only problem then is keeping your balance!

A Man-made Fish

A submarine dives under the ocean by filling its tanks with water. Once underwater, it can float just like a fish, using its propellers to push itself forward, backward, and to the sides. To bring the submarine to the surface, the crew puts compressed air into the tanks. This forces the water out, making the ship lighter and bringing it to the surface.

Putting on the Brakes

Two main types of brakes are used on bicycles today. The more old-fashioned kinds of brakes are made of pieces of metal that press against the hub (the center part) of a bike's rear wheel. Pressing backwards on your pedals makes the brake push against the hub. If you press lightly, the wheel turns slower. If you press hard, the wheel stops completely. Hand or "caliper" brakes are found on racing and mountain bikes. These have small levers that press pieces of rubber against the sides (the rims) of the front and back wheels. Again, the harder you press the slower the wheel is going to turn.

Violin Music

Violin strings are stretched across a long, thin piece of wood called the "fingerboard." Attached to this is the belly, or soundbody, of the instrument, which makes the sound of the strings louder. Instead of plucking on the strings (the way you do with a rubber band or a guitar), a violinist scrapes a bow back and forth over the strings. This makes the basic sound of the violin. The sounds can be changed by pressing down on the strings with your fingers to make them shorter or longer—this makes the sounds higher or lower in pitch. By scraping the bow across more than one string at a time, the violinist can play chords, or more than one note at a time.

Playing a Guitar

Guitar players make music by plucking the strings that stretch along the instrument's fingerboard and body. On a regular, or acoustic guitar, the body is designed to increase the sound so that it can be heard by everyone. Electric guitars, on the other hand, use electricity to increase the sound made by plucking the strings. The notes are then reproduced through loudspeakers—which is where the sound comes from when someone plays an electric guitar.

Let's Play the Piano

Despite the way a piano looks, piano music actually comes from strings. Inside a piano are dozens of strings, not very different from the ones you see on a guitar or violin. The length of each string gives it its pitch—high, low, and so on. Pressing up against each string is a "damper," a piece that rests against the string and keeps it from vibrating and making any sound. When you press down on one of the piano's keys, the damper moves away from the string. Then, a small hammer strikes the string and makes the sound. The space inside the piano increases the sound so that it can be heard all over a large room.

From Grapes to Raisins

Raisins are actually dried grapes, which are made in several different ways. Natural raisins are dried in the sun until they turn a grayish-black color. Golden bleached raisins are treated in a special liquid, then exposed to fumes from burning sulfur, and finally dried in a tunnel that slowly takes the water from them. Each of the other different types of raisins is made in pretty much the same ways.

Popping Popcorn

Popcorn pops because it has smaller, harder kernels than other corn. It also has an outer shell that surrounds a lot of moist, starchy material. When the kernels are heated, the moisture inside them turns to steam. When the steam builds up enough pressure, it inflates the starch granules. This causes the kernels to burst and turns them inside out.

Our Favorite Dessert

Ice cream is made of milk fat, sugar, air, and flavors. (Some ice creams also use eggs, but most do not.) You begin by mixing together the milk fat and sugar. This mixture is then heated to kill any germs that might have collected. Then, it is mixed together once again to break the milk fat into tiny pieces. Next, it is stored at a freezing temperature for a while. Every once in a while, the ice cream is mixed to keep it smooth and to keep pieces of ice from getting into the mixture. Then, it is put back in the freezer. Flavors—vanilla, chocolate, fruit, whatever—are usually added while the ice cream is being mixed or frozen.

◄Who Put the Holes in the Cheese?

All cheeses are made by separating the solid part, or curd, from the watery part of sour milk. Swiss cheese is made by taking the curd and heating it to around 125°F (52°C). Then, it is pressed into blocks or circles called "wheels." While the cheese is being stored, carbon dioxide gas (the same gas that we breathe out through our mouths) forms and makes the holes that have made Swiss cheese famous.

Why We Cook

When food is heated, chemicals inside of it change. This not only makes the food easier for our stomachs to work on, it also helps stop the action of germs that can cause disease. Cooking actually can use any one of a dozen methods—baking, boiling, or soaking the food in juices and chemicals that carry out the same chemical process as heating.

The History of Ovens

Long ago, people learned to cook by holding their food over a burning fire. Later, they found that they could make ovens out of stone or clay. These ovens were usually round and could be closed off from the outside in order to hold in the heat. By putting a hole in the oven to take out the smoke, people created an oven that cooked things slowly without burning. Heat either came from a fire underneath or from hot rocks placed inside the oven itself.

Cooking Made Easy

The first closed cooking stoves were invented at the end of the 1700s. These stoves let people control the amount of fire inside the oven better. By the 19th century, stoves were improved. They burned coal or gas and incorporated burners or hot plates, ovens, and boilers for heating water. In the 20th century, electric stoves became more commonplace.

A Cook's Best Friend

The food processor provides cooks with a handy machine for chopping, slicing, and mixing. In the base of the machine is a small electric motor. When the motor is turned on, it turns a shaft that sticks up inside the "work bowl," or the plastic bowl that holds the food. To chop food, the cook attaches two small blades that whirl around and cut the food into tiny pieces. These blades can also stir liquids and mix things that are already chopped up. To slice food, the cook attaches a sharp slicing blade against which the food is pressed to cut it into small pieces.

Baking pastries requires an oven.

165

The Story of Vinegar

Vinegar is made from wine in countries where wine is made, but it may also be made from malted barley, apples, sugar, or rice. Whatever alcoholic liquid is used is pumped into a vessel that is capable of holding up to 12,000 gallons (45,000 liters), although it is only half filled. In the middle of the vessel is a stage on which layers of birch twigs are placed, and below this air holes are bored in it. The liquid is then pumped over the birch twigs through a sparge, which is just like the sprinkler used for watering gardens. This way, a large amount of the liquid is exposed to the air. The process takes about six days; after this time, the vinegar is kept for some months in large storage vessels for the right flavor to be produced.

An Age-old Food

Yogurt is a food that originated in Turkey and the Balkan countries. When yogurt is produced commercially, skimmed milk powder is usually added first to thicken the milk, and bacteria called *Streptococcus thermophilus* are also added to give the correct consistency and flavor. The milk must be at a temperature of about 111°F (44°C) for the bacteria to work. When the milk has cooled to 40°F (5°C), they stop working, but by that time the milk has thickened.

Making Wine

When wine grapes are picked at the end of summer, they are crushed soon after they are picked. Their juice (called must) mixes with the wine yeast found in the grapes themselves and starts to ferment. The wine yeast works to change the sugar in the must into alcohol, although there are many ferments that may spoil the wine. The wine maker exposes the must to the air, since the wine yeast thrives on oxygen and the bad ferments do not. The temperature of fermenting grape juice is also controlled, since the wine yeast works best at 76°F (24°C). When fermentation stops (10-30 days), the juice is transferred to a large wooden vessel called a cask. Six or nine months later, the product is wine. The wine may be bottled at once or, if it is very good quality, it may be left to mature for some months in the cask.

◄Trampling Wine Grapes

Wine grapes are either crushed by treading them or by machine. If people trample the grapes with their feet, the weight is not great enough to crush the seeds and add bitterness to the juice. Grapes are still trodden in some parts of Spain and Portugal, but most are crushed by machines.

Spices and Herbs

Spices are parts of plants used to flavor food. Leaves used in the same way are usually known as herbs. Sometimes, the same plant produces both a spice and herb—for example, coriander and dill.

A Popular Flavor

Licorice is the product of the long, sweet root of a plant of the pea family. It is a perennial that grows to 3 to 5 feet (0.9 to 1.5 m) with pale blue, pealike flowers and leaves of 9 to 17 leaflets. Licorice roots are dug when the plants are three years old. When harvested, they are full of water and must be dried for six months to a year. The dried roots are then cut or sawed into pieces 6 to 12 inches (15 to 30 cm), sorted, and baled.

To prepare licorice, the roots are crushed and boiled, and the remaining liquid is evaporated. This leaves a paste or black stick licorice. Prepared licorice is used in medicines as a cough remedy, as a laxative, and to make some medicines taste better. As a flavoring, it is used in candy, chewing gum, and beverages.

Very Popular Candy

Chocolate comes from cocoa beans. The fat of the cocoa bean, known as cocoa butter, has rare properties. When it is mixed with the powder from the roasted cocoa bean and sugar, and then allowed to cool, it sets firmly and cleanly into a brittle solid. In 1828, a Dutchman named Van Houten first learned to separate the fat from the beans. Chocolate candy is now one of the most common and popular forms of modern confectionery.

Watching Bread Rise

In breadmaking, yeast plants are mixed with starch to form yeast cakes, which are combined with dough. The yeast acts on the starch in the flour, first producing glucose (a form of sugar) and then alcohol and carbon dioxide. The carbon dioxide gas causes the dough to swell or "rise." When the dough is kneaded, the bubbles of carbon dioxide are broken down. When the bread is baked, the heat expands the carbon dioxide, making the bread rise some more. Finally, the carbon dioxide, alcohol, and most of the water are driven off and light, soft bread is left.

Soaping Up

◄

Soap works to get rid of dirt because it attracts grease as well as water. Dirt is really a mixture of dirt particles and grease that sticks to clothing, skin, and just about anything else. It is also not soluble in water. When soap gets wet it forms a film. This film gets into the dirt and loosens the hold of the grease. Then, it wraps itself around the dirt, and the grease and dirt end up in the water around the soap.

Helping Someone to Breathe

Artificial respiration is a way to help people who have stopped breathing because of drowning, falling, or some other accident or illness. It is a method of breathing for another person until they can breathe on their own.

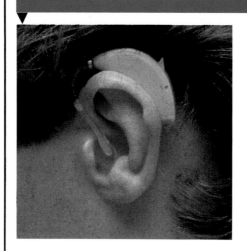

Hearing a Pin Drop

Over the years, many different kinds of machines have been used to help people who have difficulty hearing. A hundred years ago, for example, people often used "ear trumpets," which were long tubes that made sounds louder. Today, however, hearing aids are usually electronic. They increase, or amplify, sounds the same way a microphone does. The most complicated kinds of hearing aids are bone-conduction aids, which are used by people whose outer and middle ears do not work at all. This kind of hearing aid makes vibrations that pass through to the person's inner ear. This allows them to hear almost as if their ears were perfectly healthy.

In Perfect Focus

"Farsighted" people cannot see things close to them. Their eyeball is too short or the lens of their eye is not the correct shape. Eyeglasses or contact lenses help these people by making sure that the light entering their eyes is bent at exactly the correct angle. This helps the eye focus on the light in the correct way.

A Crystal-clear World

Much of what "nearsighted" people see is blurred and unclear. Either their eyeball is too long from back to front or the lens of their eye is not the correct shape to bend the light rays coming into it. Eyeglasses or contact lenses help these people by bringing the light from distant objects to the correct point in their eyeball.

►

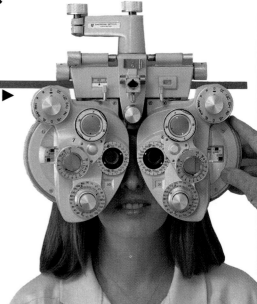

◄ Reading for the Blind

The Braille system for the blind uses raised dots to stand for each letter of the alphabet. One dot, for example, stands for the letter *A;* two dots, one on top of the other, for *B;* two dots side by side, for *C.* By feeling the dots of each letter, blind people can read everything from elevator signs to books.

Fixing Broken Bones ◄

A sharp blow, fall, or other injury can break almost any of your bones. Broken bones often heal easily. Doctors return the pieces of the bone to their normal position. Then they use a cast of some kind—plaster, plastic, or even air held inside a plastic bubble—to keep the bone from moving around. After a while, the bone begins to grow back together. Soon, the broken bone has healed. Strangely enough, bones that have been broken are often stronger than they were before, simply because the bone cells are newer and less worn.

Penicillin— The Wonder Drug!

For many years, penicillin was one of the most widely used medicines in the world because it was able to kill hundreds of different kinds of germs without harming patients. This wonder drug is actually an unusual mold that was discovered in the laboratory of Sir Alexander Fleming, a British doctor. This strange mold had the remarkable ability to stop the growth of bacteria, including those that caused such diseases as pneumonia, diphtheria, and sore throats.

Teeth for Eating

Humans have several different kinds of teeth that help us bite and chew our food. Of a person's 32 teeth, the first eight, in the front of the mouth, are incisors. These are used for cutting—pulling food apart, getting it off one surface or another, and so on. The next four teeth are the canines, which help rip food apart. Behind these are all the different kinds of molars—these are the grinding teeth. Food sits on the lower ones and is crushed as the upper and lower molars grind together. Although all of this sounds complicated—as if you had a whole factory in your mouth—you actually bite and chew without thinking. The entire process takes just a few seconds and almost no effort at all!

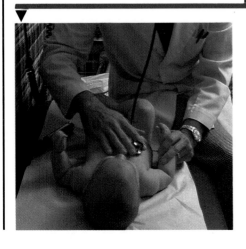

Hearing a Heartbeat

The stethoscope was invented in the early 1800s by a young French doctor, René Laennec. The idea for the invention came from watching children placing their heads to each other's chests in order to listen to heartbeats. Laennec took the idea further by using a perforated wooden cylinder. When he placed one end of the cylinder to a patient's chest and the other to his ear, he discovered that he could hear the patient's heartbeats much better.

A Painless Sleep ▶

Before major surgery, an injection in the arm puts the patient to sleep. The anesthesiologist then puts a mask on the patient's face through which he or she breathes in anesthetic gas, which is kept in special containers. The anesthesiologist operates a machine that controls the amount of gas a patient receives. While breathing the gas, the patient sleeps and feels no pain. The anesthesiologist must also monitor the patient's breathing and make sure that his or her general condition is satisfactory. The anesthetic gas, usually nitrous oxide, cyclopropane, or halothane, would kill the patient if used by itself over a long period, so oxygen must be given at the same time.

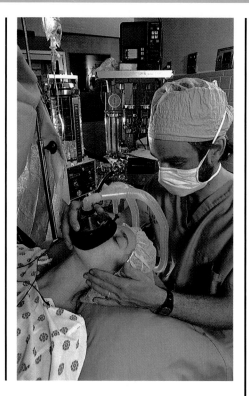

Numbing a Small Area

Special solutions are injected into the spinal canal for spinal anesthetics. Local anesthetics are injected into a nerve, or sprayed on the skin surface in the case of very short operations.

Treating Kidney Failure

There are two main treatments for kidney failure. One is *dialysis.* In hemodialysis, the person's blood is fed along tubes into an "artificial kidney machine" *(renal dialysis machine).* This filters out wastes and poisons, and then returns the blood to the body. A different form of dialysis is called peritoneal dialysis. A special fluid is injected into the abdomen, where it absorbs the wastes. It is drained away and replaced a few hours later. If kidney failure becomes long term, a better alternative is a kidney transplant. Such operations are highly successful and most patients can return to a normal live. However, as with the machines, there is always a shortage of suitable kidneys from donors.

Another Kind of Picture ▼

Ultrasonic waves travel through flesh and soft tissues and can be used by doctors in place of X rays to produce images of the internal organs and tissues of the human body. At low power, ultrasonic waves have no harmful effects on the body and are used for investigation and diagnosis. The so-called body scanner uses ultrasonics in the detection of tumors and blood clots. Ultrasonic scans are frequently given to pregnant women to make sure that the baby is growing at the right rate. The scan also checks for physical abnormalities, and whether there is more than one fetus in the womb. With modern equipment, doctors can actually obtain moving pictures of processes inside the body.

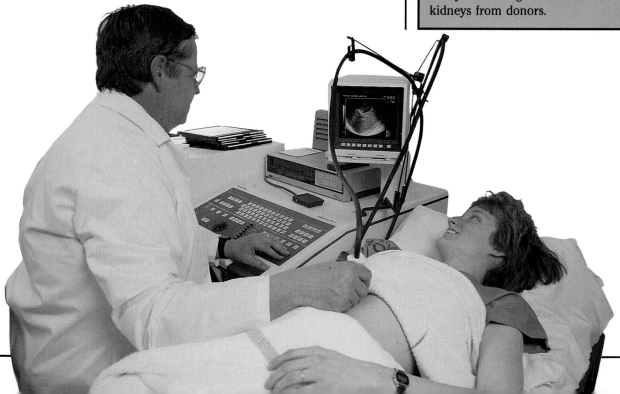

It's All in the Mind

Since the mind "lives" in the brain, illnesses of the mind are probably often brain disorders. Mental or psychiatric disorders such as schizophrenia, severe depression, and anxiety, probably have their basis in the brain's very complicated chemistry. However, researchers have a long way to go before they unravel the secret of how the brain works and how it goes wrong.

To Be Allergic

To have an allergy means to be affected by something that is harmless to most people. People can be allergic to all sorts of things, including certain foods. It is not clear why some people have allergies and others do not. Heredity seems to play a part in allergies. However, in many other cases of allergy no other member of the family has been allergic.

Powerful Drugs ▲

Depressants are drugs that slow the activity of the nervous system. They are used medically to relieve pain, bring on sleep, curb nervousness, or relieve anxiety. *Stimulants* speed up the nervous system. They include cocaine, which is used medically as a local anesthetic, and the amphetamines, which are used only occasionally to relieve mild depression. *Hallucinogens* cause hallucinations. They distort the sight and hearing. *Cannabis* in small doses may act as a mild depressant, or in large doses as a mild hallucinogen.

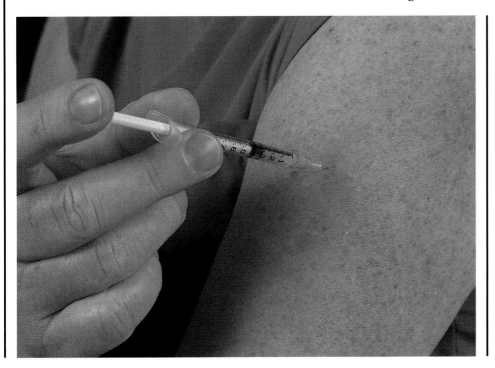

◀ Drugs Found in Nature

Some drugs have been prepared by extraction from organs of animals. Extracts of thyroid (a gland in the neck) were used in some thyroid disease. Insulin, which is used in the treatment of diabetes, was made from the pancreas of cows or pigs. Other drugs are extracted from minerals. They include mercury (for ointments), iodine (an antiseptic), and bromides (sedatives).

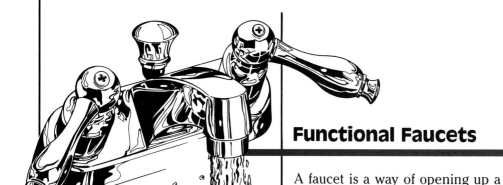

Functional Faucets

A faucet is a way of opening up a pipe to let water flow through. Turning the handle (or lifting a lever, depending on the kind of faucet you have) opens a valve that lets water pass by. The more you open the valve, the more water comes through. The water moves because of pressure inside the pipes. The pipes are filled with water, which is under pressure. When you open the valve, water comes through. Closing the valve stops the water from flowing.

Talking on the Telephone

Telephones work by using electricity to increase the signal made by the sound of the human voice. Inside the handset (the thing you talk into and listen with) is a thin piece of plastic called a "diaphragm." When you speak into the phone, the diaphragm moves in and out. Each time it moves, tiny grains of carbon get pushed together or apart. This changes the flow of electricity inside the handset. When the electricity reaches another handset, it moves its diaphragm in exactly the same way, creating precisely the same sounds that were spoken into the phone.

Telephones of the Past

In the past, telephone messages got from one place to another by wire. This meant that all phones in the world were connected by telephone wiring systems. These systems were made up of hundreds of thousands of miles of cable running over land and even under the sea.

The Wonder of Car Phones ▲

Car phones work more like radios than actual telephones, since there are no wires connecting the phones to the telephone system. Each car phone is very much like an FM radio. It sends a signal that gets linked to the regular phone system so that calls can be made.

Telephone by Satellite

Today, the telephone system uses satellites to connect one phone to another. When you dial a number, the signal for your call goes to a telephone exchange. From there, it goes to a giant tower that sends it up to a communications satellite. The satellite then strengthens the signal and beams it to a receiving station near to where you are calling. The signal is then sent directly to the phone you want to call. Although it sounds very complicated, the whole process takes just seconds to complete. ▼

Cellular Phone News

Car phones are called "cellular phones" because the cellular radio network of car and portable phones splits each area into sections, or cells. As people drive from one cell to another, their calls are routed in special ways so that the phone call continues uninterrupted.

◄ Smile and Say "Cheese"

To take a picture with a camera, you begin by pointing the camera at the person or scene you want to put on film. When you press the shutter button, light enters the camera for a fraction of a second to allow the image of the person or scene to enter the camera. The light coming into the camera acts on the light-sensitive film, putting the image onto the film. After it has been developed, the picture will show you exactly what you were pointing the camera at.

Making Cartoons Come Alive

It takes hundreds of hours of work to make today's animated cartoons, even though computers have made the job faster and easier. Cartoons are made by creating separate individual pictures for each step of an action. To show a character throwing a football, for example, cartoonists create dozens of pictures, each showing a separate step—how a football player lifts an arm, pulls it back, and then throws the ball through the air. These pictures are then photographed one after another and shown very quickly on the screen.

For Those Special Moments

The Polaroid-type camera uses a special film that can be developed inside the camera itself. This means that you can see your pictures just a few seconds after you take them. The film is coated with special chemicals that react inside the camera. When the film is taken from the camera, more chemicals react with the air and bring the finished picture onto the film.

Picture Perfect ▲

Automatic cameras have special cells that can measure the amount of light in the area around them. The camera is automatically adjusted so that it can take a picture with the proper amount of light. (Too much light makes the picture whitish; too little light makes it dark and unclear.)

Movies in Your Own Home ▲

A VCR is like a television set that has a tape recorder inside of it instead of a screen. The tape recorder can be used to record and play back programs that you would normally see on the TV screen. Or, it can be used to play back movies or other shows on tapes that you rent or buy in the store. The sights and sounds of your favorite movies and shows are turned into electronic signals, which are recorded on the tape as variations in a magnetic field. These are put onto the tape that is inside the video cassette. The VCR then reads the signals on the tape and transmits them back into pictures and sounds through a TV screen.

◄ Taking a Picture

Photographic film is coated with a thin layer (or layers) of light-sensitive *emulsion*, which consists of gelatin containing tiny crystals of chemicals called silver halides. When a picture is taken, the lens projects an image of the subject onto the film. In black-and-white film processing, the light that falls on the film causes some of the crystals in the emulsion to undergo a chemical change. When the film is soaked in a chemical solution called a *developer*, the crystals that have been affected by light change into specks of dark metallic silver and form a black *negative* image. The remaining crystals are unaffected and are washed away in a fixing bath. The developed film shows the darkest patches where most light has fallen, lighter patches where less light has fallen, and is quite transparent where no light has fallen. It is called a negative because it reverses the light and shade of the subject.

Lifelike Color Film

Color photography works on a similar principle, but the film has three individual layers of emulsion (sensitive to red, green, or blue). A silver image is formed in each layer that corresponds to the three colors of the original scene. This image is then made visible in the development process, which creates red, green, and blue areas in the film instead of black ones.

Film Editing ►

An editor or team of editors receives all of the parts of a film—sometimes in many pieces. The parts are then put together, taken apart, and reassembled until the editor and the director are satisfied. If a particular scene is too long, the editor can splice or cut out any number of frames to shorten the movie or arrange the frames in a different order. For this reason, film editors are really artists in their own right. They can remove the boring, poor scenes to make a film fast-moving and exciting, or they can change the whole way a story is told. As you might expect, it takes a crew of film editors up to six months to edit a major film.

◄ A Simple Music Machine

A music box contains tiny machinery that consists of a spring, a metal comb with teeth tuned to different notes, and a barrel studded with pins. When the wound-up spring is released, the barrel revolves and its pins strike the teeth of the comb, thus producing the tune.

Chiming and Ringing

Bells can be spherical or egg-shaped, but the typical bell most people know is the church bell, designed to be heard a long way away. There are two ways of sounding church bells—by chiming or by ringing. Chiming is a gentle method in which a wheel from below moves just enough for the clapper to hit the side of the bell. Ringing is a vigorous method in which the bell is swung full circle, starting from an upside-down position.

◄ A Traditional Instrument

Bagpipes consist of a bag, traditionally made from the skin of a goat or other animal, to which a set of pipes is attached. The bag is kept full of air, which is usually blown through the blowpipe from the mouth of the player, and is held under the left arm. Other pipes of various sizes are fixed in the bag, which when squeezed by the player's arm allows air to pass continuously to the pipes, causing them to make a sound. The sound is produced by the vibration of a reed as in a clarinet or oboe.

Making a Church Bell

The process of making a church bell is unique. After the dimensions of the bell have been worked out, a mold is made. This consists of a core of brick covered with a coating of loam or sand shaped to the inside of the bell around which the cope is constructed. The cope, also made of loam or sand, is shaped to the outside of the bell and fits over the core in such a way that a space is left between them. Molten bronze or bell metal is poured into the space at a temperature of 2000°F (1100°C). The cooling of the metal is carefully controlled to prevent the bell from cracking. After the bell has cooled (large bells may take up to two weeks), the mold is broken, and the rough casting of the bell is sandblasted and polished. The bell-founder tunes the completed bell by revolving it and grinding away bits of metal from the inside.

Let's Make Music

The harmonica is a small wind instrument consisting of a series of reeds of different pitches fixed into metal plates and mounted on a long, flat, boxlike structure. To play a tune on a harmonica, the player puts his or her lips over holes in the top. By blowing or sucking, he or she forces air over the reeds and sets them vibrating freely from side to side.

Wonders of the Human Eye ▼

To make a movie, the camera actually takes hundreds of separate, slightly different photographs. When these pictures are projected onto a screen, each of them is seen for only a fraction of a second. But, instead of seeing hundreds of different pictures, we actually see one smooth motion. The key to this is something called "the persistence of visual movement." This is a wonder of the human eye. For example, if you are in a room and turn off the lights, you still see things even after you are completely in the dark. And, when you look at a string of pictures, your eyes see each one of them for a split second, even after the next one is in front of you. This makes the series of pictures look as if it is moving.

Sound and Action

In 1927, the first "talkies" appeared, and movies changed forever. To get sound to go with the film, moviemakers record the words of the actors when the action is being filmed. This is called *synchronous,* or sync, sound. Other sound effects—such as gunshots or footsteps—are recorded later.

Perfect Sound ▲

To make a digital recording, sounds are measured thousands of times per second. They are recorded as a series of pulses on tape. This allows the recording to be absolutely faithful to the original sound, even at the very loudest and softest points.

The Sounds of Stereo

Stereo works very much like the two ears of a person. If sound is recorded with one microphone, the result is very much like a person listening with one ear. To make stereo recordings, as many as 20 microphones are used, each connected to a separate amplifier. The sounds are then blended into two different *tracks,* containing the sounds for each speaker so that each ear hears a different sound. These are the upper and lower sections of the recording tape. When these are played back at the same time, the tape gives people the sense of distance, height, and movement they would hear in real life.

Laser Power

A CD (compact disc) player uses small plastic discs to reproduce sound better than any system yet devised. Sounds are placed on the disc using digital recording techniques. When you play the disc, a laser beam inside the CD player reads the information that has been placed on the disc. The information is then processed by the amplifier and speaker. Not only is the sound quality of a CD excellent, it is also more likely to stay that way than conventional records or tapes. That is because the information is read by beams of light, so there is no needle or magnetic head to wear down the recording.

It Sounds Like You're Right There

When Thomas Edison invented the phonograph back in the 1870s, he used needles to make his recordings as well as to play them back. Today, the needle, or "stylus," as it should be called, is used to play back records you buy in a store. The needle rides through the grooves on the record and reads the sounds that have been impressed on the plastic surface. This message is then sent to the amplifier and speakers to give you the sounds of the music. On stereo records, the needle actually moves in two different directions. By moving up and down and back and forth it gives you real-life sound.

Hearing Tunes

Radios use radio waves (a type of radiation found in nature) to send sounds from place to place. When your favorite disc jockey talks into a microphone, the sounds are picked up and turned into electrical current. This current is then turned into a radio wave and transmitted from an antenna. When you turn your radio to a particular station, it picks up all of the passing radio waves and filters out all of them except the one you have chosen. Your radio increases (amplifies) that wave and separates the sounds that the DJ spoke into the microphone. Those sounds are then sent to the loudspeaker so you can hear them.

Let There Be Light

An incandescent light bulb is made up of a thin strip of metal wire inside a bulb filled with nitrogen and other gases. Electricity is used to get the metal so hot that it glows and makes light. You can change the color of the light in several ways. You can paint the bulb a certain color (blue, red, green, and so on, just like the bulbs that you see on Christmas trees). Or, you can use different kinds of metal. Certain metals, for example, give off a yellowish light; others make a light that is closer to a pure white in color.

Correcting Mistakes ▲

In the 1960s, the self-correcting typewriter was invented. When you made a mistake, you back-spaced to that place and typed the wrong letters again over a thin ribbon of chalk or chemicals. This covered the mistake and made it disappear. Then you typed the correct letter in its place. Now, electronic typewriters keep your work in their memory. You simply watch a screen and make your corrections even before the letters are printed on the page.

Old-fashioned Typewriters ___ ▲

The simplest typewriters have long "fingers," at the end of which are metal letters. Pressing a key moves the finger toward the paper. The letter then strikes an ink-soaked ribbon and leaves an ink impression of the letter on the paper. A lever lets you move the page down a line when you have reached the right-hand edge of the paper.

Typing Made Easy

Electric typewriters use electricity to print letters on paper. It takes a lot less effort to press the keys than on a conventional typewriter. And, you simply press a button to make the paper roll up another line.

State-of-the-Art Typewriters

Electronic typewriters use a spinning ball or wheel instead of the long "fingers" found on conventional typewriters. When you strike a key, an electronic signal is sent to the ball or wheel and it presses that letter against the ribbon. This leaves the mark of the letter on the paper. Because there are fewer moving parts, electronic typewriters are faster than conventional typewriters. They also break down less often.

By the Flip of a Switch▲

Getting electricity to a bulb when you need it is done through a light switch. When the light switch is in the "off" position, there is a gap in the wires through which electricity flows. Turning the switch "on" closes the gap and lets the electricity flow through. Some switches allow different amounts of electricity to go through, making the lights brighter or dimmer.

Bridging the Gap ▲

There are several different kinds of bridges. The simplest kind is made by stretching a tree or piece of lumber between two points—across a river, a stream, or over a ditch. Other bridges use an arch to give strength to the part of the bridge that has nothing underneath it. The most complicated bridges are suspension bridges. These use wires and cables to hang the bridge over a long stretch of water or space. The cables hold the bridge's roadway in place and keep it from falling down.

More Lights

Fluorescent lights, which are usually tubular in shape, work by heating gases rather than a metal strip. The inside of the tube is coated with a special powder that contains phosphorus. It also contains mercury vapor, which produces ultraviolet rays when an electric current passes through it. The powder glows when it is struck by the ultraviolet rays from the electric discharge. The light that fluorescent lights produce is more like daylight than the light produced by incandescent bulbs.

Romantic Water Wheels ▲

Water wheels were one of the earliest—and most important—machines. The wheel was set up near a stream of flowing water with buckets hooked up to it. The buckets fill with water at the top of the wheel. The water spills out as each bucket nears the bottom. Because the heavy buckets were all on one side of the wheel, the weight kept the wheel turning around and around. The wheel was attached to a large pole, or shaft. This could be used to turn other wheels or giant stones for grinding flour.

Bridges that Move ▼

Drawbridges are used wherever tall boats cannot pass under a bridge. The most common of them is called a swing bridge. The roadway of a swing bridge is mounted on a giant turntable. When a boat is to come through, the turntable twists the road out of the way. The drawbridge that is the most fun to watch is called a jackknife bridge. It has two sections that can tilt up on end. When a boat needs to come through, giant jacks (a lot like the ones you use to lift up your car when you have to change a flat tire) lift the sections into the air. When the boat has passed, the jacks lower the roadway back down again.

Do You Know the Combination?

A combination lock has one or more rings threaded onto a spindle. When the rings are turned to a particular letter or number, slots inside the rings fall into line. This allows the spindle to be drawn out and the lock to be opened.

Up and Down the Escalator

An escalator is a set of steps that has been attached to a moving chain. At the top and bottom of the chain are wheels with metal or plastic teeth. An electric motor turns the wheel at the top of the stairs. When the motor is turned on, it pulls the steps upward and, when they reach the top, sends them back down again underneath. The steps are made so that they can bend and fold as they travel down along the underside of the escalator.

Locking Up

A lock is a bolt that holds a door and door frame together. When a door is locked, pins inside keep it from being opened. Most of today's locks are based on a design made by Linus Yale, back in 1848. The Yale lock has five different pins that are pressed into a cylinder by springs. These pins keep the cylinder from turning and the door from being opened. When the key is put into the lock, it pushes the pins to the right height and allows the cylinder to turn.

Making Fire

Fire can be made in several ways. In Alaska, for example, some Indian peoples rub sulfur over two stones and then strike them together. This age-old method can be very effective, especially if the stones are flint, which sparks very easily. In China and India, people often strike a piece of broken pottery against a bamboo stick. Once a spark is made, the fire slowly builds up. The ancient Greeks and Romans used glass to make their fires. They used what was called a "burning glass" to focus the rays of the sun on some dry grass or wood. In the early days of the United States, people often carried a tinderbox. This was a metal box with a flint and steel. People struck the steel against the flint until sparks fell into the cotton placed inside the box. The burning cotton was used to light larger fires.

Taping It Together

Scotch tape is actually a brand name for just one of the many hundreds of different clear tapes that you can buy in the store. It works because a chemical called an "adhesive" is placed on one side of the tape. This chemical makes a bond with another surface that is so strong that you cannot simply lift the tape off. Many different ingredients can be used to make adhesives, including animal bones, flour, and even plastics.

Zipping It Up

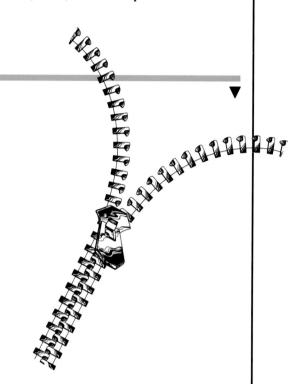

A zipper is made of two strips of metal or plastic teeth that have been sewn to the sides of an opening. (It can be an opening in a shirt, some pants, or even a suitcase.) A sliding hook is attached to the strips. To close the opening, you link the two edges together and pull the hook towards the top of the zipper. The hook pulls the edges together and locks each of the teeth to the one behind it. When you open the zipper, the hook moves downward and separates the teeth.

Learning Your ABCs ▲

The letters of the alphabet are really signs, or symbols, that stand for different sounds. As we see each letter in a word, we silently say each sound to ourselves. When we put all those sounds together, we can say the word in front of us. It took many thousands of years for people to create an alphabet. And, in fact, the very first kinds of writing used pictures to show what the writer was describing. But, since pictures can be hard to draw—and it is almost impossible to illustrate ideas—people gradually shifted to an alphabet using letters. The English alphabet uses 26 letters, although other alphabets have more or fewer letters.

The Engine Makes It Run ▲

Cars need engines of one kind or another in order to work. Internal combustion engines that burn gasoline are the most common kind of automobile engine. Other car engines have included electrical and steam motors. The car's engine provides the energy to make the car move. Its transmission joins the engine to the wheels, which actually move the car.

Cleaning Without Water

Modern dry cleaning usually uses petroleum or synthetic solvents. The petroleum type can be used in an open machine like a washing machine, but synthetic solvents evaporate quickly in the air and must be used in closed, airtight machines. Items for cleaning are sorted according to their fiber and color. The process is similar to washing and rinsing, except that the solvent is used instead of water. Since the solvent evaporates quickly, cleaning by this method is "dry," or without water. After cleaning, garments are pressed with steam to return them to their proper shape.

Using a Die

A die is a type of tool that is used in shaping, casting, cutting, or trimming materials such as metals, plastics, or fabrics. The body parts on automobiles are formed in dies built so that the top and bottom parts of the die are of the same shape. There is only enough space between the upper and lower sections of the die for a flat piece of metal. When the metal is placed in the die and pressure is applied, the sheet immediately takes the form of the die. After the part is formed, it is removed and trimmed in a trimming or blanking die. This type of die is like a pair of scissors or paper cutter. One blade passes another so that it will cut the metal instead of forming it.

Water purification plant

Technicians evaluate the water at this purification plant

Purifying a Liquid

Distillation is the process that purifies any liquid. An apparatus for distilling is usually called a still and has three main parts: the boiler, the cooler or condenser, and the receiver to catch the condensed liquid or "distillate."

The largest stills are those used on land to obtain fresh water for drinking from seawater. Fresh water is produced by stills in many places where rainfall is low. A distillation plant on an artificial island near Los Angeles is designed to produce 65 million gallons (250 million liters) a day, using nuclear reactors to supply the heat needed to change the water into steam.

Lots of Colored Images

A kaleidoscope is an instrument that shows regular patterns when you look into it. It is a tube about 1 foot (30 cm) long, with two or three plain mirrors running the length of the tube and fastened at a 60–degree angle. One end of the tube has a peephole and the other is closed with a piece of non-transparent glass. On this are several loose fragments of colored glass covered with a piece of clear glass. When you look into the peephole, several images of each fragment are seen, because the image formed in one mirror is also reflected by the other and so on. All the images together form a regular pattern that can be completely changed by shaking the tube so as to move the glass fragments to new positions.

Preserving Food the Dry Way

Freeze-drying is a form of food preservation that rapidly freezes the food in a high vacuum. Under these conditions, the ice crystals sublime and the water vapor is removed to leave the food dehydrated and in the best condition for later rehydration (addition of water) when it is to be eaten.

A Roof for Each Purpose

The roof of a building largely reflects the climate of the place in which the building stands. In dry countries, roofs are flat and can be used as an outdoor room when the sun is not too hot. In an area where it often rains, the roof usually slopes so that the water can run off it. Where there are heavy snowfalls, the roof slopes steeply so that the snow will slide off and not build up into a thick layer.

Better Than Soap

Non-soap detergents do not depend on natural edible fats as a basic raw material, since they are made from petroleum and the by-products of coal. They can be specially made to lather well in hard or salt water, to rinse easily from fabrics or from dishes, and in fact to perform many tasks for which soap is not satisfactory.

Switching Gears

A car's clutch, when pressed to the floor, disconnects the engine from the transmission. This allows you to change gears so that you can move faster or have more pulling power. The gears allow the car to travel slowly even though the engine is running very quickly.

The Ease of Automatic Transmission ▲

Automatic transmissions contain fluid that allows the car to change gears by itself, depending on how fast the engine is working and how fast the car is going.

How Fast Are You Going? ▲

A car's speedometer is connected to a set of gears inside its transmission. When the car starts moving, these gears turn the shaft that connects the speedometer to the transmission. This shaft turns a magnet that controls the speedometer's needle. As it turns, it points to the speed at which the car is traveling.

Mirror, Mirror on the Wall

▶

Mirrors have been around since the days of the ancient Egyptians, and all mirrors work in basically the same way. A mirror is a polished surface, usually metal or even a piece of glass with a special coating put on it. When light strikes this surface, it bounces off at exactly the same angle at which it first struck the surface—it reflects exactly the same image that is striking it.

184

Telescopic Vision

The simplest telescope is called a "refracting" telescope. It is made up of a hollow tube and two different-sized lenses. The larger lens, called the objective lens, gathers light rays coming from things far away. The small lens at the other end of the tube then magnifies, or makes larger, the image seen in the objective lens. A third lens in the center inverts the image—otherwise it would be upside down.

Under a Microscope

Microscopes use a hollow tube and different lenses to magnify, or make larger, things that people want to see. As light passes through the lower lens, it is concentrated by a group of lenses. You can then use the lenses just as you would a telescope. The difference is that a microscope has one set of lenses that magnifies the image produced by another set of lenses.

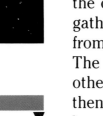

A Mirror Image

There is one slight difference between an original image and a mirror image. A person looking at himself or herself in the mirror sees an opposite picture in which the left and right sides have been turned around. That means that your left eye is looking at the mirror image's right eye; your right eye is looking at the left eye of the image in the mirror.

Blending into the Scenery

Camouflage is a way to disguise or hide things in nature as well as in the armies of the world. In nature, many animals have special colorings that help them hide from those creatures that can harm them. Soldiers have used camouflage for hundreds of years. Today's soldiers wear camouflage suits made of blotches of green, black, and brown colors. This makes the clothing look like part of the jungle or forest.

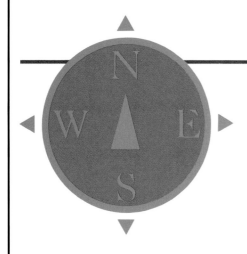

A Compass Points North

A magnetic compass is made of a magnetized needle that can turn freely—on a floating piece of cork, a sharp point, or anything similar to it. It points north because magnets attract one another. Our earth behaves as if there were a giant magnet at its center, and it attracts the tiny magnet used in a compass. The north that the compass points to, though, is not the geographic north of the North Pole. Instead, it points to what is called "magnetic north," a point about 1,000 miles (1,600 km) away from the North Pole.

Cutting a Diamond to Shape ▲

Diamonds are found in nature. But, without a lot of careful, hard work, they are really nothing much to look at. Once a diamond has been found, it is taken to a diamond-cutting center, where it is sorted according to color, size, and clarity. Then, it is cut into the best possible shape. This is a complicated job that can only be done by a skilled, experienced worker.

Powerful Lasers ▼

The laser is a machine that makes a bright light of a single wavelength and color. Unlike regular light, which goes out in all directions, the laser gives a very narrow beam of highly concentrated light. The way these beams are created and the kind of light they produce give lasers great power to light things up and even to produce heat and energy.

Computerized Typing ▲

A word processor is a computer-type machine that takes the place of a typewriter. When you type the words you want on a keyboard, electronic signals are sent to the computer "brain" where letters are formed and projected onto a video screen. Because these are electronic signals, you can change, erase, or move them using other electronic signals. Then, when you are ready to make a printed copy of your work, you simply tell the "brain" to send the work to the printer.

Lasers and Music

Lasers can "read" records or discs because there is a glass tube filled with special gases that is placed between two mirrors inside the laser machine. When electricity passes through the tube, a deep red beam of light is produced. This can be used to "read" or decode electronic signals placed on a plastic disc. The signals are then sent to be increased and broadcast through speakers.

The Mind of a Computer

Computers all work pretty much the same way. Electronic signals (from words, numbers, symbols, etc.) come into an input unit. These signals are passed to a memory unit, where they are stored. A central processing unit then carries out what has to be done—adding or subtracting, putting words on a screen, or even moving a ball around in a computer game. The new signals are then sent to an output unit, which is usually a television-type screen or a printer. Because everything happens electronically, all of this takes only a fraction of a second to carry out.

Supermarket Laser Scanners

Today's supermarkets often use lasers to "read" the prices on the things you buy. Each item is marked with a special code. (You can see it. It's the block of black lines on the outside of the package.) When you buy something, the clerk in the store passes the object over the laser scanner. The laser identifies the lines and their widths, and a small computer tells the cash register what the item is and how much it costs. That's why your sales slip not only tells you how much you spent, but what you bought and what it cost.

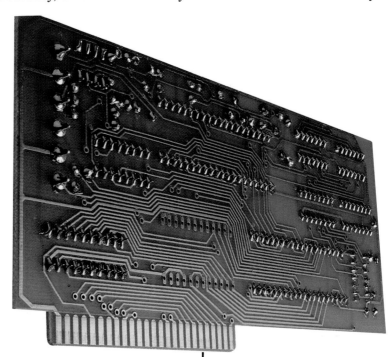

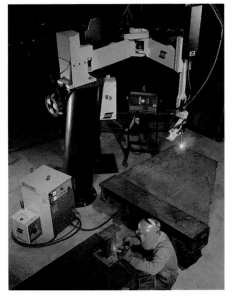

◄Working Robots

Computerized robots are computers with machines attached to them. These machines can move things, rivet or weld objects together, or even inspect the quality of things that have been made. The computer "brains" are given programs telling them what to do. There also are special sensors that let the "brain" know about things around it—other machines coming near, temperature changes, and so on. None of these machines can actually think, and they need people to write the programs that they carry out. But, they often can do jobs even better than people, as well as take on jobs that people could never do themselves.

Making a Computer Work

A computer program is a set of instructions telling a computer what to do. The program may tell it to "input," to "print," or even to let one symbol stand for another in a code. Writing a program is a matter of knowing the right language and getting the directions to the computer in exactly the right order.

Transportation

Freight cars vary greatly. There are tank cars for liquids, refrigerated cars, and "piggyback service" in which trucks and trailers are transported over great distances.

Because of their design, modern tanks can move quickly through mud, snow, rain, or rough terrain even though they weigh over 55 tons (50 tonnes).

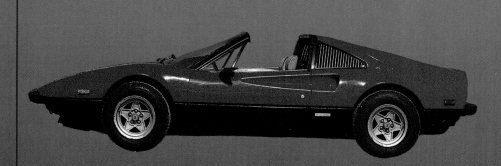

Beasts of Burden

▶

In earlier times, people tamed and trained animals to haul loads and carry riders. Some are still used today. In Tibet, for example, the yak was used. Desert people train and use the camel because it can endure extreme heat and travel for days without food and water. Its broad padded feet keep it from sinking into the sand. The elephant proved to be a powerful, intelligent pack animal used in the Indian subcontinent. Huskies, bred originally by the Inuit (Eskimos), are still used for pulling sleds in the Arctic.

A Very Strong Camel

A Bactrian (two-humped) baggage camel is very strong. It can carry a load of 600 pounds (270 kg).

People Carriers

The litter or palanquin was a vehicle used to transport people quickly through crowded or narrow streets unsuitable for wheeled vehicles or over rough country where animals were unavailable. It consisted of a box open at one side with a mattress inside on which the occupant reclined. Poles were attached to each end for porters, which could be human or animal.

Early Transport Vehicles ▲

Chariots were probably first used in royal funeral processions. Later, their use was expanded to include farming work and military purposes. The chariot revolutionized warfare by enabling armies to move faster and further than ever before. In surprise attacks, projecting scythes were sometimes fixed to the wheel hubs. Enemy troops advancing on foot would be cut to pieces. Survivors would be felled by the spears, arrows, or swords of soldiers riding beside the chariot-drivers.

An Old-fashioned Taxi

The Sedan chair was a seat in a box with a door and windows for the occupant to see out. It became popular in London and other cities in Europe and North America in the 17th and 18th centuries. It was carried by two to four men and could be hired in the street like a modern taxi.

Travel on the Santa Fe Trail ▶

The Conestoga wagon originated in Pennsylvania in the 18th century and was used on the Santa Fe Trail to carry settlers and their possessions. It had a curved floor to prevent the load (of up to 7 tons (6 tonnes)) from shifting, wheels up to $6\frac{1}{2}$ feet (2 m) high, and a white canvas cover supported on hoops to 11 feet ($3\frac{2}{5}$ m) above the ground. It was pulled by four or six horses, mules, or oxen.

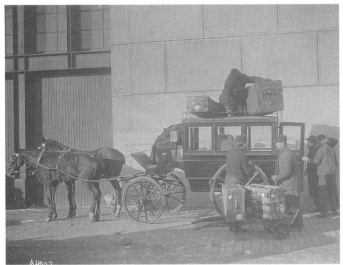

Travel with Rest Stops ▲

Stagecoaches were coaches that traveled in stages between inns, where travelers could rest and the horses and drivers could be changed. They carried passengers and their luggage. Stagecoaches were most popular between 1820 and 1850, by which time they were superseded by railroads.

Different Kinds of Carriages

Among carriages popular in the 19th century were the barouche (a four-wheeled open carriage), the victoria (a hooded carriage), and the dogcart (in which the passengers sat sideways, back to back).

Delivering the Mail

The Pony Express was a famous trans-American postal service that used a relay of horses and riders from Missouri to California between April 1860 and October 1861. It was set up by the firm of Russell, Majors, and Waddell. Along the trail they built 190 stations, or one about every 10 to 15 miles (16 to 24 km). Five hundred horses were placed at these stations to be used to relieve tired animals. Relief riders also waited at these stations. The first pony express left St. Joseph, Missouri, on April 3, 1860 and arrived in Sacramento, California, on April 13. The Pony Express lasted only 18 months—the telegraph system between the East and the West was completed on October 24, 1861. During its time, horses and riders had covered 616,000 miles (990,000 km) over the 2,000-mile (3,200-km) trail.

Uncomfortable Early Railroads

On the first railroads in the 1800s, the roadbeds, on which the tracks rested, were crudely built and there were no shock absorbers. The cars were wooden and the seats and bunks were hard. Lighting came from either flickering candles or lanterns. In cold weather, the wind blew through the cracks in the car. If there was any form of heating it could only be felt within close range of the wood or coal stoves that were used. Smoke, soot, and sparks flew around and sometimes clothes or cars were set on fire.

Freight Cars Galore

Freight cars vary greatly. There are tank cars for liquids such as milk, oil, and chemicals; refrigerated cars carry fruit, vegetables, meat, and other perishable goods. There is even "piggyback service" in which huge trucks and trailers are loaded on flatcars for transporting over long distances. At the end of their rail journey, the trailers are driven to their final destination.

The First Transcontinental Railway ▲

In 1863, work on the first American transcontinental railroad was started. The Union Pacific started building west from Omaha, Nebraska, and the Central Pacific (now the Southern Pacific) built east from Sacramento, California. On May 10, 1869, the work forces of the two companies met and the rails were joined at Promontory, Utah, in a ceremony that drove a golden spike.

Innovations on the Rails ◄

Sleeping cars were introduced in Great Britain in 1873 for first-class passengers traveling between London and Edinburgh. Four-berth sleepers for second-class passengers were introduced in 1928. Restaurant cars were started in the United States in 1867, but since there were no corridors the passengers in the restaurant car had to remain there throughout the journey.

The Importance of Trains ▶

Trains were once the primary means that got people from place to place. Long-distance trains carried people across the country; other trains carried people from city to city. Goods were also moved from place to place by train.

High-speed Trains ▼

In France and Japan, trains that can go up to 200 miles per hour (322 kph) race people from one end of the country to another. Trains are also used to carry people the short distances between most European cities.

Luxury on the Tracks

The Orient Express was a luxury train that ran from Paris, France, to Istanbul, Turkey, from 1883 to 1977. It was equipped with every comfort its makers could imagine—from Oriental carpets to wood-paneled compartments to velvet draperies. Even the food had a reputation for being the best in the world. Many writers used the train as a setting for novels and short stories, and by the 1920s, the train had become a symbol of "the high life" and the world of drama and adventure. Jet air travel, however, finally put an end to the route. Recently, luxury trains catering to the rich and adventurous are being run on parts of the old Orient Express tracks. These trains are giving the people of today a taste of what was once the most glamorous way to travel.

Getting People to Work ▲

In North America, private cars, airplanes, and trucks have pretty much replaced trains as a means of long-distance transportation. Trains are used, though, to get commuters to and from work each day.

Trains Underground ◀

The term "subway" is usually used for underground trains like the ones found in New York, London, and Paris. Other commuter trains run above the ground—usually on tracks that are elevated above the surface of the city's streets. These elevated trains have been called els for many years. Many subways include above-ground sections that are elevated above road level. As you might expect, these are still called subways.

Trains were once the primary means of transportation.

Noiseless Subways

Subways in cities such as New York and Chicago are noisy because steel wheels run on steel tracks. In some cities, however, subway cars are made with rubber or plastic wheels that run very quietly. These silent wheels and the quiet electric power that most subways use make some subways almost noiseless.

Getting Around by Streetcar ▲

Streetcars were vehicles that were pulled by horses or moved along on their own power. Many of them used electric power and were connected either to an electric rail on the ground or to an overhead wire that carried electricity. Streetcars are still used in many cities, including San Francisco, where cable cars get people up and down the steepest hills.

Let's Take a Taxi ▼

The word "taxicab" comes from two different terms. The first, "taximeter," was used to describe a machine, invented in the 1890s, that automatically figured out how much a passenger had to pay for a ride. The machine measured the distance traveled and then multiplied it by the cost of the ride per mile. The other term, "cabriolet," described a roomy vehicle used to carry passengers around the city. Saying "taximeter-equipped cabriolet" was obviously too much for anyone, so the term "taxicab" was born.

Bicycle Riding Through the Ages

Bicycles have been around since the 1800s when an odd-looking machine called the *draisienne* appeared in Paris, France. It was made of wood, and the rider moved its two wheels along by simply paddling his or her feet against the ground. It was not until the 1890s that modern-style bicycles appeared. When they did, bicycles became hugely popular. Even today, in many parts of the world, millions of people use them as daily transportation.

Special Bikes for Racing

▲

There isn't much difference between racing bikes and everyday bicycles. Racing bikes, however, are very light in weight and are often made from unusual metals like titanium. They also have very expensive gear mechanisms to help riders get up and down hills. Racing bikes have thinner, narrower tires than regular bikes, too. These tires puncture easier than regular tires, but they let riders go much faster. The biggest difference between racing and regular bikes, though, is the riders. Bicycle racers are highly trained, strong athletes who can simply pedal much harder and much faster than the rest of us.

Old-fashioned Bikes of Many Sizes ▬

Many of the bicycles of the 1870s and 1880s had giant front wheels and very tiny rear wheels. Some had front wheels that were more than 5 feet (1.5 m) in diameter—riders had to actually use ladders to get onto their bikes. They were built this way because each turn of the pedals moved this huge front wheel all the way around, causing the bike to travel a great distance on each turn of the pedals. Unfortunately, these bikes were very difficult to ride and often tipped over. Riding them took a great deal of skill and courage.

A Brand-new Tire

A great bicycle invention was J.B. Dunlop's pneumatic tire, introduced in England in 1888.

The Bicycle Craze

The bicycle was very popular in the United States and Europe during the 1890s. Everyone who could afford to buy a bike owned one. On weekdays, the streets were filled with cyclists going to and from work.

Cycle Innovations ▲

In the last century, bicycles have been improved in many ways, including the use of the free wheel, variable-speed gears, lighter wheels and tires, stronger and lighter steel, weatherproofing, better brakes and lighting, better placing of the rider for using his legs to push the pedals, and saddle designs for comfort and speed. The small-wheel bicycle invented by the British engineer Alexander Moulton and introduced in 1962 proved popular and was successful because of its rubber suspension.

◄ Functional and Fun

In Europe and Asia, the bicycle remains an important means of transportation during the 20th century. In the United States and most of Europe, however, the automobile quickly surpassed it as the primary means of transportation. During the late 20th century, bicycling has again enjoyed renewed popularity as a pollution-free means of transportation and as a healthful form of exercise.

Order on the Roads

Traffic laws began before there were even gasoline-powered cars! There have always been rules for horses and carriages. By the 1600s, many European cities had laws making it illegal to park on some streets. In 1865, the famous Locomotives (or "Red Flag") Act was passed. It was designed to do something about the people who were speeding on country and city roads in their steam-powered vehicles. The law set a speed limit of 4 miles per hour (6 kph) on country roads and 2 miles per hour (3 kph) on city roads. It also declared that a person had to walk ahead of any car and wave a red flag to warn people that an automobile was coming. By the 1890s, there were too many vehicles on the roads to make it possible to enforce the law any longer. It was repealed in 1896.

Roads Old and New

People have built roads since the times of the ancient Egyptians. In fact, the ancient Romans were probably the greatest road builders of all time. In the United States, many roads were built in the 1800s to carry wagons, carriages, and horses. When automobiles came along, they were forced to use these rough, dirt roads. Paved roads were introduced as early as the 1850s, but, until automobiles began whizzing along, they were few and far between.

The Original Highway

The first really modern highway created especially for automobiles was the Bronx River Parkway in New York. Built in 1925, it was designed to let cars travel at high speeds without stopping. After that, modern highways and turnpikes sprang up all over the world.

Different Fuels for Automobiles

Kerosene, natural gas, and even hydrogen have all been tried as automobile fuels. Most recently, engineers have been trying to use solar power. Energy from the sun would make cars pollution-free and would save precious fuel. A race is held in Australia every year to find the fastest solar-powered vehicle in the world.

Moving On its Own

A steam-powered tricycle built by Frenchman Nicolas-Joseph Cugnot in 1769 was the first vehicle built that moved along under its own power. It was powerful enough to carry up to four passengers at speeds of 2.25 miles per hour (3.6 kph).

An Automobile First

In the 1880s, the first automobile with a gasoline engine was created by Carl Benz of Germany. He patented his car in 1886, and his name is still on one of the world's most famous cars—the Mercedes-Benz.

The Original Model T ▲

Designed by Henry Ford and sold by the Ford Motor Company in 1908, the Model T was the car that made automobiles affordable for almost everyone. Model T's were so sturdy and simple to repair that many of them remained in daily use for 50 years or more. When it was finally taken out of production in 1927, over 15 million Model T's had been sold.

A Model T Replacement ▼

In 1927, the Ford Motor Company produced a second car to replace the Model T. It was called the Model A.

Electric Automobiles ▲

Electricity was used to power cars as far back as the 1880s. In fact, electric cars were fairly popular up until the 1920s. Power for the cars came from large storage batteries. The cars could run along at a fairly low speed, until the batteries ran out of "juice." Then the cars had to be plugged into a recharger so the batteries could regain their power. Electric cars were most popular among people who did not need to get anywhere in a hurry and who enjoyed having a completely silent automobile.

Gasoline Wins over Steam

The very earliest automobiles—as far back as the 1700s—were powered by steam. Even in the late 1800s, dozens of different companies made steam-powered cars, since it was the easiest way to make a car go. Finally, the safety, low price, and ease of operation of gasoline-powered cars began to drive customers away from the complicated steam cars.

Steam-powered Automobiles ▲

The Stanley "Steamer" was one of the most famous early automobiles. It was built by a company started by twin brothers Francis and Freelan Stanley, and it was manufactured for almost 25 years—from 1897 to 1921.

Automobile Facts ▶

Today's average car is made up of over 14,000 separate parts! They range from simple knobs to complicated electronic circuit boards and are made of everything from plastic to steel to silicon.

Built for a King

The world's most expensive car is the Bugatti Royale, built in the 1920s by Ettore Bugatti. The car was so expensive that Bugatti announced that only those people with royal titles would be allowed to purchase it. Unfortunately, the prices were too high even for kings, queens, and princes. Only a few of the cars were actually sold. Today, the few Bugatti Royales left are selling for millions of dollars each.

This Porsche turbo is an amazingly fast car.

Fastest Cars in the World

For the past ten or 15 years, the cars from three manufacturers—Porsche, Ferrari, and Lamborghini—have generally been considered the fastest cars in the world, with models that reach speeds of just under 200 mph (320 kph). Certain custom-built cars and racing machines, of course, are capable of even higher speeds.

Ferrari 308 GTS

Automobile Racing Firsts

People started racing automobiles almost as soon as they had them. By 1894, carefully organized races were being held in Europe. In 1895, dozens of cars ran in a race between Paris and Bordeaux, France. The event proved so popular that it was held every year until 1903, when the high number of accidents forced the organizers to cancel this race forever. By 1900, races were being held all over the world, with cars reaching speeds of up to 50 mph (80 kph). Thousands of people turned out whenever these machines took to the road.

Rolling Along

Because trucks often carry such heavy loads, they can be very difficult to stop once they get rolling down a hill. (Think of how hard it is to stop a bike that is traveling on a long, steep hill.) Drivers often have to use their brakes and gears to slow the truck down and keep it from running wildly down a hill. That's why highway departments give truck drivers lots of warning about a long, dangerous hill.

Truck Trivia

The first modern truck was built in 1896 by Gottlieb Daimler, the German carmaker whose company became the creator of the famous Mercedes-Benz automobiles. Daimler's truck had a four-horsepower engine and two forward speeds. In 1898, the American Winton Company made a truck especially designed to work as a delivery wagon.

Trucks that Tow

A tractor trailer is a truck that uses a separate towing vehicle that can be attached to a long body (a semitrailer or "semi") in which things are to be carried. The two units are connected together by what is called the "fifth wheel," a latching mechanism that allows the two parts to turn separately while keeping them from coming apart.

Let's Take a Sled Ride

Sleds are used for many things besides riding down hills on a snowy day. In Siberia, Alaska, and Canada's Northwest Territories, dogsleds have been used for hundreds of years. Most are pulled by teams of 12 to 15 dogs.

Sliding Through the Snow

A toboggan has a smooth surface—usually wood—that slides along the surface of the snow. The first toboggans were invented by American Indians, who made them of poles tied together with strips of leather. The Indians used toboggans for getting from place to place during the winter months. Later, people began riding toboggans down hills for sport. By the early 1900s, toboggans were used almost exclusively for fun, as tobogganing became one of the most popular winter sports in the world.

That's a Fast Machine ▲

Today's lightweight bobsleds can reach speeds of up to 100 mph (160 kph). These bobsleds have streamlined bodies and move on four runners that skim over the surface of the hard-packed snow of the bobsled run. The fastest bobsleds use four riders; two-rider sleds are slightly slower.

Versatile Snowmobiles ▲

Most snowmobiles are used just for fun. They take people on thrilling rides across the snow and ice, get hunters and fishermen to the best spots in the dead of winter, and help people see places they never could get to otherwise. But they are also useful. In Alaska and Canada's Northwest Territories, they are used to get people from place to place. They are even used by police for everything—from rescue work to chasing criminals.

Skiing for All Occasions ▲

Skiing has always been used as a means of transportation. A 4,000-year-old rock carving that was found in Norway, for example, shows two men skiing. They were probably hunting, and their skis were the best way to travel across the snow. The Vikings used skis for hunting and war back in the 10th and 11th centuries. Skis were even used by soldiers during World War II. Today, people still use skis to get from place to place in those parts of the world that remain covered with snow for much of the year. For the most part, though, people ski for fun—and for the excitement of rushing down a hill at top speed.

The Place to Race Is . . .

By the 1860s, ski races were being held in places as far apart as Tromso, Norway, and California.

A Very Ancient Sport

Scientists have found early skis that are probably between 4,000 and 5,000 years old. These skis, discovered in Sweden and Finland, were most likely made by hunters.

A Downhill Kind of Race ▲

Cross-country skiing is when people travel from place to place on their skis. They go up and down hills, across flat areas, and through forests. Downhill skiing, sometimes called Alpine skiing, involves a bit of jumping as well. Skiers use the steepness of a hill to give them speed. For this reason, downhill skiing usually means going to a ski slope that has some kind of lift that can take skiers back up to the top of the hill whenever they want to start a run.

Balancing at 100 mph ◀

A boat has to be going at about 20 miles per hour (32 kph) before a water-skier can get up out of the water and onto his or her skis. Expert skiers, though, are able to keep their balance at speeds of up to 100 mph (160 kph).

A Tricky Board on Wheels ▶

Skateboarding first appeared in southern California during the 1960s as a way for surfers to practice and have a good time during bad weather. The surfers simply attached roller skate wheels to pieces of wood that they shaped into tiny surfboards. The result was a fast-moving machine that could turn quickly, race along at high speeds, and even be made to do tricks. By 1965, hundreds of people were skateboarding around the roads and parking lots near California's best beaches. Within a few years, the skateboard was being seen all over the world.

Skating on Wheels ▲

A Belgian named Joseph Merlin is considered to be the inventor of the roller skate. But Merlin's skates, which appeared in the 1760s, did not work very well. In 1863, however, James Plimpton, of Medford, Massachusetts, created the first four-wheeled skates. These skates let riders move faster, stay on their feet better, and create fancy tricks. By the 1890s, there were roller skating rinks all over the country.

The Fastest Skates

Although people can move very rapidly on ice skates, roller skates are generally much faster. The spinning plastic balls on the bottom of the skates allow people to move at much greater speeds than the blades of ice skates, which must cut a thin groove on the surface of the ice.

Shall We Ice Skate? ▲

Ice skating has been around for almost 3,000 years. It has always been done mostly for fun and recreation, even though skates do help people get from place to place. Skating was extremely popular in the 1700s and 1800s, especially among the kings and queens of Europe. It was introduced to North America by British soldiers during the 1740s.

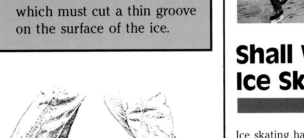

Trendy Roller Skaters ▲

In the 1970s, new plastic wheels were put on roller skates. This made the skates faster, smoother, and easier to maneuver. Roller skating became very popular. Later, these same plastic wheels were put on skateboards, helping to make that sport even more popular than ever.

Crossing the Ice by Boat ▼

If you have to cross a large area of ice—a big lake, for example—the best way to go is by iceboat. An iceboat is simply a sailboat with thin blades, or runners, fixed to the sides. A third blade, used for steering, is put at the front or back of the boat. Iceboats, which have been around for more than 2,000 years, can reach speeds up to four times as fast as the wind that is pushing them along. Speeds of 140 miles per hour (220 kph) have been recorded.

54E 5359

Crossing the Open Seas

A ship is a large floating vessel that can cross open waters. A boat is a much smaller craft.

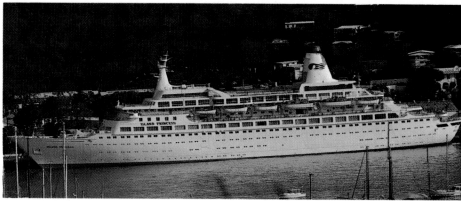

A History of Ships

Egyptian drawings made about 6000 B.C. show the earliest known ships. The ships in these pictures were made of reeds and were crescent-shaped. The first ones were rowed; later, large square sails were added. By 1500 B.C., ships were common enough for the people of Crete to build them for war and for carrying people and things from place to place. Most early ships used sails, although many also used rowers to power the craft when the wind was light.

Almost as Fast as Lightning

The *Flying Cloud* was one of the most famous clipper ships of all time. It sailed from New York to San Francisco in just 89 days. Another famous clipper, the *James Baines*, set a record by sailing across the Atlantic Ocean in 12 days and six hours. The *Lightning*, however, was probably the fastest clipper ship of all. It set an all-time record traveling 436 nautical miles (807 km) in a single day.

Egyptian sailboat

The Glory of Clipper Ships ▶

Experts consider clipper ships to be the greatest sailing ships ever built. Built in the mid-1800s by American shipbuilders, they were long, slim, graceful, and remarkably fast. They were designed especially for speed, because merchants wanted to bring the first tea of the season back from China. Speed was also important for getting mail and supplies back and forth between the East Coast and the California gold fields during the 1849 Gold Rush.

Down the River by Steamship

The first working steamship was built in 1801 by a British engineer, William Symington. His boat towed barges in the canals of Scotland. In 1807, the American inventor Robert Fulton built a steamboat that went up the Hudson River in about one-fourth the time that it usually took in a sailboat.

Floating Relics

The invention of the jet airplane put an end to most travel by ocean liner. By the late 1960s, most of the famous ocean liners were sold and turned into scrap metal, tourist attractions, or even floating schools.

Making Ships Go

Most ships today are powered by diesel engines. A few nuclear-powered ships have been built, but almost all ships still use gasoline as a source of fuel.

Submarine Specifics

The **Turtle**

The first working submarine was built in 1776. At that time, an American named David Bushnell built the *Turtle,* a tiny submarine used to attack British ships during the Revolutionary War. Submarines were also used in the 1860s during the American Civil War. By the 1890s, submarines were able to cruise for long distances under the sea.

Staying Underwater

Early submarines could stay underwater for only a short time. By World War II, submarines could stay under for 12 hours or more. There were several reasons why these submarines had to come to the surface: to store air for use under the sea and to recharge the giant batteries that powered the ship underwater. Today's nuclear submarines have solved these problems. As a result, they can stay underwater for weeks and even months at a time.

Fighting Power of Submarines

Submarines have always been used almost exclusively for warfare. They attack surface ships, launch missiles, or set floating bombs (called mines) in areas where they could be hit by passing ships. Submarines are usually too small and too slow to be really useful for carrying cargo or passengers.

Exploring the Bottom of the Sea

Scientists explore the undersea world with a machine called a "bathyscaphe." The bathyscaphe was invented by a Swiss scientist, Auguste Piccard, to study life in the very deepest parts of the ocean. It is made up of a super-strong steel capsule, which holds the divers and scientists. Above this is a tank filled with liquid that is lighter than water. This tank gives the bathyscaphe the "lift" it needs to come back to the surface after it dives. During the 1960s, Piccard's son Jacques set many diving records in the bathyscaphe *Trieste,* eventually reaching a depth of 35,810 ft (10,916 m).

Practical Pontoons ▲

The first practical seaplanes were created in 1911 by Glenn Curtiss, an American engineer and pilot. His planes were standard, lightweight planes with large floats, or pontoons, in place of landing wheels. These pontoons kept the plane afloat while it was on the water.

Boats that Fly

"Flying boat" was the term often used for a certain type of seaplane. The entire bottom of a flying boat was designed like a boat, and smaller pontoons, or floats, were attached to the plane's wings. This made it possible for the flying boat to float whenever it was in the water.

The Heyday of Seaplanes

All through the 1920s and 1930s, the fastest and largest airplanes were seaplanes, which set dozens of records for flights across the Atlantic, the Pacific, and around the world. After World War II, though, planes were able to fly far enough that they no longer had to stop on the water to refuel. As a result, seaplanes were needed only for special uses—like bringing mail or medical help to out-of-the-way places.

▼

Flying on a Cushion of Air

Hovercraft, or air-cushion machines, fly on a cushion of air between the machine and the ground or water surface. Experiments with hovercraft began back in the 1870s, but the first useful air-cushion machine was not built until 1959. This machine, called the SR.N1, was built by Christopher Cockerell of Great Britain and could carry three passengers.

Crossing the English Channel

Hovercraft are primarily being used to carry passengers back and forth across the English Channel. These large hovercraft can carry up to 400 people at speeds of almost 60 knots (70 mph).

A Different Kind of Ferry ▲

A "hydrofoil" is an underwater fin that can lift a ship out of the water. As a ship's speed increases, this fin gradually forces more and more of the boat clear of the water. This allows a ship to move at far greater speeds than it could in the water. During the 1950s, hydrofoil ships began to appear in many parts of the world. Today, they are often used as ferries—even carrying commuters back and forth from the office.

◄Airfields at Sea

Aircraft carriers are airfields at sea with many special features. To facilitate short takeoffs and landings, airspeeds over the deck are increased by turning the ship into the wind. Catapults flush with the flight deck assist in launching the aircraft. For landing, aircraft are fitted with retractable hooks that engage special wires on the deck, braking them to a quick stop. The control centers of a carrier are situated in a location at one side of the flight deck. Aircraft landings are guided by radio, radar, and hand signals from the deck.

Picking Up Freight

Most ships carry freight. They travel either on regular runs or as "tramps." The tramp steamer carries with it a bit of the romance of the old days of sailing. It wanders from port to port, picking up cargoes and not knowing where it will go next.

Saving Lives at Sea

Modern lifeboats have twin engines for safety reasons. They are fitted with radar, radio, and echo-sounding equipment. They also carry line-throwing apparatus, a breeches buoy (special canvas seat for rescue work), stretcher, first aid equipment, emergency rations, and a scrambling net.

A Ship for Every Purpose ▲

Many ships—oil tankers, for example—are built especially for certain kinds of cargo. Other special ships include refrigerator ships, tugs, lumber schooners, grain ships, ore boats, ventilated ships for tropical fruits, colliers for coal, ferryboats that are usually double-ended, icebreakers that are designed to ride up over the ice and crush it with their weight, and container ships whose cargo is placed inside many large boxes made of aluminum alloy.

A Different Kind of Lighthouse

A lightship is a floating lighthouse, anchored near a sandbank or other hazard where a lighthouse cannot be built. One of the best-known American lightships is the Nantucket lightship moored about 41 miles (65 km) out off Nantucket Island, east of New York City.

Rules on the Seas

The "rule of the road" on the water is that rowing and sculling boats (as well as steam and motor-driven ones) must give way to sailboats, while rowers and scullers out for pleasure or practice must give way to those racing. On a river, the general rule is to keep in the middle when going with the stream and to one side when going against it. On a lake or at sea, two boats traveling in opposite directions should pass port side to port side. (The port side is the left side looking forward; the right side is called the starboard.)

A Long History at Sea ▲

A catamaran is descended from a type of boat that has existed in the Pacific islands for thousands of years. The name comes from the Tamil (southern Indian) word *katta-maram* meaning "tied tree," and was originally used for rafts made by lashing together tree trunks. Nowadays catamarans are craft with the weight equally shared between two hulls.

◀Romantic Gondolas

Gondolas are the best-known means of transportation in Venice, Italy. They are flat-bottomed boats, with raised stern and bows, and are often 30 feet long (9 m). They are usually propelled by one oarsman, the gondolier, who stands at the stern.

Ships of the Air

Dirigibles are large flying machines. The early ones consisted of a compartment for passengers and crew and a giant balloon filled with lighter-than-air gas. Propellers were used to move the ships through the air.

Uses for Dirigibles

During World War I, dirigibles were used for anti-submarine warfare and for bombing London and Paris. By the 1920s, dirigibles were in service for long-distance air travel. German dirigibles were the most successful, with the *Graf Zeppelin* making almost 600 flights. Passengers liked the quiet, stable ride of the airships and did not seem to mind their slow pace. People became concerned about the safety of dirigibles, however, when the hydrogen-filled balloon of the German airship *Hindenberg* exploded in Lakehurst, New Jersey, in 1937. Since then, dirigibles have been used occasionally by armies and air forces. Today, nonrigid dirigibles, or blimps, are used for advertising by companies such as Goodyear Tire & Rubber and Fuji Film. They are also sometimes used for sight-seeing and scientific observation. These blimps are filled with nonflammable helium, making them much safer than the hydrogen dirigibles of the past.

The First Flyers

Flight began when two Americans, Wilbur and Orville Wright, began work on an airplane in 1899. By 1902, they had created a successful two-winged glider. In 1903, the Wrights added a 12-horsepower engine and two propellers. On December 17, 1903, the Wright Brothers' *Flyer* (as they named it) flew for 59 seconds. By 1905, their third *Flyer* was flying, turning, making circles, and staying in the air for up to half an hour at a time. Within a few years, Europeans were also building planes—the age of flight had begun.

From One Wing to Two

In 1909, a single-winged plane became the first airplane to cross the English Channel. Between then and 1914, many of the world's best airplanes had only a single wing. But a number of accidents with monoplanes (as the one-winged airplanes were called) convinced engineers that wings needed a great deal of support. For this reason, they started using two and even three wings, all held together with wood or metal struts and strong wires. These braces managed to hold the fragile wood and fabric planes in the air.

Memorable Atlantic Crossing

Charles Lindbergh was the first person to complete a solo, nonstop flight across the Atlantic Ocean. Although people had crossed the Atlantic before, they had done so by making several stops. Lindbergh, however, left Roosevelt Field, outside New York City, and, a little more than 33 hours later, landed outside of Paris, France. The flight, which took place May 20-21, 1927, captured the public's imagination. Overnight, Lindbergh became one of the most famous and honored people in the world.

A Famous Woman Pilot

The most popular early woman flyer was Amelia Earhart. Earhart had been an army nurse during World War I where she became interested in flying. In 1928, she became famous for flying across the Atlantic Ocean as a passenger. Determined to earn respect as a pilot, she made a series of flights around the United States to attract attention to herself and to the growing airline industry. In 1935, she made a solo flight from Hawaii to California—the first person to ever successfully make that flight. In 1937, she set out to fly around the world. After completing two-thirds of the flight, her plane vanished in the middle of the Pacific Ocean and she was never found.

Flying Around the Globe

On April 6, 1924, four United States Army Air Service planes left Seattle, Washington, in an attempt to become the first to fly around the globe. Although one plane was forced to make a crash landing off the coast of Alaska, and another one was lost in the North Atlantic, two of the planes returned to Seattle 175 days and over 26,000 miles (41,850 km) later.

The Story of Jets

A jet engine works by pushing hot gas out of itself. This gives the engine the power to move things through the air or off the ground. The first jet aircraft was created in Germany, in 1939, just before World War II. By the late 1940s, jets were used in most of the world's air forces, and by 1952, the first jet airliners were in service.

The Job of a Pilot ◄

Either the pilot or copilot is always seated at the controls during every moment of flight. Flight plans must be created, reviewed, and registered for each flight. Weather must be checked constantly so that the plane can avoid dangerous weather conditions. The pilot must also be on the lookout for other aircraft to make sure that there are no midair collisions. A plane's pilot and copilot are also at the controls for most takeoffs and landings, just to make sure that everything goes smoothly. The captain is even in charge of maintaining law and order on the plane—just like a captain on a ship.

The First Commercial Airline

An American named Tony Jannus established the world's first commercial airline in 1914. Jannus's airline, which had a full schedule of flights between St. Petersburg and Tampa, Florida, could carry only one passenger at a time. People, however, were not really ready for air travel at that time, and Jannus's airline went out of business after a few months. After World War I, however, people were more willing to accept the idea of air travel. Slowly, airlines began to be organized, and, by the 1930s, adventurous and wealthy people were traveling by air.

The Busiest Airports

Surprisingly, the busiest airports are not always in the largest cities. Some airports serve as "hubs"—they are used hundreds of times each day by people who change from one plane to another in order to get to where they are going. Someone going from Boston, Massachusetts, to Dallas, Texas, for example, would probably fly from Boston to Atlanta, Georgia. There, he or she would change planes and fly to Dallas. Consistently, Chicago's O'Hare Field and Atlanta's Hartsfield Airport are among the very busiest in the world.

The Effects of Wind

An airliner's progress is affected by the wind. A headwind slows up its speed over the earth, while a tailwind increases speed. A wind blowing from either side causes it to drift to the other side as it travels forward.

Jumbo Jets

The first of the wide-bodied jets, the Boeing 747, has a wing span of 197 feet (60 m) and a length of 185 feet (56.4 m). Powered by four very large turbofan engines, it cruises about 600 miles (970 km) per hour.

The Famous "Black Box"

The so-called "black box" flight recorder automatically records every detail of the flight, and recordings can also be made of conversations on the flight deck. Should anything go wrong, and the aircraft be forced to suddenly land or even crash, these records are invaluable in helping experts to discover the cause of the failure.

Keeping in Contact

An aircraft is hardly ever cut off from contact with the ground, even when it is flying high above the clouds or over the ocean. Radio messages are constantly passing between the airplane and the ground radio stations as the aircraft flies along airways—corridors about 9 miles (15 km) wide that are marked out over land with radio navigation beams. It is the job of the crew to see that the airliner flies along these airways.

Helpful Helicopters

Because they can hover in the air and lift straight off the ground without a runway, helicopters are extremely useful. They are used in warfare to carry troops into battle as well as to attack enemy positions. They are also widely used for rescuing people, especially at sea and in hard-to-reach areas. Today, they are also popular for making short air flights, often from the middle of one city to another. Many passengers, for example, are willing to pay a high price for the privilege of having a helicopter take them from a city's downtown area to a nearby airport.

Helicopter Statistics

The first real helicopter was built by the famous Russian engineer, Igor Sikorsky. By 1910, Sikorsky had built two helicopters, and, within a few years, other people had made their own versions of these flying machines. The first helicopter that was actually good enough to be used for practical tasks was built in Germany during the 1930s. In 1938, Hanna Reitsch flew it and established several world records—proving that helicopters would soon be an excellent form of transportation.

Vertical Takeoff and Landing ▶

Since being able to take off and land without a runway is useful, engineers worked for many years to develop a plane capable of vertical takeoff and landing (VTOL). Several such planes have been made for the world's air forces. However, they are usually not fast enough to be all that practical for passengers.

◄The Alaskan Pipeline

The trans-Alaska pipeline, completed in 1977, carries petroleum 800 miles (1,300 km) from Prudhoe Bay on Alaska's Arctic coast to the Pacific coast port of Valdez. Work was done over rugged terrain and in Arctic weather and plans had to include ways of preserving the environment. Other uses for pipelines include carrying water from lakes and rivers for irrigation and drinking purposes and transporting coal.

A Very Long Pipeline

One of the longest pipelines in the world is the trans-Siberian, which carries natural gas from northern Siberia approximately 3,750 miles (6,000 km) to western Europe.

A Truly Vast Undertaking

The construction of the Panama Canal took seven years and was directed by John Stevens and George Goethals. Close to 65,000 men were employed at one time, and more than 200 million cubic yards (153 cubic meters) of soil and rock were moved. The canal opened to ships in August 1914, and effectively cut the sailing distance from New York to San Francisco by 8,000 miles (13,000 km).

A Famous Waterway▶

The Panama Canal is a great international waterway connecting the Atlantic and Pacific Oceans through the Isthmus of Panama in Central America. The canal is located near the geographical center of the western hemisphere and is a vital link in the world's ocean trade routes. Just over 11,000 ships pass through its locks each year, saving a vast amount of money in shipping costs by reducing the distances that goods must travel by sea.

Mountain Travel

▶

A form of transportation common in some mountainous areas is the aerial cableway. This uses very strong steel ropes that are winched electrically back and forth onto cable drums, or worked on the "endless belt" principle, similar to the San Francisco cable cars. Where the land allows, the cables may be supported on towers. Cableways are used to pull or carry skiers and tourists up mountain slopes.

Two Types of Monorails

Monorails are single-track rail systems that can carry passengers or freight. They fall into two types. The train may run on top of the rail supported on wheels, an air cushion, or magnetically, or it may be suspended below the rail, supported by its drive wheel.

A Monorail First

The first successful "over-rail" monorail was invented by Charles Lartigue in 1883 and built at Ballybunion, Ireland. It consisted of a twin-boilered steam engine and carriages that ran on wheels, and straddled the rail that was supported on trestles 2 feet (60 cm) above the ground. Loads had to be very carefully balanced to prevent the monorail from overturning. Modern versions are found in Seattle and Tokyo.

Using a Magnetic Field

Magnetic levitation, or "Maglev," has been used for the monorail link to Birmingham International Airport in England. The train is supported above a flat steel rail by a magnetic field. Propulsion is by linear motor—similar to a conventional motor that has been flattened out to give motion in a straight line instead of a circle.

216

Sketching for the Future

Leonardo da Vinci, the great Italian artist and inventor, made sketches of a man-propelled tank in 1482. It was not until the gasoline engine had been developed, however, that there was a compact source of power able to move a heavy gun and armor about the battlefield.

Tank Duties ▲

The first tanks were developed in World War I (1914-18). They were developed from motorized caterpillar-tracked tractors. In World War I, the task of tanks was to clear a way for the infantry through the barbed-wire entanglements and to overrun trenches and machine-gun positions.

Moving on All Surfaces

In all modern tanks, the engine turns wheels engaging in steel links called tracks on each side. As a result, a tank's weight is spread over the underside of both tracks, giving better grip. Despite a weight of over 55 tons (50 tonnes), the tank can move at speed through mud, snow, rain, or rough terrain.

Modern Tank Capabilities ▲

The main weapon of a tank is its long-barreled and very accurate gun. A "ranging" machine gun is often mounted alongside the big gun. It fires tracer bullets in bursts; these are easily seen so that the gunner can correct the aim of the big gun. A modern tank uses laser beams for range-finding and may also be armed with guided weapons. Its armor is designed to deflect enemy gunfire. Its infra-red system enables the crew to see in the dark, and a filtered air supply allows them to remain inside for up to 72 hours with the hatches closed.

Geography

Mount Rushmore in South Dakota contains four 60-foot high sculptures of former presidents George Washington, Thomas Jefferson, Theodore Roosevelt, and Abraham Lincoln.

Ireland is called "the Emerald Isle" because of its very green grass. This vibrant color is caused by limestone beneath the soil.

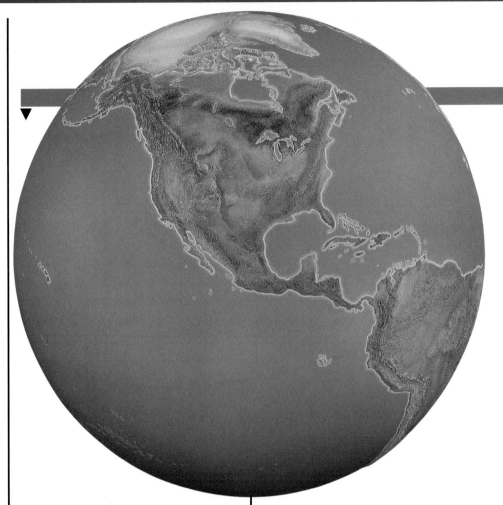

The Earth's Bulge

Although the earth is basically round, it does have a bulge at the equator. The reason for this bulge: As the earth spins round and round on its axis, the spinning motion causes it to bulge out at its center. This phenomenon is called "centrifugal force." The proper name for the earth's shape is *oblate spheroid*—this means that it is flatter at the North and South Poles than it is in the middle.

Measuring the Earth

The earth is really very big—measured at the equator, it is 24,902 miles (40,076 km) in circumference. At the equator, the earth's diameter, which is the distance through its center, is 7,927 miles (12,757 km). And it weighs about 6.6 sextillion tons!

The World Is Round

Almost 2,300 years ago, the Greek mathematician Eratosthenes figured out the distance around the earth. He learned that at Aswan in Egypt the sun's rays came down vertically at exactly noon—there was no shadow. He then noticed that 500 miles away in the city of Alexandria, Egypt, the sun's rays came down at an angle of $7\frac{1}{2}°$ and there was a bit of a shadow at noon. Using simple geometry, he figured out the distance around the world almost exactly. But it took almost 1,600 years before people in Europe believed that the world was round.

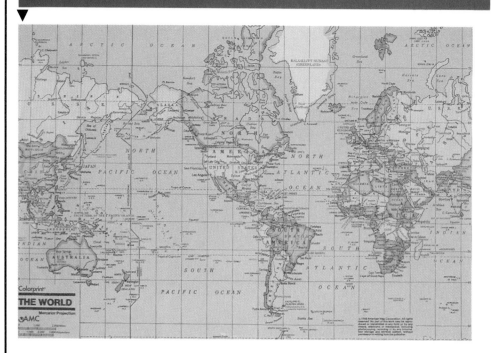

The Long and Short of It

Latitude measures the distance of a place from the equator. All lines of latitude are exactly 69 miles (111 km) apart. *Longitude* records the distance of a location from the prime meridian at Greenwich, England, which is 0° longitude. These calculations take into account the curvature of the earth when measuring and showing distances.

Round Earth on a Flat Map

A mercator projection is a way of showing the earth's curved surface on a flat piece of paper. It is named after Gerardus Mercator, a Flemish mapmaker, who first discovered a way to do this in 1569. As amazing as it seems, the mercator projection map is still in use today—over 400 years after it was first invented!

Measuring the Earth

Most maps are made from measurements that come from airplanes or orbiting satellites. These provide photographs and other information about locations, geographical features, and even the distances between places and objects. This data is then transferred to paper using standard markings and distances.

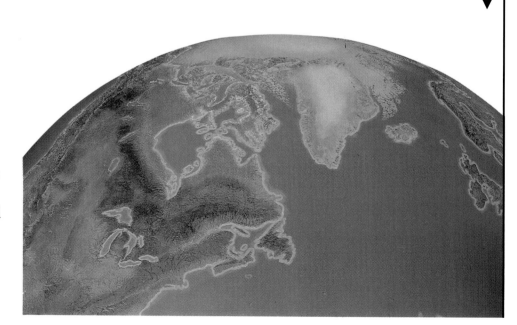

The World's Highest Point ▶

The world's highest mountain is Mount Everest, which is located in the Himalayas between Tibet and Nepal. The mountain actually has two peaks: Everest, which is 29,028 ft (8,848 m) high, and South Peak, at 28,700 ft (8,748 m). Since it has very difficult surfaces and bad weather conditions, it was impossible to climb for many years. However, on May 29, 1953, Edmund Hillary of New Zealand, and Tenzing Norgay, his local guide, became the first people to stand on top of Everest, the highest point on Earth.

A Very Lofty Second Place

The second highest mountain in the world is Everest's neighbor in the Himalayas, K2. Sometimes called Mount Godwin Austen and Dapsang, it stands 28,251 ft (8,611 m) and is considered by many experts to be even more difficult to climb than Mount Everest.

Presidents Immortalized

Mount Rushmore, located in the Black Hills of South Dakota, about 25 miles (40 km) southwest of Rapid City, contains four sculptures carved in stone on the side of the mountain. Each sculpture is almost 60 feet high. They show the heads of our first president, George Washington (signifying the nation's founding); our third president, Thomas Jefferson (representing the nation's political philosophy); our 26th president, Theodore Roosevelt (exemplifying the expansion and conservation of the country's land); and our 16th president, Abraham Lincoln (symbolizing the preservation of the Union).

The Depths of the Ocean

The average depth of the world's oceans is 2.3 miles (3.7 km). There are, however, several trenches (or deep craters) that are considerably deeper. The Marianas Trench in the northwest Pacific Ocean is believed to be the deepest known point—it measures over 6.8 miles (11 km). That's almost three times as deep as the average depth of the ocean!

Some Very Salty Water ▲

The Dead Sea, located in the hills of Judaea, has been called "dead" for at least 2,300 years. In actuality, nothing ever "killed" it at all. It got its name because the water of the Dead Sea is so salty that the only things that can live in it are certain tiny, salt-loving bacteria. In fact, fish carried into it from the Jordan River nearby die almost instantly from the salt, as do most other forms of plant or animal life.

Yellow Waters

The Yellow Sea off the coast of China is actually yellowish in color. The unusual color is caused by clay that is carried down to the sea by rivers.

▼

Colorful Seawater

Although seawater itself is usually a deep blue color, it can be colored by clouds overhead, by mud, or by tiny organisms called *plankton*, which can make the water look brown, green, or even red.

The World's Longest River

The Nile River, located in Africa, is the longest river in the world. Starting in Lake Victoria in Uganda, it flows northward to the Mediterranean Sea for 4,132 miles (6,648 km) through many countries. The Nile is so large that the land around it has a special name—it is called the Nile River Basin and makes up almost 10 percent of all the land in Africa.

A Sprawling River

If you include its two main tributaries, the Missouri and Ohio Rivers, the Mississippi River touches all or part of 31 different states, as well as two Canadian provinces. It's almost hard to believe that more that half of the states in the United States border on this mighty river!

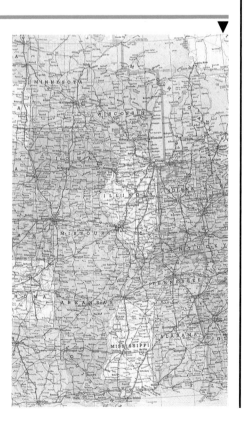

The Riddle of the Nile

The riddle: Why does the Nile River flood each year during the driest time of the year? This question remained unanswered until the late 1800s. The answer: In the high forests of Ethiopia, far south of Egypt, the Nile's main tributary, called the Blue Nile, swells with water during the Ethiopian rainy season. Those floodwaters are carried hundreds of miles downstream and they finally cause the Nile to overrun its banks during the hot, dry Egyptian summer.

A Great Shortcut

The Northwest Passage is a direct sea route that links Europe and Asia. For centuries, explorers searched for such a course that would link the Atlantic and Pacific Oceans without a long, dangerous voyage around Africa or South America. Ever since the time of Columbus, numerous expeditions set out in search of such a route. The Norwegian explorer Roald Amundsen finally found a passage through the Arctic in 1906—it took more than three years to get through the heavy ice. Since then, many other explorers have made this same voyage in a lot less time. Today, jet planes just fly right over this area in minutes.

The Father of Waters

The Mississippi River in the United States is called "the father of waters." The name "Mississippi" ("father of waters" and "big river") comes from the Illinois, Kickapoo, Ojibway, and other Indian tribes that lived along this famous river.

A Very Cold Place

The first thing that comes to mind when you hear the word "Arctic" is a COLD place. However, the Arctic isn't a particular place at all. It is an area made up of parts of Canada, Alaska, the former Soviet Union, Norway, and the Atlantic Ocean. It has no boundaries that would set it off from other places. Scientists generally agree that the Arctic begins at the point at which trees no longer grow on the land.

Not One, But Three

You may be surprised to know that there are actually three North Poles! The geographic North Pole is in the Arctic Ocean, about 450 miles (725 km) north of Greenland. There is also a magnetic North Pole (compasses point to this one) and a geomagnetic North Pole. Both of these are some distance from the more famous geographic North Pole. Contrary to popular belief, however, there is no real pole standing at the top of the world.

The Prime Meridian ▲

One meridian is no different than another. But in 1884, the nations of the world agreed that Greenwich, England, a few miles east of London, would be the point of 0° longitude, or the prime meridian. All lines of longitude are measured east and west of this imaginary line.

An Unanswered Question

Between 1909 and 1914, both Frederick Cook, a New York doctor, and Robert Peary, of the United States Navy, claimed to have been the first person to reach the North Pole. The United States Congress actually investigated the matter because the two men disagreed so violently. They decided in favor of Peary after analyzing the data from both expeditions. In the past few years, however, evidence has been found to suggest that Peary's expedition never actually reached the Pole. It's a question that may never be answered.

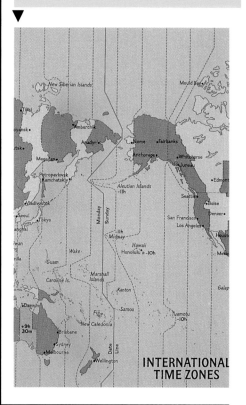

INTERNATIONAL TIME ZONES

Helping the World Keep Time

The International Date Line is an imaginary line between the North and South Poles at approximately 180° longitude. It is used to help adjust the world's timekeeping system. Since this system is based on time zones that are one hour apart, travelers going eastward across the line set their calendars back one day; those going westward, forward a day. Can you imagine—just by crossing the International Date Line you can be one day ahead or behind of where you were before you started your trip.

Calling It By the Same Name

Naming a place is not as simple as you may think. It would be a real mess if there were no rules by which places were named. So the Board on Geographic Names hands out official place names in the United States. They decide on a place name, how the name is spelled, and how it is pronounced. This way there is no confusion—everyone who hears "New York City" thinks of the same place!

Giving a Place a Name

Places get their names in a variety of different ways. Sometimes, a place is named after the people who live there. Other times, a location is named after the person who discovered it or for a famous person. There are even places that are named after the way they look.

An Icy Place Called Greenland

When the Viking sailor Erik the Red returned to Iceland in 986 A.D., he wanted to attract people to the settlements he was creating on a large island to the west. He came up with a name that appealed to people living in Iceland's cold climate: Greenland. People were intrigued by a name that made them think of warm, sunny days and green grass. The name stuck, despite the fact that Greenland's summertime temperatures average only about 45°F (about 7°C) with much of the island covered with ice 12 months of the year.

The Grass Is Always Green

Ireland is called "the Emerald Isle" because of the color of its grass. The grass is so green because the limestone beneath the country's soil makes the grass brighter green than in most places.

The Naming of America

A German geographer by the name of Martin Waldseemuller was the first person to use the name "America." This was in 1507. Waldseemuller did not know about the voyages of Christopher Columbus, so he used this name in honor of the Italian navigator Amerigo Vespucci, who explored the coasts of South America and the Caribbean in 1499-1500 and 1501-02.

Scottish Lands and Lakes

Scotland is a place of jagged coastline, twisting waterways, wide rolling countryside, and towering mountain peaks. In addition to the mainland, the country also includes over 700 islands that lie off the northern and western coasts. The natural beauty of this small land brings thousands of tourists each year. Perhaps the most well known features of the landscape are the lochs, such as Loch Lomond and the infamous Loch Ness. "Loch" is actually the Scottish word for lake. These deep lakes are found mostly in the western highlands.

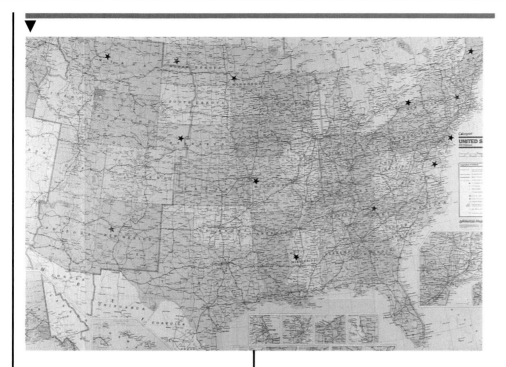

The Winners Are *M* and *N*

Many state names begin with the letters *M* and *N*, which are tied at eight state names. *M* is found at the beginning of Maine, Maryland, Massachusetts, Michigan, Minnesota, Mississippi, Missouri, and Montana. *N* starts the state names of Nebraska, Nevada, New Hampshire, New Jersey, New Mexico, New York, North Carolina, and North Dakota.

Duplicate Nicknames ▼

Both Florida and South Dakota are called the "Sunshine State," making it the only state nickname repeated among the 50 states. However, South Dakota has another nickname, too. It is also called "Coyote State," a name that is not shared with any other state.

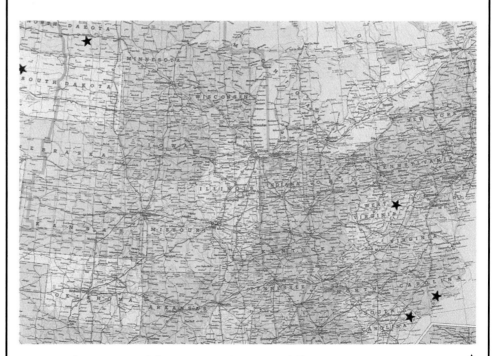

West, North, and South ▲

Five state names come from directions—West Virginia, North Carolina, South Carolina, North Dakota, and South Dakota.

The boardwalk in Atlantic City, New Jersey, is always crowded.

A Pretty Crowded Place

Although several states have a larger population, New Jersey is officially the most crowded, or densely populated, state. According to the United States Census Bureau, not only does New Jersey have the highest number of people per square mile, 89 percent of the population lives within what are considered metropolitan areas.

A Town Called Normal ▲

Normal, Illinois, is a town of more than 35,000 people located in the central part of the state. It was originally called North Bloomington, but changed its name when Illinois State Normal University was established there in the mid-1800s. Today, its biggest businesses are the state university, which is still located there, as well as agriculture and tire manufacturing.

The Exotic Corn Palace ▲

Located in Mitchell, South Dakota, the Corn Palace is a building that was built in 1921. It looks like something out of an Arabian Nights fable, complete with towers, minarets, and complicated, gold-colored paintings on its walls. It is used each year as part of Mitchell's annual corn festival.

228

Apartments Under the Cliffs ◄

The Mesa Verde apartments are astonishing Pueblo cliff dwellings located in the Mesa Verde National Park in southwestern Colorado. They are up to 1,300 years old. Built under overhanging cliffs, the largest of these apartments contain hundreds of rooms, including ceremonial rooms and living quarters. No one knows exactly how many people lived in these dwellings, but they have been deserted since 1906 when the area became a national park.

The Grand Canyon

The Grand Canyon's width ranges from one-tenth of a mile up to 18 miles (0.2 to 29 km). It is almost 277 miles (443 km) long. Of this, about 57 miles (91 km) of canyon are part of the Grand Canyon National Park.

▼

Snowy Stampede Pass

Stampede Pass in the state of Washington is the "snow capital" of the United States. It has an average snowfall of 430 inches each year. In contrast, a well-known winter resort like Mount Washington, New Hampshire, gets only 250 inches of snow each year.

Our Northern Neighbor

Canada is an extraordinarily large country. It stretches over 3,000 miles (5,000 km) from east to west and almost as much from north to south. Canada spans six time zones, and it borders three oceans. Most of its population lives in cities and towns that are within 185 miles (300 km) of its border with the United States. Most of the rest of the land has almost no population at all.

Many Natural Resources

Canada is very rich in natural resources. Mining of iron, copper, nickel, zinc, gold, silver, and uranium produces 30 percent of the value of Canada's mineral sales to other countries. Crude oil and natural gas account for about half of Canada's sale of mineral products to other countries. One-fifth of the things that Canada sells to other countries come from its forests.

A Rocky Mountain State

The state of Colorado has all 54 peaks in the Rockies that top 14,000 feet (4,300 m). Its average elevation is 6,800 feet (2,073 m).

A Beautiful Mountain Range

The Cascade Range is one of the most beautiful mountain ranges in the northwestern United States. It extends from southern Canada across Washington and Oregon into northern California for a distance of 700 miles (1,100 km). Many volcanoes, including Mt. St. Helens and Mt. Shasta, form the highest peaks of the Cascades. The Cascade forests supply the largest timber industry in the United States.

Water, Water Everywhere

The five North American lakes of Superior, Michigan, Huron, Erie, and Ontario are called the great lakes. Lake Superior is the world's largest freshwater lake, and the five together cover an area greater than that of the United Kingdom.

Our Fiftieth State

The multi-island state of Hawaii is unlike any other in the United States. It is the only state consisting entirely of islands. It is the only state not part of the North American mainland. It was the last of the 50 states to be admitted to the Union. It is the only state ever to have been a monarchy or to have a royal palace. Hawaii is the only state not dominated by Americans of European ancestry.

A Growing Island ▶

Hawaii, the southernmost and largest of the Hawaiian archipelago, is constantly being increased in size by volcanic activity. It is composed of three mountain masses, with Mauna Loa, Mauna Kea, and Hualalai being the highest peaks. Kilauea Crater, on the side of Mauna Loa, is the world's largest active volcano.

Many Pineapples

Lanai Island of Hawaii is owned by the Dole Corporation. Nearly all of the island's residents are employed by this company, which harvests about 120 million pineapples a year.

◀ Brrrr!

Montana is the fourth largest state in area, but in population density it ranks 48th. The state was once called the "icebox of the nation," before Alaska took away that distinction. The lowest temperature ever recorded in the United States (except Alaska) was –70°F (–57°C) at Rogers Pass, Montana, in January 1954.

A Very Wealthy State

Nevada is the driest state in the United States and one of the hottest. It is also one of the wealthiest states in terms of individual income. This has been made possible by its minerals and a remarkable tourist trade. The fantastically rich Comstock Lode, near Virginia City, was discovered in 1859. It was once the single largest source of gold and silver in the world. In the 20 years after its opening, more than half a billion dollars worth of the precious metals had been extracted.

Minerals Galore

New Mexico is the fifth largest state in area, and it has less surface water than any other state. Only irrigation makes productive farming possible. However, the state is very rich in minerals. The state produces about 85 percent of the nation's potash, and it leads in uranium production.

Dangerous Capes

Off the coast of North Carolina there are three capes—Cape Hatteras, Cape Lookout, and Cape Fear—that jut into the ocean. This area is known as the "Graveyard of the Atlantic" because of all the ships that have gone down in the treacherous waters.

The Smallest State

Rhode Island, the smallest state, is one-fourth the size of Los Angeles County in California. By population density, it ranks second in the nation, with 898 persons per square mile (347 persons per sq km).

More Cattle Than People

Wyoming is the second most sparsely settled state in the United States. There are ten times as many cattle and sheep grazing its millions of acres (hectares) of grasslands than there are people.

Finding Chalk in Kansas

Chalk is a very pure, soft white limestone, often containing curiously shaped small lumps of hard black flint. Wide areas of land in Kansas are made of chalk, as are stretches of southern England and northern France.

A Very Hot Place

Death Valley is a long, narrow basin in southeastern California. It is famous as the lowest place in the Western Hemisphere and also as the driest part of North America. The highest temperature ever recorded in the United States, 134°F (56.6°C), occurred in Death Valley in 1913.

The Peak of Extremes

From the peak at Death Valley known as Dantes View, it is possible to see the lowest point in the United States (near Badwater) and one of the highest (Mount Whitney).

The Grand Canal in Venice, Italy

Two Grand Canals

There are two famous Grand Canals. One of them is the main waterway through Venice, Italy, a city with dozens of canals and waterways (and very few streets). The other Grand Canal is in northern China. It links the city of Hang-chou with the capital, Peking. More than 1,050 miles long (1,700 km), it is the longest man-made waterway in the world.

Little Island with a Big Name

Grand Turk is an island located in the Caribbean Sea. It was once in the business of making salt from seawater. Today, tourists and banks are its main source of income.

A Tall Teton

Grand Teton is the highest peak in the Teton Range, located in northwestern Wyoming. It is 13,766 feet high (4,196 m). The mountains are part of the Grand Teton National Park.

Taking a Hike ◄

The Appalachian National Scenic Trail is a footpath that begins at Mount Katahdin, Maine, and ends 2,034 miles (3,254 km) away at Springer Mountain, Georgia. Created during the 1920s and 1930s for people who love hiking, it passes through 14 different states. Along the way are shelters and campsites, all maintained by hikers themselves.

Going to the Sun ▼

The Going to the Sun Highway is one of the main tourist attractions in Glacier National Park.

A Historic Trail

The Oregon Trail began in Independence, Missouri, and extended for more than 2,000 miles (3,200 km) to the Columbia River region of Oregon. It was originally used by fur traders and trappers. During the 1840s, the Oregon Trail was a very important route for people going west— it was crowded with the wagons and horses of thousands of miners, farmers, and pioneers.

235

Man-made Structure Seen from Space

The Great Wall of China was one of the greatest building projects ever undertaken. Started in the 3rd century B.C., it was built to guard the border between China and its neighbors, the Hsuing-nu, who were nomadic tribes living north of China. It extends east to west for almost 4,000 miles (6,400 km) from Po Hai, near the Yellow Sea, to central Asia and is so large that it can be observed from space.

How to Get to Timbuktu

Timbuktu in Mali, Africa, on the edge of the Sahara Desert has a reputation for being the most out-of-the-way place in the world. Founded around 1100 A.D., it was at one time an important trading city. However, it was often attacked by neighboring peoples, and by the 1600s it was mostly in ruins. The French government finally took it over at the end of the 1800s and rebuilt it. Even then, however, there was no railway or paved road to link Timbuktu to the rest of the world. As a result, people began to think of it as the most hard-to-get-to place on earth.

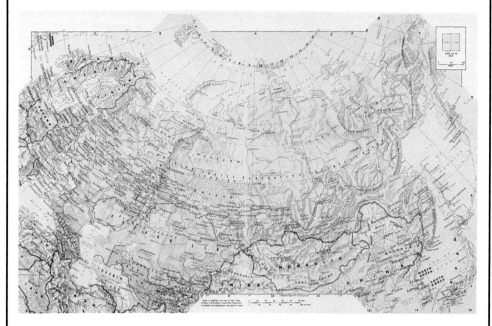

The Largest Area in the World ▲

What was once the Union of Soviet Socialist Republics, or the Soviet Union, was the largest country in area. It covered almost one–sixth of the earth's land. But, with a population of a little under 286 million people, it was only the third largest country in population.

The Real Russia

Although the term "Russia" is often used to mean all of what was once the Union of Soviet Socialist Republics (U.S.S.R.), Russia was really only part of the U.S.S.R. It was one of the fifteen Soviet republics in that union, which was referred to commonly as the Soviet Union.

The Famous Red Square ▲

The large open square in Moscow, Russia, has been called Red Square since the 1600s. The name comes from the Russian word *krasnaya*, which means both "red" and "beautiful." Red Square has a long and colorful history. Originally a market place, it has also housed churches, Moscow's first public library and university, a theater, Lenin's tomb, and a printing establishment. It has also been the scene for demonstrations, riots, parades, speeches, and even executions.

More People Than Anywhere Else

The world's most heavily populated country is the People's Republic of China, which has a population of slightly more than one billion. China is also large, ranking as the third largest nation behind the former Soviet Union and Canada.

▼   ▶

The Red Fort in India

The Red Fort, which stands in Old Delhi, India, was built by the famous Shah Jahan, who also built the Taj Mahal to honor his wife. Finished during the mid-1600s, the fort has bright red sandstone walls that protect its palaces, gardens, soldiers' quarters, and other buildings.

◄ C-O-L-D

Verkhoyansk and Oymyakon in northeastern Siberia, with winter temperatures falling to a record low of −89.9°F (−67.5°C), are the coldest inhabited places in the world.

Now That's a Deep Lake

The deepest lake in the world is Lake Baikal in Siberia at 5,314 feet (1,620 m). It is also larger than any other freshwater lake in Asia or Europe.

The Largest Power Plants

The Siberian power plants at Krasnoyarsk on the Yenisei and at Bratsk on the Angara River further east are the largest in the world.

Timber Rich

Siberia is the richest timber region in the world and has lumber camps and sawmills in many places.

A Land of Extremes ◄

Asia, the largest continent, is a land of extremes. It has the world's highest mountain peaks, including Mt. Everest, and most of the world's longest rivers. Yet it also has the earth's lowest land surface, the shore of the Dead Sea. It includes one of the world's wettest places (Cherripungi, in India) and some of the driest deserts. Verkhoyansk and Oymyakon in Siberia are two of the coldest places in the world, and some of the hottest temperatures on the earth's surface have been recorded near Aden, in the Arabian Peninsula.

Lots of Trees

Some 500 miles (800 km) off the southeastern coast of Asia between Taiwan and Indonesia is a large group of islands called the Philippines. Forests cover more than one-third of the total land area, containing some of the finest forests of hardwood timber in the world. There are also some 800 species of orchids.

Warm, Salty Water ►

The Red Sea lies between Africa and Asia almost separating the two continents. Little fresh water reaches the Red Sea so its waters are very salty. They are also very warm, with temperatures reaching 84°F (29°C) towards the southern end. The numerous coral reefs and banks are mostly near the coast but include the dangerous Daedalus Reef, which is just below the surface and right in the middle. These reefs and the irregular currents make navigation in the Red Sea difficult.

Potato vender in Nepal.

◀ High and Lofty Nepal

Nepal is one of the world's most geographically isolated countries. It lies between the northeast frontier of India and Tibet, extending about 500 miles (800 km) southeast to northwest, and roughly 115 miles (185 km) north to south. Most of Nepal is mountainous and along the northern border rise some of the highest peaks in the world, including Mt. Everest and Kanchenjunga. Nepal is one of the least developed countries in the world.

A Much Shorter Route

The Suez Canal is one of the most important artificial waterways in the world. It is in Egypt and connects the Mediterranean Sea with the northwestern arm of the Red Sea. It is about 100 miles (160 km) long. The Suez Canal provides the shortest route for ships voyaging between Europe and the Persian Gulf, Pakistan and India, Australia, and the Far East, although the largest tankers are too big to pass through the canal. It is also the shortest sea route between the eastern seaboard of North America and ports on the Indian Ocean.

Oil and Pearls ▶

The chief product of the Persian Gulf is oil. The Gulf and neighboring countries produce about 30 percent of the world's oil. Even though many of the Persian Gulf's traditional industries have declined as the production of oil grew in importance, divers still bring pearl oysters up from 66 feet (20 m) deep without the aid of diving suits. The climate is one of the hottest in the world.

Mining for Gold

Johannesburg is the largest city in South Africa and the center of the world's wealthiest gold-mining industry. It is sometimes called the "city of gold"; its African name is *egoli*, "the place of gold."

Accounting for Copper

Nine-tenths of the world's known copper deposits are in four regions: south-central Africa (Zambia, and Shaba in Zaire), Chile, the western United States, and the Canadian Shield.

A Country in West Africa

Ghana in West Africa is a country about the size of Britain. An important feature of its Volta River Basin is Lake Volta, one of the largest artificial lakes in the world, covering more than 3,000 square miles (8,000 sq km). The Ashanti plateau, to the southwest of the Volta Basin, is the region where most of Ghana's chief crop, cacao, is grown.

A Very Lofty Mountain

The highest mountain in Africa is Kilimanjaro at 19,341 feet (5,895 m). It is located in northeastern Tanzania, near the frontier that divides it from Kenya. Kilimanjaro is made up of three extinct volcanoes. It has three peaks—ice-covered Kibo, made of solidified lava; Mawensi, with stupendous walls of rock; and the grassy Shira ridge.

Africa's Largest Lake

Lake Victoria, located in Tanzania, Uganda, and Kenya, is Africa's largest lake and the second largest freshwater lake in the world. It occupies a shallow depression in the East African plateau, and its greatest depth is only 262 feet (80 m).

The Largest Falls in the World ▲

Victoria Falls are among the largest falls in the world. They are located on the boundary between Zambia and Zimbabwe and are more than twice as deep and twice as wide as Niagara Falls. At the widest point, they are more than 5,500 feet (1,675 m) across. Fine spray is flung up from the Falls, and in the sunlight or even moonlight rainbows gleam among the tiny drops. The spray leaps more than 1,000 feet (300 m), and is visible 40 miles (65 km) away.

◄The True Southernmost Point

The Cape of Good Hope is often thought of as the point furthest south in the continent of Africa. Actually, Cape Agulhas, about 100 miles (160 km) further southeast of the Cape of Good Hope, is the southernmost point of Africa.

Making Lots of Aluminum ▶

The island of Jamaica in the West Indies contains one of the largest-known deposits of bauxite (from which aluminum is made) in the world. Jamaica is the world's second-largest producer after Australia, accounting for nearly a fifth of the total world production.

Impressive Petroleum Output

The largest production of petroleum is in the area that was once the U.S.S.R. with nearly one–fifth of the world output. It produces slightly more petroleum than it uses. The United States (the world's largest importer of oil) and Saudi Arabia (the world's largest exporter) come second and third in the world production league.

Rich in Nickel

Cuba is the largest island of the West Indies. It lies only about 90 miles (145 km) south of Florida. Although chiefly an agricultural country, Cuba has some minerals and is one of the world's principal producers of nickel. Much salt is also produced by the evaporation of seawater in shallow coastal pools.

Spicy Products ▶

Grenada in the West Indies is known as the Isle of Spice. Nutmeg, cinnamon, pepper, cloves, ginger, and vanilla are some of the chief products.

A large crowd gathers by the clock tower in Venice, Italy.

The Facts on France

France is the largest country totally within Europe. The climate of France differs very much from one part to another. The northern part of France has cool to cold winters, warm summers, and plenty of rain. On the southern coast, it rarely rains in the summer and is usually sunny in winter. The highest mountains of the Alps, which include Mont Blanc, the highest peak in Europe, are snow-covered all year.

Land Very Far North ▶

Lapland consists of the northernmost districts of Norway, Sweden, and Finland together with the west part of the Kola Peninsula. It is not a separate country, although the Lapps are a distinct people. Most Lapps live north of the Arctic Circle, where snow lies on the ground for more than seven months of the year. Northern Lapland is a "land of the midnight sun." Between May 22 and July 23 the sun can always be seen moving along the horizon at midnight.

▼ A Highly Populated Place

Europe is one of the most thickly populated areas of the world. About one-seventh of the world's population (about 785,700,000 in 1990) live on the continent. The heaviest concentrations of people are in Italy and in an area extending from England through northern France and the Low Countries into Germany. The thinnest population is in the northern lands of Scandinavia, Finland, and northern parts of the former U.S.S.R.

A Land of Lakes

There are about 90,000 lakes in Sweden. The best known are Lake Vattern, Lake Malaren, and Lake Vanern.

An Island with a Past

Corsica is the fourth largest island in the Mediterranean Sea after Sicily, Cyprus, and Sardinia. It has been part of France for over 150 years, even though the people speak a kind of Italian—most of their ancestors came from Italy. The chief town, Ajaccio, is famous as the birthplace of Napoleon, who made himself emperor of France.

On the Beautiful Blue Danube ▲

The Danube River is the second longest river in Europe and has by far the greatest flow of water. Eight countries and three national capitals stand on its banks and it flows for 1,755 miles (2,824 km) from the Black Forest mountains of southwest Germany to the Black Sea.

Special Islands

The Azores in the Atlantic are about 800 miles (1,300 km) from Portugal. They are actually the visible peaks of the massive underwater Mid-Atlantic Ridge. This region is prone to earthquakes. About 35 years ago a volcanic eruption increased the size of Faial—one of the nine islands.

A Very Rough Bay ▲

The Bay of Biscay is found where the Atlantic Ocean takes a great bite out of the west coast of Europe. It is bounded by France to the east and Spain to the south. It is notorious among sailors for its rough seas, with gales of over 70 miles per hour (110 kmh) recorded.

245

A Very Barren Place ▲

Patagonia is a vast region of desert, semidesert, and treeless scrubland taking up most of the southern land area of South America. With an area of 260,000 square miles (673,000 sq km), it is the largest desert in the Americas.

The Capital in the Sky

La Paz in Bolivia is the highest capital city in the world at an altitude of between 10,650 and 13,450 feet (3,250 and 4,100 m).

Hats Made in Ecuador

"Panama" hats are woven in Ecuador from the leaves of the toquilla plant. The hats were given their name by gold-hunters who traveled from the eastern United States to California via Panama (before the Panama Canal was built), as that was easier than the long overland route across the United States. They saw "Panama" hats for sale in Panama City.

The Largest South American Lake ▶

Lake Titicaca, on the borders of Peru and Bolivia, is the largest lake in South America. It is 12,500 feet (3,810 m) above sea level.

The Smallest Continent

Australia lies between the Indian Ocean and the South Pacific, on the opposite side of the world from Europe. The Commonwealth of Australia is both the largest island in the world (although it is not usually counted as an island) and the smallest continent. It covers an area of 2,966,200 square miles (7,682,300 sq km).

Separating the Land

In eastern Australia, from Cape York peninsula in the north to Bass Strait in the south, stretches a broken belt of highland. It runs for 2,300 miles (3,700 km) through Queensland, New South Wales, and Victoria. It is called the Great Dividing Range or Great Divide because it separates the coast from the interior of Australia and causes one set of rivers to flow to the Pacific Ocean and another set to flow inland.

Amazing Hot Springs ▲

Rotorua is about 150 miles (240 km) southeast of Auckland, on the North Island of New Zealand. It is one of the country's most popular tourist resorts. Geysers, boiling pools of mud and water, and steaming hot springs in the earth amaze the visitor. The natives of Rotorua use the natural hot water of the pools for cooking and washing, while many of the hotels and houses are centrally heated by water piped from the boiling springs.

The Most Southern City ▼

Melbourne, Australia, is the world's most southerly urban area to have a population of more than one million people. It was the capital of Australia from 1901 to 1927 and is rivaled in size and importance only by Sydney.

History

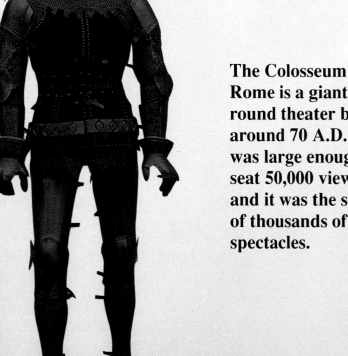

The Colosseum in Rome is a giant, round theater built around 70 A.D. It was large enough to seat 50,000 viewers, and it was the scene of thousands of spectacles.

Mayan "glyphs," or picture-writings, describe the Mayans as being a warlike people who practiced a violent religion that included both human and animal sacrifice.

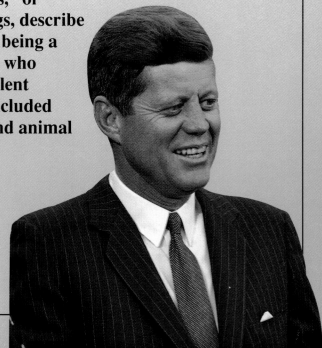

A Wonder of the World

The pyramids were built to remind the citizens left behind just how rich and powerful the Pharaoh had been. Since the ancient Egyptians believed in life after death, they wanted people to be as comfortable as possible in the afterlife. As a result, a person's favorite belongings, as well as much-needed items like clothing and food, were buried with him or her. Egypt's kings and queens obviously wanted to live well in the afterlife, since they put everything they might possibly want, including gold and jewels, ships, and servants, in their tombs. To hold all of this—and to keep all of these things safe from robbers—they built large, safe tombs.

Many workers were needed to construct a pyramid.

The Pharoahs of Egypt ◀

The Pharaohs were the kings and rulers of ancient Egypt, governing more than 5,000 years ago. These rulers had complete, total power and were even treated as gods and goddesses by their people. Despite many wars and conquests, the Pharaohs ruled Egypt until the coming of the Roman Empire, 3,000 years later.

The Curse of the Tomb

Not long after King Tut's tomb was found, the leader of the expedition who discovered it, Lord Carnarvon, died from the effects of a mosquito bite. Other members of the group also met mysterious fates. As a result, some people began to believe that the ancient Egyptians had placed a curse on the tomb. According to this curse, anyone who disturbed King Tutankhamen's tomb would soon meet a violent and terrible fate. No one today, of course, takes the curse very seriously.

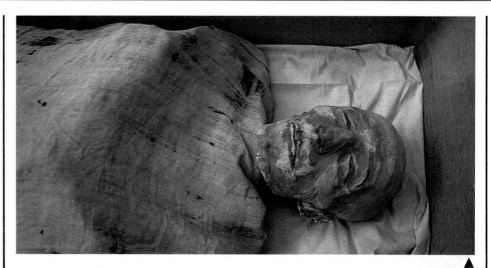

Preserving Mummies

Because they believed that people could live after death, the Egyptians preserved the bodies of those who had died. They first soaked these mummies in herbs and chemicals, wrapping the bodies in bandages and placing them inside a coffin. The coffins were often painted to show the face and body of the person whose body was inside. The Egyptians also made mummies of people's favorite pets, so they could accompany their masters to the afterlife. These pet mummies were then set out close to the main coffin.

The Amazing Tomb of King Tut

King Tutankhamen (or "King Tut" as he is called by modern people) ruled Egypt 2,400 years ago. He died young, at about the age of 18, and was buried with all of the riches and goods he would need in his afterlife. His tomb was discovered in 1922 by an English archaeologist, Howard Carter. The things that were found—as well as the young King's preserved body— created a sensation. Many of these things can now be seen in the world's best museums.

The Persian Empire

The Persian Empire was one of the largest and most powerful kingdoms of the ancient world. Founded in 553 B.C. by the emperor Cyrus, it eventually stretched from Asia Minor to India and relied on good roads and a complex military and political system to maintain its power. The Persians produced some of the greatest pottery, porcelain, and literature of that period in history, and they were known for their fair treatment of the nations they conquered. Until the time of Alexander the Great, Persia was the greatest empire the world had ever seen.

A Very Mighty Empire

Alexander was the King of Macedonia, a small, warlike country to the north of Greece. He became one of the greatest conquerors in the history of the world. Educated in Athens by the great philosopher Aristotle, Alexander became ruler of Macedonia and Athens in 336 B.C. He then set out to conquer the world. He led his armies across to Asia and, in 333 B.C., defeated the Persians, who had the largest empire in the world at that time. He then proceeded south and east, conquering almost all of the known world of the time. By the time he died at the age of 33, his empire spread from Greece to Egypt and as far as India.

The Fall of an Empire

Wherever he went, Alexander spread the Greek culture and way of life. However, his empire was not able to survive without him. After his death, his generals divided the empire among themselves. Soon, it was nothing more than a group of small, weak nations fighting against one another.

The death of Alexander the Great

251

Reading the *Iliad* ◀

The *Iliad* is the story of the war between one group of city-states and the great city of Troy, which was located in what is now Turkey. The book is a long poem that describes the battles and events, as well as the heroes of that war.

Odysseus feigned madness by plowing the seashore.

Adventures of Odysseus

The *Odyssey* tells of the adventures of one of the Trojan War's great heroes, Odysseus, as he made his way home from Troy.

Government of the People

Unlike other ancient nations, Athens was not ruled by a king or emperor. Instead, it had a special governing council. All male citizens were also part of an assembly that made Athens' laws. This meant that everyone—nobles, merchants, and even simple farmers—had a voice in their government.

These people are looking at the objects that Schliemann found at Troy.

The Height of Greek Civilization

In the 400s B.C., the city-state of Athens reached new heights of strength and civilization. Art, plays, and philosophy were flourishing. Athens also had a great deal of military power. Unfortunately, Athens grew too confident and was led into a war with another Greek city-state, Sparta. It was defeated and never quite recovered its glory.

A Great Discovery

In 1873, a German scientist named Schliemann discovered the ruins of Troy—a city whose citizens fought a ten-year war with ancient Greece. Over the years, dozens of scientists have examined the ruins. Finally, an American expedition concluded that the walled city was in fact the Troy of the *Iliad*.

Hippocrates was the father of modern medicine.

Ancient Greek Learning

In ancient Greece, learning and knowledge were highly valued, especially in the city-state of Athens. In fact, Greek philosophers and scientists made contributions to knowledge that we are still using today. Democritus, for example, came up with the idea of atoms 2,400 years before the atomic bomb. Pythagoras helped create the geometry that we still study in school today. Herodotus wrote the world's first history books, trying to find out the truth of what happened in the past. Hippocrates started modern medicine, showing people how to cure injuries and illnesses scientifically, instead of with prayers and magic.

Rome's Most Famous Ruler

Julius Caesar was one of ancient Rome's greatest soldiers and leaders. After an early career in politics, Caesar set out to become a military leader. In less than ten years, he had conquered what is now France, Belgium, and parts of The Netherlands, Germany, and Switzerland. He even led troops across the English Channel to invade Britain. Later, he turned his attention eastward and added territories in the Middle East to Rome's growing empire. In 45 B.C., he was made permanent head of Rome's government and began to be treated as a god by the people. This made other politicians jealous and led to his murder by a group led by one of Caesar's closest friends, Marcus Brutus.

Mark Antony and Cleopatra

The Queen of the Nile

For thousands of years, Cleopatra has been a symbol of beauty, power, and romance. She became a queen of Egypt at the age of 17, but it was her love affairs with Julius Caesar and, later, Mark Antony, that made her so famous. Cleopatra and Antony joined together to try to take over the entire Roman Empire. They were unsuccessful, however, and they both committed suicide.

A Roman Extravaganza

The Colosseum was a giant, round theater built around 70 A.D. It was large enough to seat 50,000 viewers, and it was the scene of thousands of battles between gladiators, fights between men and animals, and other spectacles. At times, it was even flooded with water so that navies of gladiators could battle one another. Lightning, earthquakes, and vandalism have left it a ruin, but it still stands in Rome today.

Ruling the Roman Empire

During the early days, Rome was a Republic, ruled by a Senate and consuls who were elected to office. As Rome grew weaker, however, the Republic became weaker. Professional soldiers often helped bring leaders to power by force of arms. Senators and business people took power in order to make profits for themselves. By the time of Julius Caesar, political battles in Rome often led to civil war. Finally, Julius Caesar's adopted son, Octavian, took power. He ruled Rome for 45 years and brought peace. By the end of his life, the Republic was over, and Rome had become an Empire ruled by an Emperor.

A Terrible Emperor

The worst Roman emperor was probably Caligula, who came to power at the age of 25. He began his rule quite well, but illnesses seemed to bring about a mental breakdown after a few months. After that, he behaved in a dangerous and violent manner. He murdered his relatives, made his favorite horse a high public official, and fought in the arena as a gladiator. In one of his more outrageous acts, he made a bridge of ships across the Bay of Naples. He filled the ships with houses and trees, and announced that he was now able to cross the sea on dry land. To celebrate his accomplishment, he threw a giant party on the ships and had hundreds of his guests thrown into the sea and murdered. Four years later, he was murdered by an officer of his imperial guards.

Respected Roman Emperors

The emperors Trajan and Hadrian brought good government back to Rome after years of corruption. Marcus Aurelius was another excellent emperor, a wise man who was a successful politician and general as well as a philosopher.

Marcus Aurelius

Vicious Vikings ▲

Between the years 700 and 1000 A.D., warriors from Norway, Sweden, and Denmark called Vikings attacked people all through northern Europe. Sometimes, they simply attacked and stole whatever they wanted; other times, they took over land and settled themselves as farmers and landowners. These Vikings were among the most fierce and cruel fighters the world had ever seen. Viking attacks usually meant that homes were burned, churches and other buildings were robbed, and dozens of people were killed or taken away as slaves. As you might expect, people were terrified whenever they heard that Vikings were near.

Viking Settlements ▲

Unlike other conquerors, the Vikings never built up a single organized empire. They did, however, sail all the way to Greece and Turkey, using the rivers and seas of Eastern Europe. They traded with Greek and Arab merchants there and brought many goods back home to Scandinavia. They also set up settlements in Iceland and Greenland. Many experts believe that they sailed as far as North America, building settlements in Labrador and Newfoundland.

Fierce Genghis Khan

Genghis Khan was the son of a Mongolian chief who led his armies halfway across the world in the early 1200s. After conquering several small Mongolian tribes, he led his army of light horsemen into China, which he quickly conquered. In 1217, he sent one army to capture Korea and another into Chinese Turkestan. By 1219, his armies were invading parts of what was formerly the Soviet Union, and by 1223, they had conquered much of Russia. After he died in 1227, Genghis Khan's forces kept marching westward, eventually reaching the Dnieper River in southern Russia.

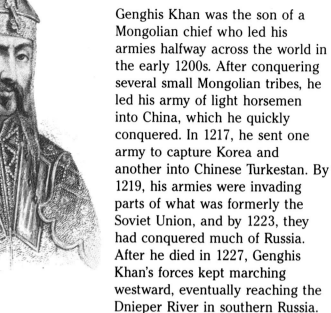

Leif Eriksson.

Vikings Everyone Knows

Erik the Red, who founded the Viking settlement in Greenland, is one of the best-known Vikings, as is his son, Leif Eriksson. Leif is supposed to have been the leader of the Viking expedition that reached North America.

Renowned Mongol Soldiers

Unlike other armies of the time, Genghis Khan's soldiers wore lightweight armor and rode small, fast horses. Most of his soldiers were born horsemen, able to ride for days at a time without rest. (In fact, stories say that they often did not even stop to cook food; they merely drank a little horse's blood and rode on.) They were also fierce warriors, totally destroying the cities and lands they conquered. When the city of Herat, Afghanistan, rebelled against the Mongols, Genghis Khan's soldiers burned and looted for a week, killing over 1.5 million people. Their violent actions made them the most feared fighters in the history of the world.

Popular Kublai Khan

Kublai Khan, the grandson of Genghis Khan, became the ruler of the Mongol empire in 1259. Not content with the kingdom that had been passed down to him, Kublai Khan sent armies to the south, finishing the conquest of China. He was a superb ruler, but he was also intelligent and tolerant. He was very popular with his Chinese subjects, as well as among his own Mongol people. Kublai Khan admired Chinese culture so much that he gradually adapted himself and his own people to it.

Knights fought bravely in the Crusades.

An Honorable Knighthood

By the year 1000, the Church began to put forward a new kind of knighthood. Laws were passed that protected people from the actions of knights. The idea of knights as protectors of the less fortunate was spread. Most importantly, the knights themselves were convinced to join in a great Crusade to free the Holy Land of Palestine from Muslim rule. All of these factors worked to change Europe's knights from rough, violent bullies to more well-behaved and noble individuals.

On Becoming a Knight ▼

Once a young man had become a knight, he was supposed to live a model life. According to his vows, his primary job was to help make the world a better place to live. This meant fighting against his master's enemies, following the rules and regulations of his religion, and helping those in need. Since knights were still supposed to fight, much of their time was spent making themselves stronger and better fighters.

A young man is knighted.

Life in the Middle Ages

The Middle Ages began when the Roman Empire fell apart, and went on for almost a thousand years. This was a rough, violent time in Europe. Almost 90 percent of the people were peasants—farm laborers who worked on the lands of rich nobles. These peasants were not free at all, bound to their lords and the land from birth. Food and clothing were scarce, and life was always a battle for survival. The nobles, as you might expect, lived better, but they certainly didn't have an easy life. They had clothing and food, but little else. Their homes were cold, they had little entertainment, and they were almost constantly at war with foreign invaders or greedy neighbors who wanted to take over their land. All of this made life so hard that few people ever lived a very long life.

Games, Dances, and Song ▲

Knights and nobles kept themselves busy with games, dances, and, especially, singing. By the 1200s, most knights were well trained in singing, playing the lute, and writing their own songs. (If a knight was not especially talented in music, he could hire a professional singer to provide the voice and music.) Other forms of entertainment included festivals, banquets, and contests that tested knights' skill with the lance and sword.

Fighting the Holy Wars

The Crusades were a series of religious wars that took place between 1095 and 1270. Their goal was to keep the Turks and other Muslims from invading Europe and to return the holy city of Jerusalem to Christian control. Over the years, there were many Crusades, and battles were fought everywhere from Egypt to Jerusalem to Constantinople (the present-day city of Istanbul). In the end, the Muslim armies proved too strong and they eventually gained complete control of the Middle East by the 1500s.

Knights defended their castle fiercely.

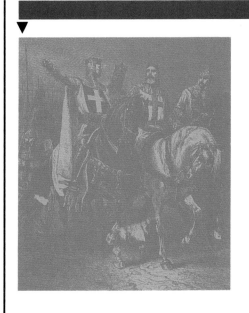

King Richard the Lion-hearted

King Richard I of England was nicknamed "Lion Heart" because he was a brave and successful soldier. Whether he was as well loved by his people as legends say is not known, especially since he spent most of his life away from England—at one war or another. What we do know is that he won many battles in France, Italy, and Palestine and that he was killed attacking a castle in France.

Armor protected knights in battle.

259

The Queen of the Golden Age

When Queen Elizabeth I came to power, England had been through several years of unrest. She quickly brought order and set out to make England the greatest power in the world. She also loved music, poetry, and dance. Under her rule, England enjoyed a time of great cultural triumph. Even in her own time she was applauded as the queen of England's "golden age."

The Famous King Henry VIII

Stories describe King Henry VIII as a fat man who had many wives. In truth, Henry was a handsome young man when he came to the throne in 1509 at age 18. Moreover, he was well educated and was a talented poet and musician. He was also a skilled athlete who often won contests that were held at the royal court. His marriage problems were caused by his desire to leave England a male heir who would become king after him. Because his first wife had no sons, he divorced her to marry someone else. This put him in conflict with the Pope, starting years of problems. Unfortunately, Henry did not always find peaceful solutions to problems, sending many men and women to their deaths. Surprisingly, despite all these troubles, he remained quite popular with the people—and the nobles—for most of his life.

Men Who Should Not Have Been King ▲

King George III was one of the worst kings of England, since his policies helped bring about the American Revolution. Another poor ruler was Richard III, who is supposed to have killed his own young nephews in order to make his way to the throne. Going further back in history is another very bad king, King William II, the son of William the Conqueror. William II came to the throne at the age of 31, already famous for his wicked life. His years on the throne were spent making plots against his brother Robert, the Duke of Normandy, and setting up harsh new taxes in England. His rule ended when he was found killed by an arrow at the age of 44. No one confessed to the murder, but most people believed that it was ordered by William's brother, who later became King Henry I.

The Long Reign of Queen Victoria ▼

Queen Victoria had the longest reign of any British ruler. Coming to the throne in 1837 at the age of 18, she ruled for 64 years until her death in 1901. She was among Britain's most popular monarchs, despite the fact that people seemed annoyed at her way of hiding from the public. The 50th and 60th anniversaries of her coronation were treated as major national holidays, with celebrations going on all through the vast British Empire.

The Sun Never Sets on the British Empire

By the middle of the 1800s, when Queen Victoria was named Empress of India, the British Empire stretched all around the globe. In fact, one of the old sayings was that "the sun never sets on the British Empire"—meaning that the sun was always shining at some point in the world where the British flag flew.

Britain's Famous Leader

Winston Churchill was a symbol of Great Britain's refusal to surrender to its enemies during World War II. He broadcast speeches on the radio, made public appearances, and convinced the United States to provide as much aid as possible. His words urged people all over the world to fight the Nazis (whose name he insisted on mispronouncing, as a kind of insult) and their allies. In one of his most famous speeches he told the world that "we shall defend our island whatever the cost may be, we shall fight on the beaches...we shall fight in the fields and in the streets, we shall fight in the hills; we shall never surrender." After the war, the British people wanted a change and voted his Tory party out of power in 1945.

The Three Napoleons

Besides the famous Napoleon Bonaparte, there were two other French emperors named Napoleon. Napoleon II (1811-1832) was the only son of Napoleon I (Bonaparte) and his second wife, the empress Marie-Louise. At birth, he was named King of Rome. When his father abdicated the throne, Napoleon II was named his successor. He never ruled France, however, since the French people chose to be ruled by Louis XVIII instead. Napoleon III (1801-1873) was the nephew of Bonaparte. After two unsuccessful attempts to overthrow the monarchy, he fled to England. After the Revolution of 1848, he returned to France and was first elected to the National Assembly and later to the presidency. He crowned himself emperor of France as Napoleon III in 1852.

Coronation of Napoleon and Josephine ▲

In December 1804, Napoleon crowned himself Emperor of France. He also crowned his wife, Josephine, Empress of France.

The Height of the French Empire ▬ ▲

At one time, Napoleon's conquests stretched from the English Channel in the west all the way to Moscow, Russia. Italy, Spain, and even Denmark and Norway were tied to him. This gave him one of the largest empires seen in Europe since the days of the ancient Romans.

Napoleon's Famous Pose ▬▬▬ ▼

Pictures of Napoleon often show him with his right hand stretched across his stomach and placed in his coat or shirt. In fact, this picture is so familiar that people have been making jokes about it for over a hundred years. The reason for this pose is that portrait painters thought it looked dignified and saved them from the job of drawing someone's hand (which can be quite a difficult task). If you look at the portraits in an art museum, you will probably see dozens of other people holding their hands in exactly the same way.

Liberty, Equality, Fraternity

The French Revolution was fought because the peasants and workers decided to throw off the rule of the royal family and the whole system that seemed to keep them poor, overtaxed, and attacked. Hundreds of France's nobles, including the king and queen, were killed, and a new government—a Republic—began.

Let Them Eat Cake

According to stories told in the late 1700s, Marie Antoinette, the Queen of France, was a spoiled woman who loved luxury. When she was told that the people of France had no bread to eat, she replied, "Let them eat cake," a message that seemed to say that there was no problem of hunger and that everyone lived as well as she did. Marie Antoinette, who was particularly disliked, was beheaded during the French Revolution.

A Famous French Statesman

Many people consider Charles de Gaulle the greatest hero of modern France. When Germany invaded France at the beginning of World War II, de Gaulle refused to admit defeat. France itself surrendered, but de Gaulle gathered thousands of Frenchmen in England. Calling themselves the "free French," they continued to fight. When the Allies invaded Europe and marched to free France from the Nazi armies, de Gaulle's free French army marched with them. After the war, de Gaulle helped organize a new French government. During the 1950s, the French people called on de Gaulle again. He came out of retirement to lead France one last time.

A Civilized King

Frederick the Great was King of Prussia from 1740 to 1786. (At this time, there was no Germany, only a group of different states of which Prussia was the largest and strongest.) A wise and strong ruler, he was known as a skilled military leader and for his fondness for literature and the arts. In fact, when he was young he tried to run away from the royal court so that he could pursue his scholarly interests. Throughout his life, Frederick worked hard to develop and modernize his country. He encouraged agriculture and education. He also did much for primary education and the study of science. He called himself "the first servant of the State" and made the Prussian government extremely efficient.

The Iron Chancellor

In Germany, the chief political leader is called "chancellor," and the "Iron Chancellor" was Otto von Bismarck, the man who led Germany for almost 30 years. He was a firm leader who often overruled the German emperor (or "Kaiser"). His policies made Germany into a strong, wealthy country. In 1890, however, the young Kaiser Wilhelm II decided that he wanted to rule without the advice of his strong Chancellor and threw Bismarck out of office.

Heil Hitler!

The word *Nazi* is an abbreviation for the German words meaning "National Socialist German Workers' Party." Adolf Hitler became president of the group in 1921. Hitler took advantage of the hard times Germany had after World War I to convince the German people that only he could restore German power and wealth. Part of his plan, however, were racist policies that declared that all other nationalities, races, and ethnic groups were inferior to Germans. He also believed that Germans would ultimately rule the world. The actions of the Nazis led to World War II and the death of millions of people.

The Age of the Aztecs ▼

The Aztecs, arriving in Mexico during the 1200s, were one of the most important people in North America before the arrival of Europeans. Although they started out as a poor, weak tribe, they soon began conquering the land of other groups in the area, as well as making new farmland by creating man-made islands in the giant lakes of central Mexico. By 1325, they were building their great capital city near what is now Mexico City. They remained powerful rulers until the Spanish defeated them in the 1500s.

The Aztec Way of Life ▲

The Aztecs were a highly advanced people. They built marvelous cities, had a successful system for draining lakes and making new farmland, and were excellent astronomers—predicting eclipses and seasons. They were also a fierce people with a very strong army, which allowed them to use captives as human sacrifices to their many gods.

Reading Mayan Glyphs ▲

For many years, scientists believed that the Maya were peaceful farmers, quite different from their violent Aztec neighbors to the north. Recently, however, scientists have learned to read Mayan "glyphs," picture-writings that they left on buildings and stone tablets. These writings give us a different picture of Mayan life. They describe a warlike people who practiced a violent religion that included both human and animal sacrifice.

The Mayan Years ▲

The Maya were an important group living in America before the coming of Europeans. Their empire reached from southern Mexico to Guatemala and Belize. The Maya reached their height between 300 A.D. and 900 A.D.

The city of Cuzco today
▲

A Place for Everyone ▲

The Inca were a highly organized people. Every group of ten families had a leader who reported to a captain. The captain was responsible for five leaders—a total of 50 families. The Inca himself was the ultimate ruler. Everything belonged to the state in the Inca system. Everyone worked, and a certain amount of everything the people produced went to the Inca himself and to his government.

Inca and the City of the Sun

The "City of the Sun" was Cuzco, the capital of the Inca Empire in South America. Around the year 800 A.D., the Inca people began building a wonderful civilization. At its peak, it stretched from Bolivia to parts of Argentina and Chile. They were ruled by a king called the Inca, who was believed to be a god descended from the sun. This ruler, who had total power of life and death over his people, lived in the sacred "City of the Sun."

The End of the Inca

In the 1500s, the Spanish leader, Francisco Pizarro, had the Inca rulers killed so that Spain would be in complete control of the Incan people, land, and gold.

The Ruins of Machu Picchu ▼

In 1911, Hiram Bingham of Yale University discovered an Incan city. High in the Andes mountains, between two high, rough mountain peaks, he came upon the city of Machu Picchu where a temple, a fortress, and terraced gardens were found.

Vikings on American Soil

For many years, American children were taught that Christopher Columbus discovered America in 1492. Evidence, however, points to settlements on this continent long before that time. According to ruins and records, it seems that Vikings landed in North America around the year 1000. According to the "Tale of the Greenlanders," which tells many stories of the Vikings' voyages, Leif Eriksson learned of a place called "Vinland" (Wine-land) and set out to find it. The tales say that he landed in that area, setting up a fort for Viking settlers. Later trips were made by Leif's brother and another Viking explorer, Thorfinn Karlsefni. For years, people looked for proof that Vinland existed. Recently, ruins were found in Newfoundland and Labrador, Canada.

The Landing of the *Mayflower*

The Pilgrims were one of several groups in England who wanted to break away from the country's official church, the Church of England. They made plans to set up a new home for themselves in North America—on the Hudson River, in what is now New York State. However, when their ship, the *Mayflower*, finally reached the New World, it landed at Cape Cod, in Massachusetts. Since the captain of the ship was unwilling to risk taking the ship any farther along the coast, the Pilgrims set up their colony at Plymouth, Massachusetts.

History Repeats Itself

The first *Mayflower* carried the Pilgrims from Southampton, England, to Massachusetts in 66 days. In 1957, a copy of the ship was built and sailed from England to the United States in honor of that first voyage. The *Mayflower II* proved faster than its ancestor, making the journey in just 53 days. Since then, it has been used as a floating museum and tourist attraction.

The Mayflower braved treacherous seas to reach the New World.

Organized Minutemen

By 1774, feelings against Great Britain were so strong that the militia of Worcester County, Massachusetts, decided that part of their militia should always be ready to fight at a moment's notice. The men soon got the name "Minutemen." After the Minutemen fought against British soldiers at the Battles of Lexington and Concord, other colonies began setting up Minutemen units of their own.

The Green Mountain Boys

The Green Mountain Boys were a militia set up in the early 1770s in Vermont. Originally, they got together to keep New York from claiming land in Vermont. When the Revolution broke out, they actually took part in the first real military action of the war. Led by Ethan Allen and Benedict Arnold, 100 Green Mountain Boys, along with 100 other volunteers, captured Fort Ticonderoga, on May 10, 1775.

The Father of Our Country

George Washington was a rare individual, able to be both a skilled general and a brilliant politician. As commander in chief of the American forces during the Revolution, he managed to win a victory against England, the most powerful army in the world. Much of the credit was in Washington's ability to get people to work and fight together despite differences of opinion. Later, when Washington became the first president of the United States, he faced an even more difficult job. The Constitution described what kind of government the country would have, but it was up to Washington to actually set up that government.

The Site of Washington, D.C. ◀

The people writing the U.S. Constitution decided that the capital of the nation should not be in either the North or the South. George Washington himself chose the site for the new city, Washington, D.C., selecting the French architect Pierre Charles L'Enfant to plan it.

A Famous American Fighter

Andrew Jackson was famous as a fighter long before the War of 1812. As a boy during the Revolution, he was struck with a saber by a British officer when young Jackson refused to clean the officer's boots. Later, he became a general in the Tennessee militia. In 1814, he put down a rising of Creek Indians and became famous as an Indian fighter. It was this reputation that led to his command at the Battle of New Orleans. In 1818, he led a group of soldiers into Florida, chasing a group of Indian raiders. Even though this action caused problems since Florida was a Spanish territory, the arguments over the situation eventually led to Florida's becoming part of the United States.

Attacking the Nation's Capital

During the War of 1812, U.S. forces invaded Canada several times. To get even, the British sent a force of 4,000 soldiers to take the American capital, Washington, D.C. In August 1814, they arrived by ship and captured the city easily, burning the Capitol, the president's house, and other important buildings. The attack came as a complete surprise, and it was a terrible blow to the young nation's pride.

The Defeat of Tecumseh ▼

Tecumseh was a Shawnee leader who tried to save Indian lands from being completely taken over by white settlers. In the early 1800s, he organized the Ohio, Michigan, and other tribes to act against white settlements. In 1811, warriors led by his brother were defeated by General William Henry Harrison, and Tecumseh's power was broken. He was finally killed during the War of 1812.

Thomas Jefferson

America's 50th Anniversary ▲

July 4, 1826, was the 50th anniversary of the Declaration of Independence, and celebrations went on throughout the United States. On that day, however, two former presidents died— Thomas Jefferson, the author of the Declaration of Independence and the nation's third president, and John Adams, one of the leaders of the Revolution and the country's second president.

John Quincy Adams

John Adams

The Celebrated Adams Family

The Adams Family of Massachusetts was one of the most remarkable groups in the history of the United States. It included two presidents, John Adams and John Quincy Adams; Charles Francis Adams, a member of Congress and a diplomat; Charles Francis Adams, Jr., a president of the Union Pacific Railroad; Henry Adams, a writer and historian; Brooks Adams, a historian and radical thinker; and Charles Francis Adams III, Secretary of the Navy during the 1920s.

The March of the Nez Perce

Chief Joseph was the leader of the Nez Perce Indians who tried to lead his people all the way from their home in the Northwest to Canada. For three months, an army of more than 5,000 soldiers chased the 500 Nez Perce over Oregon, Washington, Idaho, and Montana. When Chief Joseph finally surrendered, his people had marched over 1,000 miles.

Putting Up a Good Fight ▲

A leader of the Chiricahua Apaches, Geronimo was famous for his raids on white settlers. Although he was caught many times, he also managed to escape on numerous occasions. In all, 5,000 soldiers and 500 Indians chased after Geronimo and his band of 35 men, eight boys, and many women. He was finally captured and sent first to Florida and then to Alabama. Although he tried to escape several times, he finally settled into a life of peace and quiet.

Custer's Last Stand ▲

When gold was discovered in South Dakota, hundreds of white settlers entered the area. This led to Indian attacks, and a large army was sent to protect the settlers against the Indians. Lieutenant Colonel George Armstrong Custer, along with 600 men, was sent out to scout for Indians. One group of Custer's force attacked a group of Indians near the Little Bighorn River in Montana. They found, to their horror, that instead of a few hundred warriors, there was a force of almost 2,500. They retreated, as did another group of soldiers. Custer, along with 226 soldiers under his command, attacked. In the fighting that followed, Custer and all of his men were killed. This battle was called Custer's Last Stand.

Honest Abe

From his youth, Abraham Lincoln was known for his personal honesty. According to some sources, the nickname "Honest Abe" was given to him in childhood; others say that Lincoln was given this name for his integrity as a young lawyer. In any event, Lincoln was known as "Honest Abe" by the time he first served in the United States Congress in 1847.

All Men Are Created Equal

In 1863, Lincoln issued the Emancipation Proclamation, which freed slaves in all of the states fighting against the Union. It did not officially end slavery, since some of the states remaining in the Union still had laws permitting slavery. It did, however, give the states that had joined the Confederacy a strong message that the days of slavery were over.

The Death of a President

Lincoln was shot on the night of April 14, 1865, just a few months after the final surrender of the Confederate armies. The man who shot the president while he was at the theater was an actor named John Wilkes Booth. Born in Maryland, Booth had devout Southern sympathies and saw Lincoln as a man who would destroy the defeated states. He had originally planned to kidnap Lincoln and hold him for the ransom of Confederate soldiers held in prison camps in the North. Since this scheme failed, Booth decided to assassinate the president. Eight people were found guilty on June 30, 1865, of conspiring with Booth to kill Lincoln.

Our Fallen Heroes

Lincoln was the first United States president to be murdered in office—unfortunately he was not the last. On July 2, 1882, President James Garfield was on his way through the train station in Washington D.C., when a stranger came up and fired two shots. The murderer, a man named Charles Guiteau, shot the president because he had not been given a job as U.S. Consul in Paris. Nineteen years later, another president was murdered. On September 5, 1901, President William McKinley gave an important speech at the Pan-American Exposition in Buffalo, New York. The next day he attended the fair again, taking a tour of the Temple of Music. While McKinley was shaking hands with people in the crowd, a man named Leon Czolgosz reached out his hand and shot the president. Eight days later, McKinley died. The most recent president to be murdered was John F. Kennedy, who was shot on November 22, 1963, while driving through the streets of Dallas, Texas. The man who was arrested for the murder, Lee Harvey Oswald, was shot a few days later.

A Square Deal

The words "square deal" were made famous by Theodore Roosevelt, the 20th president of the United States, when he declared that he would make sure that there would be a "square deal" for everyone, rich and poor alike.

The New Frontier

While he was running for president, John F. Kennedy used the words "New Frontier" as he urged Americans to think of the future in the same way as earlier Americans had—and to accept the challenge to change the world for the better.

The New Deal

When Franklin D. Roosevelt was elected president, the United States was suffering from hard times. To confront the problems, Roosevelt declared that there would be a "new deal"—new policies that would make things better for everyone. For many years, Roosevelt worked to make the "new deal" a reality.

Exploring for France

In 1534, the French explorer Jacques Cartier sailed up the St. Lawrence River, exploring the area. He returned there later and set up a fort on a piece of high ground that he named *Mont Real,* or "mount royal." The place has been called Montreal ever since.

ARRÊT STOP

Canada's Two Languages

The area of what is now Canada was originally explored and settled by the French, and for many years the area belonged to France. At the end of a series of wars between France and Britain, the territory was given to Great Britain. As one of the terms of the treaty, Britain promised that the Canadians (or French-Canadians, as they are sometimes called) would be allowed to keep their own religion, laws, and language. As a result, there are many French-speaking areas in Canada today.

The Royal Canadian Mounties ▲

You probably have seen pictures of Canada's famous "Mounties," their national police, in their bright red coats. Although the Mounties do not wear these uniforms for their everyday work, they do wear them on dressy occasions.

Friendly Neighbors

Although the United States and Canada have had good relations for the past one hundred years, this was not always the case. During the American Revolution, American forces invaded Canada several times. During the War of 1812, part of Canada became a battleground between American and British soldiers. In the 1800s, there were several disagreements over borders in Maine and Oregon. At one point, the United States seemed willing to go to war over its borders in the Northwest. Since the 1870s, however, any disagreements that have come up have been handled without threat of war or violence.

Heroes of Mexican Liberty

Pancho Villa and Emiliano Zapata were important leaders of the Mexican Revolution. Beginning in 1909, Villa helped overthrow several Mexican dictators, including the much-hated Porfirio Diaz. Zapata was a *mestizo*, a peasant who made his living training and raising horses. He organized other peasants into a powerful political party that fought for the liberty and rights of the Mexican people. Villa was killed in 1923. Zapata was murdered by political enemies in 1919. Both are considered heroes of Mexican liberty.

Pancho Villa

Emiliano Zapata

The Halls of Montezuma

The "halls of Montezuma," words made famous by the official song of the U.S. Marine Corps, were the domain of the Aztec Indians, near what is now Mexico City. Montezuma was the last king of the Aztecs, the people who ruled Mexico before the Spanish invaders arrived in the 1500s. Stories differ about what happened when the Spanish leader, Cortez, arrived in Mexico City. Some say that Montezuma was killed by his own people because they were angry that he did not fight against the Spanish. Others say that it was the Spanish themselves who killed the Aztec king. Either way, after Montezuma's death, the Spanish had little trouble in conquering the huge country once ruled by the Aztecs.

The Liberator of South America

Simon Bolivar, a Venezuelan born in 1783, was the great liberator of South America. Through his efforts and advice, Bolivia, Colombia, Ecuador, Panama, Peru, and Venezuela were all able to overthrow their Spanish masters and become independent countries. An idealist and unselfish man, Bolivar died penniless.

Setting South America Free

Through the efforts of Simon Bolivar and General Jose de San Martin, South America was free of Spain by 1826. At the same time that Simon Bolivar was helping free the nations of northern South America, General Jose de San Martin was defeating the Spanish in Argentina, Chile, and Peru. While fighting against the Spanish in Argentina, San Martin realized that Argentina would never be free of Spain unless Peru and Chile were also free. So, he marched his Army of the Andes across the mountains and freed Chile from Spanish rule. He then led his men up the coast of Peru, where Bolivar helped him free that country.

Simon Bolivar

The Many Faces of Brazil

Unlike most of the other countries in Latin America, Brazil was discovered and colonized by Portugal, not Spain. As a result, Portuguese, not Spanish, is the official language of the country. Many other languages are spoken by the Indian groups who still live there and the immigrants who came to Brazil from Italy, Germany, Spain, and even Poland and Japan.

Evita Peron

Hugely popular, Eva or "Evita" Peron was the wife of Juan Domingo Peron, who took power in Argentina in 1946. She organized labor unions, worked to get Argentine women the right to vote, and helped raise money to build schools and hospitals. She also forced the closing of newspapers and radio stations that opposed the Perons. She died in 1952, a few years before her husband's dictatorship was overthrown.

Dr. Livingstone, I Presume

In 1866, the Scottish explorer David Livingstone set out on his third expedition into the heart of Africa. Soon, however, all word from him stopped. The *New York Herald,* one of the leading newspapers in the United States, sent its best reporter, Henry Morton Stanley, to find out what had happened to Livingstone. After marching through the jungle for many months, Stanley finally found Livingstone on the shores of Lake Tanganyika. Livingstone was seriously ill and was grateful for the food and medicine Stanley brought, although he was not yet ready to return to civilization. Eighteen months later, Livingstone died. Stanley took up Livingstone's work, exploring the land and waterways of Central Africa for the next 15 years. His adventures made him one of the best-known and admired men in the world.

Henry Morton Stanley

David Livingstone

South African Freedom Fighter

The name of Nelson Mandela is linked to the cause of freedom in South Africa. The son of a South African tribal chief, he became a lawyer in the 1940s and began working against the South African government's policy of "apartheid"—the system that kept black and white South Africans completely separate from one another. Mandela's activities led to his trial for treason in 1961, which found him innocent and set him free. He was arrested again in 1962 and sent to prison for five years. While he was in jail, he was also charged with planning to use violence to overthrow the government of South Africa. In 1964, he was sentenced to life in prison, although he was released in 1990.

The Land Down Under

Although people had lived in Australia for thousands of years, Europeans first learned of the continent in the 1500s. Between 1516 and 1530, Portuguese sailors mapped part of the coast. Later, Spanish, Dutch, and English explorers also visited the area. Captain James Cook, the most famous of these adventurers, explored the area in the 1770s.

Gem of a Business ▲

Besides being a South African politician, Cecil Rhodes was the organizer of the famous De Beers diamond mining company. After many years of struggle, he managed to create the world's largest diamond company, gaining almost complete control of the diamond mining industry. Without him, there would have been far fewer diamonds mined in the world.

Fascinating Aborigines

When Europeans first arrived in Australia, there were almost 300,000 native people, or "Aborigines" as they were called. These people had come to Australia thousands of years before and lived by hunting, gathering food, and fishing. Conflicts between the new settlers and the Aborigines almost always ended up in the settlers' favor.

Australian Independence

Australia did not become an independent country until January 1, 1901. On that day the different provinces and areas were joined together into a single nation and were made a part of the British Commonwealth.

Sports

Basketball is the only major world sport that began and developed in the United States.

The number a football player wears can be a matter of personal choice as long as it is not yet worn by a teammate. There is, however, a system behind the numbers. Quarterbacks and kickers, for example, wear 1 through 19 and running backs wear 20 through 49.

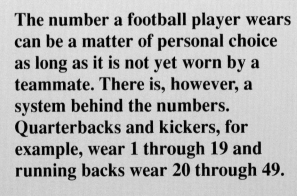

Early Olympic Games ►

The first Olympic Games were held in ancient Greece in 776 B.C. Athletes, artists, and even poets gathered at the temple of Zeus (the chief god of the ancient Greeks) at Olympia. There, writers and artists shared their works, and the athletes held a race that was roughly 191 yards (175 m) long. As time went on, the festival became more complicated and more and more athletic events were added. The main events were running, wrestling, boxing, horse racing, and a pentathlon (five different events). In the early games, valuable prizes were awarded. Later, the prize was a branch of wild olives.

The Spirit of the Olympics ▲

Any citizen of a country who is an amateur, nonprofessional (nonpaid) athlete is allowed to compete for his or her nation in the Olympic Games. In recent years, there has been a lot of discussion about whether or not many athletes are really amateurs or not. As a result, there is pressure to allow any athlete, whether or not he or she is ever paid to perform, to compete in the games.

Modern Olympic Games ▼

After the Roman emperor Theodosius banned the games in 393 A.D., the Olympic Games disappeared for almost 1,500 years. In the late 1800s, a member of the French nobility, Baron Pierre de Coubertin, suggested that the games be brought back. In 1894, he organized a meeting of athletic groups from nine different countries, and they decided to hold a new Olympic Games. The first of the modern games was held in Greece in 1896, and since then, they have been held every four years—except during times of war.

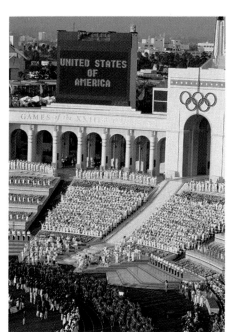

Daley Thompson was a famous decathlete.

An Ancient Way of Doing Things ▶

The torch is a symbol of the peaceful competition that signifies the Olympics. Before each set of Olympic Games, runners carry a torch all the way from Greece to the site of the games. This is done to remind people of how the games began. It also reminds them that the games are run in the same spirit as the games of ancient Greece—which were created to show that people's bodies should be as fit and healthy as their minds.

Testing an Athlete's Skill

In ancient Greece, the pentathlon event tested an athlete's all-around strength and ability. It was revived for the modern games as a similar test taking place over five days. From 1912 to 1924, the pentathlon consisted of a sprint, long jump, discus throw, javelin throw, and a long-distance run. Later, the pentathlon was changed to be a test of "military" skills. It includes horseback riding, fencing, pistol-shooting, swimming, and cross-country running.

The Biggest Challenge

The decathlon is thought to be the most challenging of all Olympic events. It takes up two days and includes ten different events. It consists of a sprint, long jump, shot put, high jump, and a run on the first day. On the second day, athletes compete in the hurdles, discus throw, pole vault, javelin throw, and a long-distance run. Athletes receive scores for each event and receive their points on the basis of a complicated scoring system.

Row Your Boat ▶

Oars to row boats were used as far back as ancient Egypt and Phoenicia. The Romans also used great numbers of rowers to move their giant warships. From the time of the Middle Ages, people in Europe used oars to move boats up and down rivers. Races between these ferrymen, as they were called, were held whenever two rowers bragged about their skills. The first organized rowing events were modeled on these races. Since then, people have rowed against each other in many different kinds of boats. In England, in particular, hundreds of people turn out to see rowing contests between schools and universities.

Olympic Rules

Each Olympic Games lasts about two weeks. Every participating country is limited to three entries (four in Winter Games). Competitors must be citizens of the country they represent, and each must sign a statement that he or she is an amateur. There is no age limit, and medals are awarded for individual events.

Very Successful Olympics ▲

The XXIIIrd (23rd) Olympic Games proved to be the most successful financially, and the most highly attended with some 5 million spectators overall. It is estimated that as many as 2.5 billion viewers watched at least some of the Olympics (between July 27 and August 13, 1984), making this the highest worldwide television audience ever recorded.

Let the Winter Games Begin ▲

Unlike the modern Summer Games that began in 1896, the Winter Games were begun in 1924. They include various forms of skiing, skating, ice hockey, and bobsledding.

Controversial Site

There was considerable criticism when Mexico City was awarded the 1968 Games. Many people believed that the high altitude (7,500 feet (2,300 m)) would adversely affect the athletes.

Unusual Competitive Swimming

Competitive swimming has been an Olympic event since 1896. In the early 1900s, some unusual events were part of the Games. In 1900, for example, when the Games' swimming events were held on the Seine River in France, a 200-meter obstacle race involved climbing over a pole and a line of boats and swimming under them.

Meters over Yards ▲

When the Federation Internationale de Natation Amateur (FINA) took over competitive swimming, race lengths increasingly came to be measured in meters. In 1969, world records for yard-measured races were abolished.

Diving Difficulty ▲

Diving is an Olympic event that includes both springboard and high board competitions. Divers are awarded points for the success with which they perform dives of varying degrees of difficulty. The sport requires immense concentration and superb coordination.

A Swimming Feat

The first person to swim the English Channel was Captain Matthew Webb. In 1875, he covered the distance from Dover to Cape Cris Nez in 21 hours 45 minutes, swimming breaststroke. By the 1980s, the fastest time for the crossing was cut to about 7$^{1}/_{2}$ hours.

One Oar or Two?

Sculling is a rowing-style sport in which the rower uses two oars—one in each hand. In rowing, each person uses just a single oar.

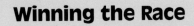

Winning the Race

American yachts won the race for the America's Cup 24 straight times—from 1870 until 1983. That year, however, it was won by the Australian boat *Australia II.* Since then, it has been won back by the Americans, although the future home of the cup is in doubt because of legal problems.

Mastering a Sailboard

The simplest kind of sailboat—a sailboard—is also one of the hardest to use. It only has a few simple parts: the sail, the mast, a wishbone for steering, and a surfboard to stand on. Mastering a sailboard demands a good sense of balance, strength, and patience.

The America's Cup ▲

The America's Cup is awarded to the winner of a best four-of-seven set of races between swift sailboats. It was first offered as part of a racing challenge by the Royal Yacht Squadron of Great Britain in 1851. When it was won by the American yacht *America,* the cup became known by that name.

Polo in the Water

While polo is played on horseback, water polo players don't use horses at all. The game is played by swimmers, and its object is to throw a ball into the opponent's goal in order to score points.

Who Invented Ping-Pong?

No one knows exactly who invented ping-pong—the common name for table tennis—but there are two likely candidates for the honor. One is a group of English college students. Another possibility is soldiers of the British army, who, while stationed in India, began hitting small balls over a line of books. In either case, table tennis was popular by the 1890s.

The East Reigns Supreme

For many years now, China has had the best table tennis players in the world, and its teams have been able to defeat ping-pong players from almost every other country. Recently, Japan has begun to supply the world with many top-notch players as well.

Rules of the Game

The basic rules of tennis and table tennis are very similar except for the scoring. Table tennis uses a simple one to 21 system, with a serving change after every five points.

Scoring Points

In tennis, "love" means that there is no score. Tennis uses other unusual words and numbers for scoring. Points are not counted in simple numerical order. For instance, the first point is scored as 15; the second point is 30; the third is 40; and the fourth is the game-winning point. To make it more confusing, when two players are tied at 40, it is called "deuce," a word that usually means "two." Despite all this confusion, people somehow still manage to play tennis.

For Men and Women

Women have been playing tennis since at least the Middle Ages. They were also quick to join the ranks of top players. In 1884, just seven years after the first British games were held at Wimbledon, Maud Watson became the first woman champion there.

A Different Kind of Tennis

"Real tennis" is the term for the game of tennis that was played as long ago as the Middle Ages. Unlike today's game, it was played on a walled-in court that had overhanging roofs. People used a pear-shaped racket and a tightly wound ball that did not bounce very high. The players had to hit the ball onto the roof that hung over the court, and they scored points by making the ball bounce twice before the other player could get to it.

The Grand Slam ▲

A player who wins the "Grand Slam" has won each of the four most important tennis competitions in a single year. Those championships are the ones held in Great Britain (Wimbledon), France, the United States, and Australia. It is a feat that has been accomplished by only a handful of players, and it is considered the supreme achievement for any tennis champion.

England's National Pastime

The phrase "it isn't cricket" means that something is unfair or not very sporting. It comes from the game of cricket, which is generally considered to be England's national summer game. The phrase took on new meaning in 1981 at a match between Australia and New Zealand. Toward the end of the match, the Australian team performed an unusual maneuver, which made it impossible for the New Zealanders to have a fair chance to catch up and tie the match. Criticism of the Australians' behavior was fierce, and such "uncricketlike" play has been banned from future matches.

A Sticky Wicket

Since one of the objects of the game of cricket is to knock the bails off the wicket, a "sticky wicket" is one from which the bails won't fall off.

Playing Cricket

In cricket, a wicket is made up of three stumps, each about 28 inches (70 cm) high and 1.25 inches (3 cm) in diameter. On top of a wicket are two small pieces of wood called bails.

Croquet on the Lawn ▶

Croquet is a lawn game that began in France during the 1700s. It reached Britain, the United States, and other countries during the middle of the 1800s. The game is played by hitting wooden balls with a wooden mallet, or hammer. The object of the game is to hit balls through a series of curved hoops that are stuck in the grass. It is played for fun by families and friends as well as on a more serious and professional level.

From Town Ball to Baseball

The most likely inventor of baseball was a man named Alexander Cartwright. Cartwright was a devoted player of a game called town ball, which was often played in small towns during the early 1800s. In 1845, Cartwright is supposed to have written down a full set of rules for a game very much like the game of baseball we know today. Cartwright himself played as an amateur on a team called the New York Knickerbockers. On June 19, 1846, the Knickerbockers played the New York Nine in what is often thought to be the very first organized game of baseball in the world. The New York Nine won by the score of 23-1.

Baseball Scandal

In 1919, eight members of the Chicago White Sox were accused of taking bribes. This was called the "Black Sox" scandal. Gamblers, it was charged, paid the players to deliberately lose certain games of the 1919 World Series. The players were found innocent in their trial, but the Commissioner of Baseball barred them from the game for life. Since then, people have argued furiously about whether any or all of the players were actually guilty, especially since some of them played spectacularly well during the World Series.

"Shoeless" Joe Jackson of the 1919 "Black Sox"

Let's Play Ball ◄

To figure out the maximum number of players on a baseball field, simply add the nine players of the team in the field, the three possible runners from the team at bat, and one batter. That gives a total of 13 players. Umpires, obviously, do not count; neither do managers and coaches, even though they may come to the field to talk to the pitcher or other players.

A Winning Team ▲

The first baseball team to admit that it was made up of full-time, professional players was the Cincinnati Red Stockings of 1869. The Red Stockings played teams all around the country, from Massachusetts to California. They went undefeated for 93 games—for well over a year—until they were finally beaten by a team from Brooklyn, New York, in June 1870.

Say It Ain't So, Joe!

One of the eight accused players in the "Black Sox" scandal, "Shoeless" Joe Jackson was one of the great baseball heroes of his time. During the trial, a young boy came up to Jackson as the players were leaving the courthouse. According to legend, the boy looked up, with heartbroken tears in his eyes, and said, "Say it ain't so, Joe," hoping to hear that his hero was actually innocent of any wrongdoing.

Home Run Record

▼ For 35 years, one of the great records in baseball was Babe Ruth's feat of hitting 60 home runs in a single season. Many players came close to tying the record, but until 1961, no one had done it. That year, Yankee outfielder Roger Maris began getting close. Ruth, however, had accomplished his feat when the baseball season consisted of 154 games. In Maris's day, a season had 162 games. Maris did not hit home run number 61 until the end of the season. Ford Frick, the Commissioner of Baseball, ruled that Maris's accomplishment did not equal Ruth's, and both were accepted. In time, Ruth's special designation was erased, and Roger Maris is now recognized as the single-season home run king.

The First Ball

When the president or vice-president throws out the first ball of the season (a tradition that goes back more than 50 years), he must go to Baltimore, the home of the nearest major league team.

It's a Strike

A strike is called in baseball either because of a foul ball or an unhit pitch that passes the batter lower than his armpits and higher than the tops of his knees.

Hall of Fame Firsts ▲

The first baseball players inducted into the Hall of Fame were Ty Cobb, Babe Ruth, Christy Matthewson, Honus Wagner, and Walter Johnson. Ty Cobb was the one with the most votes. During his 24-year career with the Detroit Tigers and the Philadelphia Athletics, he had a lifetime batting average of .367 and 892 stolen bases. His record for the most hits in a career was finally broken by Pete Rose in the 1980s.

The Amazing Babe Ruth ▼

As a youth, Babe Ruth had the reputation around Baltimore, Maryland, as being a "natural" player, since he was outstanding at every single position on the baseball diamond. After playing for a brief time for the Baltimore Orioles, Ruth joined the Boston Red Sox in 1914. There, he quickly became one of the strongest pitchers in professional baseball. In the first year with the team, he won 18 games and lost only seven. The Red Sox, however, realized that Ruth was far too good a hitter to use only every fourth or fifth day, so they asked him to play the outfield. And that was where he stayed, even after being sold to the New York Yankees in 1920. At the end of his career, he played for a brief time for the Boston Braves in the National League. There he was used as a pinch hitter and outfielder.

The Finest Footballs

The first footballs were made of pigskin—a leather that is famous for being strong and durable. It can also be made to have a fairly rough surface, making the ball easier to hold, throw, and catch.

Football Game Officials

Professional football games usually have six officials: A referee, who is the person in charge of the officials; an umpire; a field judge; a head linesman; a back judge; and a line judge. College games sometimes are held without a line judge, giving them five officials.

Half Time

Traditionally, there is a 15-minute rest period between the second and third quarters of a football game called half time. During that time, marching bands perform to keep spectators amused while the players rest and plan for the rest of the game. Recently, however, audiences have been so interested in these intermission shows that they have started to become longer and longer. The traditional 1-minute break between the first and second quarter and the third and fourth quarter may also become longer in the future.

Who Wears the Towel?

Usually the quarterback—the person who passes or hands off the ball—receives the ball directly from the center. In order to handle the ball well, the quarterback wants hands that are free of sweat, mud, rain, or snow. Sometimes, the quarterback tucks a towel into his own pants. Other times, the towel is tucked into the back of the center's pants, so the quarterback can reach it while he is setting up each play.

A Super Bowl First

In 1959, the American Football League was founded to compete against the established National Football League. The first Super Bowls were played between the championship teams from the two different leagues. When the leagues joined together in 1970, the tradition of a big game between two champions—a kind of World Series for football—continued.

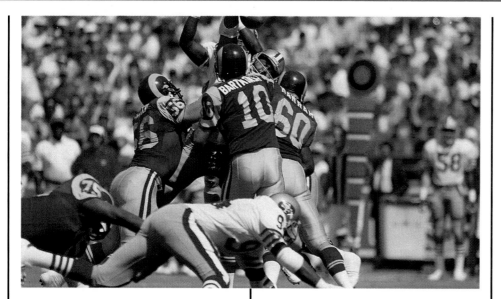

Loaded Down with Equipment

Football players wear quite a bit of equipment, and even though it is made to be as light in weight as possible, it still gets to be quite a load. Helmets are fairly light, but the face guard that covers the mouth and nose gets in many players' ways. Shoulder pads are worn under the shirt to protect the player's body. There are also pads under a player's pants to protect hips and thighs. Even the shoes, with their strong cleats, are heavier than normal.

Offense and Defense

The offensive team in football is the team trying to score. The defensive one is the team trying to keep the other side from scoring.

Old-fashioned Football

Football has been played in North America since the 1600s. Early games were very different from the football we play today. By 1869, though, the first modern college game was held. It took place in New Brunswick, New Jersey, and the game was between Princeton University and Rutgers University. Within a few years, games were played on a regular basis between many colleges. Professional football followed quickly. In 1895, a team from Latrobe, Pennsylvania, beat one from Jeannette, 12-0. By the early 1900s, professional teams from many different cities and states were playing against each other for the world championship.

Substituting Players

Years ago, football players played for almost an entire game. Today, however, each position is highly specialized, with carefully trained players for offense and defense. Rules allow almost unlimited substitutions (letting one player take another player's place), which is why you see so many players going on and off the field between plays.

Players' Numbers

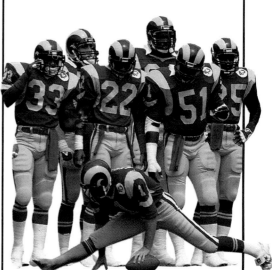

Exactly which number a player wears can be a matter of personal choice (a player might be superstitious about a particular number) or of what number is not yet worn by another player. However, there is a system behind the numbers. The following system is used in the National Football League as well as in most colleges and high schools: Quarterbacks and kickers wear numbers 1-19; running backs—20-49; defensive backs—20-49; centers and linebackers—50-59; gaurds—60-69; tackles—70-79; ends—80-89; and defensive linemen—60-89.

Kicking the Ball

In football, the players use their feet more for running than for kicking. The ball is kicked for a kickoff at the beginning of each half and after each touchdown. Feet are used again when a team wants to try to score a field goal by kicking the ball between the two goal posts. The ball is also kicked for a punt, when a team is giving the ball over to the other team.

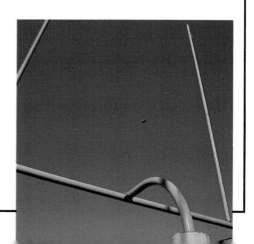

Football Called Soccer

In most of the world, soccer is called football. The name, in fact, is much more logical than it is for the American game, since soccer is played almost completely with the feet. Players, of course, can hit the ball with their heads, too, but only the goalkeeper is allowed to pick up and throw the ball. Since no one ever actually "socks" a ball, exactly how the name "soccer" came about is really a mystery.

Kicking that Ball

Soccer players usually kick the ball with the inside of their foot. This allows them to dribble the ball and to kick it with more power. In the past, football players kicked with their toes. Beginning in the 1960s, soccer-style kicking became popular, probably because it sent the ball farther and more accurately. Some players even went so far as to play barefooted. They claimed that this helped them get the feel of the ball better.

The History of Soccer

Soccer has been played, in one form or another, since ancient times. The Romans, for example, seem to have had several games that were quite a bit like today's soccer. During the Middle Ages, a game resembling soccer was very popular. The play was so rough, however, that seven different English kings made laws against the game. Soccer and football got their modern rules during the 1860s. So, even though soccer goes further back in history than football, today's versions of the two games are about the same age.

Hacking Problems

Hacking, in soccer, is kicking wildly to get the ball. It has always been a problem in soccer to figure out exactly when a player is hacking and whether or not it should be allowed. Modern soccer really didn't become popular until rules against hacking were made up during the 1890s.

The World Cup of Soccer

The World Cup is the international championship of soccer. It is held every four years, usually with a different country acting as host each time. The first World Cup was held in South America in 1930. That year, only four European countries showed up, and the Cup was won by Uruguay. Now, dozens of countries send teams, and winning the championship is a matter of pride for everyone from that country. Millions of people watch the matches live and on television, since the competition goes on for several weeks.

A Soccer Team

In soccer, each team is allowed 11 players. In addition to these 22 people, there are three officials—a referee and two linesmen. This makes a total of 25 people on the field.

Possible Positions

Strikers are the forwards of a soccer team. They are the players who usually score the goals, and, for this reason, it is often considered to be the most glamorous and exciting position to play. Most teams play with four forwards. Two of them play at the far left and right of the field and are called wings. The two forwards in the middle are called center forwards or simply strikers.

Roughing It in Rugby

Rugby is a game something like soccer and American football. Each team has 15 players, and they use an oval ball, which is easier to catch than a round one. The point of the game is to score tries by touching the ball down on the ground inside the other team's goal line. Each try is worth four points.

A Very Fast Game

In rugby, the only ways to gain ground and win are to run with the ball or kick it. This makes rugby a fast-paced game.

A Very Competitive Game ▲

Tackling is legal in rugby. Unlike American football, a tackle in rugby is really a matter of having the ball touch the ground. Therefore, players must bring the player with the ball down and then make sure that the ball touches the ground. However, the kind of blocking that is part of American football isn't usually done in rugby. Still, the game strikes most people, especially Americans, as very rough and competitive.

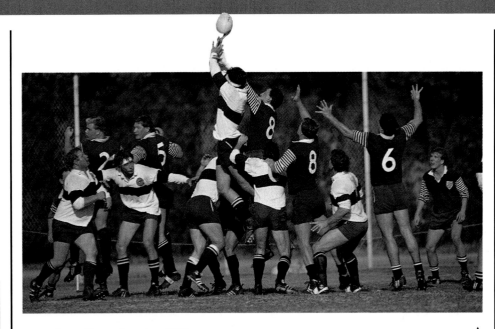

Get That Ball! ▲

Rugby's rough reputation primarily comes from the "scrums" that are used to begin play. This consists of some of the players arranged in a circle trying to get the ball. This activity often leads to wild, rough behavior that some people consider legalized fighting.

Two Kinds of Hockey ▶

There are two kinds of hockey. One is played on a field and the other on ice. Field hockey goes back thousands of years to ancient Greece. Ice hockey is a fairly new sport that started to become popular after World War I.

Hockey Puck Statistics

An official hockey puck is 3 inches (7.62 cm) in diameter and weighs between 5.5 and 6 ounces (156 to 170 gm).

Fascinating Field Hockey

In the United States, field hockey is often played by girls' physical education classes. In the rest of the world, it is a fast-paced, action-filled sport in which men and women compete. National teams were formed as early as the 1890s, and there has been a World Cup for field hockey since 1971. So far, there are no real professional leagues or teams.

Basketball Beginnings

Basketball was invented in 1891, and, by 1896, the first college basketball game was held. The National Basketball League was started in 1898, and professional basketball was born.

Inventing Basketball

In 1891, James Naismith was a physical education instructor at the YMCA training school in Springfield, Massachusetts. He was asked to create a game that would be interesting to play and watch and that would not have a great deal of physical contact. After trying to revise existing games, Naismith finally decided to come up with a completely new game. The result was basketball.

In the Penalty Box

Hockey has always been considered a rough sport, and officials use penalties to control the violence of the games. A player's penalty is often spent in the penalty box—an area off the ice. At this time, a player's team is working without his or her help for a given number of minutes, giving the other team a great advantage. Other penalties lead to penalty shots in which a team gets a free shot at the goal.

Keeping the Game a Noncontact Sport

When it was invented by James Naismith, basketball was supposed to be a game of quick movements and talent rather than a game of physical strength. As it turned out, however, there is a great deal of physical contact in today's basketball games. Rules and referees work to keep the game a noncontact sport.

The 24-second Rule

To keep the teams from stalling and to keep the game fast-paced, professional basketball players play with what is called a "24-second rule." This means that the team with the ball has to take a shot at the basket within 24 seconds or turn the ball over to the other team. A clock is usually located near each basket so players can see how much time has gone by.

◄An All-American Sport

Basketball is the only major world sport that began and developed in the United States.

Winning the Gold

The United States has won the gold medal in basketball each time since 1936, with the exceptions of 1972 and 1988. They also boycotted the 1980 Olympics in Moscow.

Similar to Basketball

Netball is a popular team sport for women and girls in Britain and other countries. It developed from basketball. The first rules for netball were published in 1901. However, the International Federation of Women's Basketball and Netball Associations was formed, and a new code of rules for the game was drawn up.

Canada's National Game ►

Ice hockey is regarded as the national game of Canada, the country that organized the sport into its present form in 1875.

Volleyball is a popular team sport in more than 100 countries. It was invented in 1895 by William G. Morgan, physical director of the YMCA in Holyoke, Massachusetts. He wanted a game for businessmen that was less strenuous than basketball.

Fast and Furious ▶

Hurling is an ancient national game of Ireland. The Gaelic name for it is *iomain*. It is an outdoor stick and ball game, rather like a blend of field hockey and lacrosse between teams of 15 players. Hurling is a very fast game, requiring much skill and apt to be dangerous. It is little played outside Ireland.

Incredible Cycling Speed ▼

The highest speed ever achieved by a cyclist is 140.5 miles per hour (226.10 kmh). An American, Dr. Allan Abbott, achieved this speed in 1973 at Bonneville Salt Flats, Utah, riding behind a windshield mounted on a car.

Cycling through France ▶

The most famous massed-start cycling race is the Tour de France, first held in 1903. This race is divided into about 21 daily stages and lasts for three weeks. The cyclists race all over France, covering a total distance of 2,500 miles (4,000 km), which includes grueling climbs over the mountain roads of the Alps and Pyrenees.

The Fastest Human

The current record-holder at 100 meters is generally considered to be "the fastest human." Holding that title have been such champions as Eddie Tolan, Jesse Owens, Bobby Morrow, Bob Hayes, and Carl Lewis (all of the United States) and Valeriy Borzov (of the U.S.S.R.).

Carl Lewis

The Oldest Sports

Athletics, or track-and-field sports, are the oldest form of organized sport. They developed out of man's most basic activities—running, walking, jumping, and throwing. They are the most international of sports, since nearly every country in the world engages in some form of competition.

Three VERY Long Jumps

Three distinct landmarks stand out in the history of long jumping. First, Jesse Owens jumped 26 feet 8¹/₄ inches (8.13 m) on May 25, 1935. The second landmark was at the Mexico City Olympics when Bob Beamon lept 29 feet 2¹/₂ inches (8.9 m), exceeding the world record by 21¹/₂ inches (55 cm). Finally, at the Tokyo World Track and Field Championships in 1991, Mike Powell jumped 29 feet 4¹/₂ inches (8.95 m), smashing Beamon's 23-year-old record.

Breaking the Four-minute Mile

British athlete Roger Bannister was the first person to run a mile in less than four minutes. He achieved his feat at Oxford on May 6, 1954.

Great Leaps

World-class standards in track and field have improved dramatically. For example, it took 70 years for the world record in the mile to improve from 4 minutes 10 seconds to 4 minutes. But it was only a further 21 years before New Zealander John Walker became the first to run the mile in less than 3 minutes 50 seconds in 1975.

For Men and Women ▶

It was not until 1969 that women first raced at 1,500 meters in international competition. The 3,000 meters followed in 1974 and the marathon in the late 1970s. Recognized running events for women are now the same as for men, except for the steeplechase.

◀ Varying Courses

There is no official record for the marathon because the severity of the courses varies. The best Olympic time is 2 hours 9 minutes and 21.0 seconds by C. Lopes of Portugal. Abebe Bikila of Ethiopia is the only man to have won the Olympic marathon twice (in 1960 and 1964).

A Popular Pastime

Bowls, a type of game played on a smooth green turf, is one of the oldest of English sports that was being played some 700 years ago. According to a well-known story, Sir Francis Drake was playing bowls with his sea captains on Plymouth Hoe when news was brought that the Spanish Armada had been sighted. Turning to his fellow players, he calmly suggested that they should finish the game first and beat the Spaniards afterwards.

An Undefeated Champ ▲

In 1937, Joe Louis, known as the "Brown Bomber," became heavyweight champion. His reign lasted until 1949 when he retired an undefeated champion. During those years, he defended his title a record 25 times.

The Color of the Belt

How good someone is in judo is shown by the color of the belt that he or she wears. There are six *kyus*, or student grades. The colors of the belts in ascending order of skill are white, yellow, orange, green, blue, and brown. The hardest step in judo is entry into the *Dan* or master grades, which is shown by a black belt.

Breaking Bricks ▲

An expert at karate can break several thick planks of wood or bricks with one blow of his or her bare hand or foot.

Skiing on the Water ▲

Water skiing as a sport began in France in the 1920s. A water skier uses one or two skis, which are wider than skis used on snow. Most water skis also have a stabilizing fin underneath, although the special skis used for tricks are flat underneath to allow the skier to make a complete 360-degree turn.

Fast and Clever

The sport of orienteering began in Sweden in 1918. It is like cross-country running with a map and compass. The key to success is accurate navigation at speed. But since the fastest runners are not always the most clever map readers, you do not need to be a top-class athlete to be a successful orienteer.

Speeding Along

The Cresta Run at St. Moritz, Switzerland, is a toboggan run that is 1,326 yards (1,213 m) long with a fall of about 460 feet (140 m) and steeply banked corners. Speeds of about 80 miles an hour (125 kmh) are reached on the Cresta Run. The riders wear crash helmets, padded clothes, and boots with steel spikes that help in steering and braking.

Another Game on Ice ▼

Curling is a game played on a flat ice rink using flat-bottomed stones that have metal handles attached to them. At each end of the rink a "tee"—an iron pin—is fixed in the ice. The aim of the game is to slide the stones from one end of the rink to the other, getting them as near as possible to the tee. Curling probably originated in Scotland and is popular in Canada and the northern United States.

Different Styles of Wrestling

There are several different styles of wrestling, such as the Cumberland and Westmorland, the Cornish, and the Lancashire. Of these styles, the Lancashire style, known as "catch-as-catch-can," or freestyle, is the most popular. With some variation, it is practiced in North America and other English-speaking countries, as well as in India and Pakistan.

Take Any Hold ▲

In catch-as-catch-can wrestling, the opponents may take any "hold" on each other, but a grip or an attack used to cause pain or injury is forbidden. The object is to bring about a "fall." This is done by forcing both the opponent's shoulder blades to touch the mat at the same time.

◀ A European Favorite

Greco-Roman wrestling is the favorite style of wrestling in Europe. Tripping and holding below the hip are forbidden.

A Lively Spectacle

All-in wrestling is a sport mainly practiced by professionals who make a living by staging bouts. It is spectacular and allows a number of dangerous tricks that are barred from other types of wrestling. In all-in wrestling the thrills and brutality of many of the contests are rehearsed. The struggles are rarely as severe as they seem.

The 18-Hole Course ▲

In the early 19th century, there was no agreement on the number of holes on a golf course. Localities differed widely in the matter. When St. Andrews with its 18-hole course became very popular, the round of 18 holes was established.

Feathery Golf Balls

In the early 17th century, golf balls were made of feathers. They consisted of boiled feathers that were compressed through a hole left in pieces of stitched leather that made up the cover. The feathers were stuffed first with a wooden tool, then with a stuffing iron. When the leather case was crammed completely, the hole was stitched up, the ball hammered and made as round as possible, and painted white. The whole process was very slow and the "feathery" quickly became disabled in bad weather and destroyed by hacks from iron clubs.

◄Golfing Champ

By the 1980s, Jack Nicklaus not only was golf's all-time money winner, he had also won a remarkable 20 major championships—more than anyone in golfing history.

A British Pastime

The development of golf as an organized sport is distinctly British, and Britain produced the first great players of the game.

British Open Winners

U.S. dominance of the men's British Open from 1970 to 1983 was broken only twice. The first time was by Gary Player of South Africa (1974); the second time was by Severiano Ballesteros of Spain in 1979.

Playing Badminton

A shuttlecock is the lightweight conical object with a rounded, rubber-coated nose that is used in badminton.

Many World Cups

There are many World Cups in sports. The Jules Rimet Trophy is awarded for soccer. There is also a four-day, 72-hole stroke competition in golf, which is awarded to the two-man team with the lowest score. In skiing, male and female alpine skiers receive this prestigious award as well. There are also World Cup competitions in cricket, rugby, and track and field.

Another Tennis Trophy

The Wightman Cup is a trophy awarded to the winner of tennis matches held annually between teams of women from England and the United States. A competition comprises five singles and two doubles matches. Matches are played in the United States in odd-numbered years and in Great Britain in even-numbered years.

Once an Olympic Event

Tug-of-war was an Olympic event from 1900 to 1920, with five men to a side. It is primarily a rural pastime in England and Scotland.

A Sport of Swords ▶

Fencing grew out of the practice of settling quarrels or avenging insults by dueling or fighting with swords. The modern sport is carried on with three distinct weapons—foil, epee, and saber. With all of them the fencer tries to hit his opponent without being hit, and the winner of a match is the one who first scores five hits (four hits in women's matches).

Mind and Body Working Together ▶

Quick thinking and movements are more important in fencing than strength. As a result, the sport can be enjoyed by women and children as well as men. Fencing makes a person swift and supple and helps mind and body to work together.

A Very Fast Game

Jai alai is one of the world's fastest games. It is the native ball game of the Basques—a people who live in the Pyrenees Mountains in France and Spain. It is like handball played on a larger court.

Speeding Balls

Jai alai balls have been timed as traveling over 150 miles per hour (240 kmh).

Jumping over Fences ▶

Show jumping is the sport of riding horses over a course of fences. The number of points is the only thing that affects the result. The style of riding is not taken into account, although the rider must be a good horseman.

Moving to Perfection

The word *dressage* is French for "training." In a dressage competition, horse and rider carry out a wide range of movements. The horse's natural gaits (walk, trot, canter, and so on) are shown to their most perfect level in the form of schooling practiced at the Imperial Spanish Riding School in Vienna.

Lots of Money to be Made

The sport of racing thoroughbred horses is divided into flat racing and jumping. Flat racing offers the richest prizes and attracts the most valuable racehorses. Millions of pounds and dollars are spent at the annual sale at Newmarket. The chief buyers are Arabs and Americans. Kentucky and California are the main centers of horse breeding in the United States.

◀ Racing with a Handicap

In "weight-for-age" races, older horses carry more weight than younger ones so that the younger ones are not at a disadvantage. In handicap races, the past performance of horses is taken into account and different weights are allotted to try to give each horse an equal chance of winning. The weight a horse is set to carry is made up of the weight of the jockey, the saddle, and, if necessary, lead carried in a weight-cloth under the saddle.

The Ancient Game of Chess ▶

Chess is an ancient game, though when and where it began is not certain. Both old Persian and Indian writings prove that it was known in both of these countries at least as long ago as the early part of the 7th century.

Long-distance Matches

Chess matches are often played by cable, radio, telephone, and computer, since chess is one of the very few games in which it is not necessary for the opponents to be in close contact. The first match by trans-Atlantic cable took place between Great Britain and the United States in 1896. The first chess match by radio was played between the U.S.S.R. and the United States in 1946.

Chess Champions

All world chess champions in recent years (with the exception of American Bobby Fischer, 1972-75) have been players from the U.S.S.R.

Keeping the Moves Recorded

Unlike in other sports, it is a simple matter to keep a record of the moves of a game in chess exactly as they are played. All games in important contests are recorded. For many years, books containing collections of games played by experts have been published for the ordinary player to enjoy at leisure. ▼

Early Gamblers

People have gambled since the earliest times. Gaming boards were used 3,500 years ago, and spinning disks were used in China for a form of the game known as roulette. The ancient Greeks and Egyptians gambled with knucklebones painted as four-sided dice, and the Arabs were the first people to use the six-sided dice.

Early Laws ▶

Among the first laws ever made were laws against gaming. In 1388, the English parliament passed an act to prevent men from spending Sundays on games of dice, quoits, and tennis, in order that they might use the time to practice archery instead.

Cards We All Know

The pack of cards that we know today arose from the tarot cards in France. The trump cards were gotten rid of and the designs were simplified so they could be printed more cheaply. The two knights were combined to give one card, now known as the jack. The pack had 52 cards and 4 suits—pikes, hearts, squares, and trefoils. The English adopted this pack but called the symbols spades, hearts, diamonds, and clubs. It is now used in almost all countries.

Popular Horses

Betting on horse races is the main form of gambling in the English-speaking countries and in France.

Games on a Billiards Table ▶

Several games may be played on a billiards table, but the main ones are billiards, snooker, and pool. Billiards is by far the oldest—it probably dates back 600 years.

An Impossible Situation

To "snooker" one's opponent in the game of snooker means to make a stroke so that the ball the opponent has to strike at is obstructed by another ball and he or she cannot strike at it.

Picking from the Bone Yard

A "bone yard" in the game of dominoes is the pool from which each player draws a domino after the dominoes or "bones" have been shuffled face-down on the table.

◀ Playing Dominoes

The domino game of Muggins, or All Fives, is a scoring game in which the players must match their bones so that the total adds up to five or a multiple of five.

Early Dice

The word "dice" is the plural of "die," a word rarely used except in expressions like "the die is cast." Knucklebones (the anklebones of sheep) were probably the first dice.

People, Places, & Things

In ancient myths, a sphinx was a creature with a human's head and a lion's body. The most famous statue of a sphinx still stands at Giza, Egypt.

The largest sand dunes located in the Sahara Desert are over 500 feet (150 m) high. Even camels have difficulty walking on them.

Soft Drinks and Hard Liquor

Drinks, such as sodas, are called "soft" because they do not contain any alcohol. Drinks with alcohol in them are called "hard liquor" by most people. Most soft drinks are carbonated and have sweeteners added. Non-alcoholic drinks like coffee, tea, milk, and fruit juices are usually not called soft drinks.

Man's Oldest Friend▼

One of the oldest of all dog breeds is the chow chow. It originated in China as far back as 200 B.C. Curiously, people in England used to call any load of goods coming to Europe from China a "chow chow."

Taking a Ride in a Sulky

"Sulky" is not just used to describe a person who is in a bad mood. Actually, that's not even what the word originally meant. A sulky is a two-wheeled cart that is pulled by a horse for trotting races. Its name came from its inventor—an English doctor who was famous for his sulky behavior and bad moods. Stories say that this doctor invented the small, single-seated vehicle so that he would be able to travel completely alone whenever he went to see his patients.

Eating with Chopsticks

Chopsticks are the main eating utensil all over the Far East. In China, they are called *kuai-tzu* (meaning "quick ones"). Over the years, however, the word "chop" came to mean "quick" among many Chinese living abroad. Thus the word "chopsticks" (meaning "quick sticks") was born.

Getting the Hiccups

Hiccups are a spasm, or sudden movement in the chest. They are caused when a person has a breath of air cut off by surprise—it can be from an upset stomach, nervousness, or even allergies. Many different remedies are suggested to get rid of hiccups. You may have had people tell you to hold your breath or to drink water. People sometimes even try to scare a person with hiccups out of having the hiccups. Whatever you do, hiccups usually go away very quickly.

Tall and Short

How tall we grow is to a large extent controlled by *heredity*—the traits that we inherit from our parents, grandparents, and other family members.

Nothing But a Tin-horned Gambler

A "tin-horned gambler" is a person without class, morals, or even good manners. The phrase was originally used for a very specific type of gambler. The story claims that on the American frontier, one of the most popular games that gamblers played was a game called "Chuck-a-Luck." The game consisted of players throwing three dice from a cone-shaped chute made of leather or metal. Since the leather chutes were more expensive and better looking than the metal ones, gamblers who could only afford the metal chutes were looked down upon and called tin-horned gamblers.

A Sure Sign of Christmas

During the Middle Ages, carols were songs that were sung by a group of people singing and dancing in a ring or chain. Since these songs were extremely popular, the tradition continued to this day. During the Christmas season, you will often see a group of people going from place to place singing carols.

A Mythological Creature

In ancient myths, a sphinx was a famous creature with a human's head and a lion's body. The most famous statue of a sphinx is a giant statue that still stands at Giza, Egypt.

The Riddle of the Sphinx

According to legend, a winged sphinx, who was the monster of Thebes in ancient Greece, demanded that people answer the following riddle: What has one voice and yet is four-footed, three-footed, and two-footed? Anyone who could not answer the riddle was supposedly eaten by the monster. The riddle was finally solved by Oedipus who announced that the answer was "man," since people crawl on all fours when they are babies, walk on two legs when they are grown, and lean on a staff when they are old.

Reading Your Mind

ESP, or extrasensory perception, is the ability to perceive things other than through the senses of sight, hearing, touch, smell, and taste. The most famous kind of ESP is *telepathy*, which is the ability to "read" another person's mind. Scientists have studied ESP for many years, trying to discover once and for all whether it actually exists. Even today, scientists are not sure. Some scientists believe in ESP. They attempt to use it in simple mind-reading experiments and in searches for missing persons. Other scientists dismiss the idea as impossible. Experiments going on today, may, in time, help decide the issue.

The First Art

Finger tracings, usually done on cave walls or on pieces of clay, are the oldest art on earth. Scientists believe that thousands of years ago people used footprints and fingerprints to imitate the tracks and marks made by animals. After a while, ancient people began to make these marks in designs that were interesting and decorative to adorn their cave walls.

Inventing Coca-Cola

Coca-Cola was invented in 1886 by a druggist in Atlanta, Georgia. It was originally sold as a medicine that contained caffeine and cocaine. Since it quickly became more popular as a refreshment than a medicine, cocaine was removed from Coca-Cola in 1905. In recent years, a caffeine-free version of the drink has also been introduced.

311

A Marsh Mallow Plant

Believe it or not, there actually is a marsh mallow plant. Originally raised in marshy areas in eastern Europe and North Africa, it has been grown in North America for many years. Growing as tall as 6 feet (1.8 m), it has large pinkish flowers that are almost 2 inches (5 cm) across. The roots of marsh mallows were originally used to make candy marshmallows that people toast over a fire or float in a cup of hot chocolate. Nowadays, they are mostly made from corn syrup and sugar.

Fish that Fly ▲

There really are about 40 different kinds of flying fish. Most of them are small—usually no more than 18 inches (45 cm) long—and have winglike fins and an unevenly forked tail. They do not flap their "wings" like birds in order to fly. Instead, they build up speed underwater and lift themselves out with their tails. Then they glide through the air.

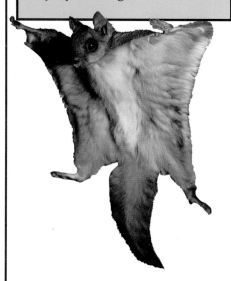

A Bat Called a Fox ◄

The European flying fox is not a fox at all. It is a bat that looks a bit like a fox.

Squirrels in Flight ▲

Flying squirrels are able to glide through the air because of thin membranes connecting the front and back legs on each side of their bodies. These membranes act like parachutes. They hold the squirrels in the air as they leap from branch to branch.

The Yellow Spitting Spider

The yellow spitting spider of the eastern United States actually hunts its prey by "spitting" a gluey saliva at them. Flies and other insects caught in the saliva can then be gobbled up whenever the spider is hungry.

Flying for Your Dinner

Among the most unusual reptiles in the world are the flying or "golden tree snakes" of southern Asia and the East Indies. These black and green snakes with yellowish markings leap into the air by straightening out their bodies. Then they hollow out their undersides to give themselves a lift to glide short distances. The snakes find this ability quite useful for capturing bats, birds, lizards, and small rodents.

The Smallest Bear in the World

The sun bear, at 3.3 to 4 feet (1 to 1.2 m) long, is the smallest bear in the world. It makes its home in the forests of Asia. The sun bear makes an excellent pet while it is young, but usually must be let loose when it becomes an adult. Fully grown sun bears apparently have a nasty temper and cannot be kept around the house.

Natural Bath Sponges

Most of the sponges we use today are made in factories from artificial materials. But there are natural sponges living in nature. These so-called bath sponges are mostly found in the Mediterranean Sea and the Gulf of Mexico, where they are harvested on hooks or harpoons.

Tales of Mermaids

There are several strange sea mammals that sailors might have mistaken for mermaids. Dugongs, for example, live in shallow waters along the Red Sea, eastern Africa, and parts of the Pacific. They usually grow to between 7 and 11 feet (2.2 to 3.4 m) in length and often "tail stand" with their heads and shoulders out of the water. Manatees, which are found in the Caribbean, Florida, and the Amazon, are large water mammals that live in shallow waters along the coast. They live in small groups and pet or nuzzle each other in ways that seem quite human at times.

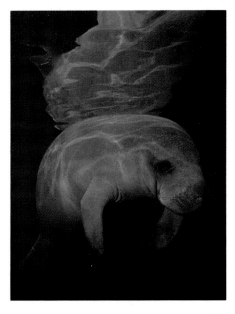

Manatees

313

Strange-looking Dogs ◄

Dachshunds—those strange-looking creatures that resemble hot dogs—were deliberately bred to be that size and shape. By interbreeding different types of hounds and terriers, German hunters created a dog specifically designed to be able to chase badgers and other animals into their underground homes. Although today's dachshunds are generally kept as house pets, some are still used for their original purpose—hunting.

Landing Squarely on Their Feet

Cats have an amazing sense of balance. Their legs are short in proportion to the rest of their body and their back can be moved about in all directions. As a result, when a cat is dropped from a height, it can twist in midair to land on its feet. Its tail helps it to change into a landing position, while the muscles of the legs and haunches absorb the shock of landing.

A Lion's Roar

Lions usually roar a couple of times during the day. One of their favorite times for roaring is the evening—just before going for a nighttime hunt. Lions also tend to roar when they wake up in the morning. In addition to roaring, lions also cough, grunt, and growl.

Fog, Mist, and Haze

Fog is a cloud of small water droplets floating near the ground. When it is foggy outside, it really is difficult to see anything. Mist and haze are simply conditions that do not reduce visibility quite so much. Mist, like fog, is made up of water drops; haze is made up of more solid particles.

Low tide at the Bay of Fundy

Swimming in the Bay of Fundy

The Bay of Fundy, which is located between New Brunswick and Nova Scotia, is one of the most beautiful areas of shoreline on the Atlantic coast. Swimming, however, can be difficult. In the first place, the water rises and falls as much as 70 feet (21 m) with each high and low tide. Also, the water rushes in and out at speeds of up to 20 feet (6.5 m) per second, making the current too fast for many swimmers.

The Graveyard of the Atlantic

Cape Hatteras, a long curved piece of sand that sticks out in the Atlantic Ocean off the coast of North Carolina, is called the "Graveyard of the Atlantic." Hundreds of ships, big and small, have been wrecked in the deadly seas of this area.

Taking the Hippocratic Oath

The Hippocratic Oath is a two-part code of conduct for doctors, supposedly created by the ancient Greek, Hippocrates. The first part spells out the things doctors and their students should do for each other. The second, and more famous part, pledges doctors to do only those things that will help their patients and to make sure they never do their patients any harm.

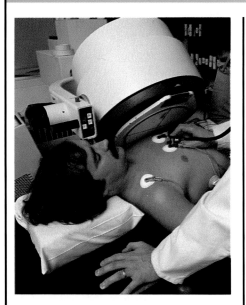

Hearing Your Heartbeat ▲

Although stethoscopes are designed to help doctors hear, they only transmit sounds from inside the body. Even the earpieces are designed to block out normal sounds so that doctors can only hear what they need to hear. If you tried talking directly into the small metal circle at the end of a stethoscope, your doctor still would not hear what you are saying.

A Bark that Sails

A bark (sometimes spelled barque) is a type of sailing ship that usually has three or more masts.

The Most Famous American Pilot

The most famous American pilot was Captain "Eddie" Rickenbacker. One of the country's most successful race car drivers in the years before World War I, Rickenbacker entered the army in 1917 and was assigned to drive a car for Colonel William Mitchell. With Mitchell's help he became a fighter pilot, scoring 26 air victories and winning the Congressional Medal of Honor. After the war, he became an executive with several different automobile and airline companies.

Sailor Bells

Five hundred years ago, sailors started ringing bells at the end of each half-hour of a "watch" to let everyone on the ship know what time it was. The system divides the sailors' day into six watches, or tours of duty. Each of these is four hours long. This means, for example, that at 12:30 the ship's bell is rung once for "one bell." At 1:00, the bell is rung two times, and at 1:30—three times. The maximum number of times the bell is rung is eight. After that, it starts over again with one ring.

Port and Starboard ▲

Port, on a boat or ship, is the left-hand side when you are facing forward. Starboard is the right-hand side. To this day, no one is really sure why sailors don't simply call them left and right.

Would You Like a Piece of Gum?

Chewing gum is usually made up of 20 percent gum base, 63 percent sugar, 16 percent corn syrup, and about 1 percent flavoring oils. When a mass of chewing gum is still warm, it is run between pairs of rollers, which thin it down into a long ribbon. Powdered sugar is added to both sides to prevent it from sticking. The last pair of rollers contains knives to cut the ribbon into sticks. Machines wrap these sticks separately, later putting them into packages.

A Natural Gum Base

Most of the gum base now used for chewing gum is made in factories, but some still comes from the chicle of wild sapodilla trees in Mexico and Guatemala. The people who look after these trees are called *chicleros.* In a forest, they gash the tree trunks in a criss-cross pattern. A milky white sap oozes down into a bucket. The *chiclero* gathers it, boils it down, and molds it into 25-pound (10-kg) blocks to be shipped to chewing gum factories.

In Rain or Shine ◀▼

A parasol is used to keep off the sun; an umbrella is made to keep off the rain. The word "umbrella" comes from the Latin word *umbra,* which means "shade". The first parasols were probably used in China in the 12th century. In the East, the umbrella was long regarded as a sign of rank. In medieval Europe, umbrellas were used for ceremonial purposes. It was only in the 17th century that the ordinary everyday umbrella was used. A heavy, clumsy thing covered with leather or with sticky oiled silk, it was usually carried by a servant. Finally in the 18th century, umbrellas became lighter and more elegant in design.

The First Chewing Gum

People in Central America chew chicle straight from the tree. In New England, early settlers learned to chew spruce gum. This was the first chewing gum to be sold in the United States in the early 1800s. At first, chicle was imported in the 1860s as a substitute for rubber. It was only in the 1890s that it was used in the chewing gum industry.

Origins of the Christmas Tree

The Christmas tree, which is common today in many countries, is thought to have originated in Germany. Before Christianity was introduced, pagans worshipped oak trees as a symbol of their gods. St. Boniface, the missionary who brought Christianity to Germany, is said to have introduced the evergreen in place of the oak tree, since the evergreen was a traditional Christian symbol of resurrection and everlasting life. Some legends even say that Martin Luther was the first person to cut down a fir tree and bring it indoors as a Christmas decoration.

Christmas Customs

In countries where Christmas weather is hot and sunny, Christmas is celebrated by decorating houses with flowers. Picnics, boating trips, and other outdoor activities are popular.

Standing Under the Mistletoe

Mistletoe is an evergreen bush that has pale green leaves. It flowers in February and March with small yellow flowers. There are many superstitions and legends about the mistletoe. Some people believe that it will bring happiness, safety, and good fortune as long as it does not touch the ground. There is a Christmas tradition that says that mistletoe will bring good luck to the people who kiss under it.

Easter Symbols

The Easter lily, the symbol of resurrection, is the special Easter flower. Hares, rabbits, and colored eggs are ancient symbols of new life that have become associated with Easter.

Eating Easter Buns

Many people eat hot cross buns on Good Friday, the Friday before Easter. Greeks, Romans, and Saxons ate bread marked with a cross during certain festivals. Early Christians took up the custom, since the cross represented the cross on which Christ died.

Eggs of All Sizes

The smallest egg laid by a bird is the size of a pea. It is laid by a hummingbird. The largest, laid by an ostrich, measures up to 7 inches (17 cm) across and weighs up to 4 pounds (1.75 kg).

Very Many Eggs

The very small eggs of fish, insects, and other small animals are laid in much greater numbers than those of birds, reptiles, or certain mammals. Cod lay about 6 million eggs a year; turbot—9 million; and ling—28 million. Since they are generally left to look after themselves, large quantities of them are eaten by other animals.

320

Pretty Unusual Eggs

Dogfish eggs are found in a thick, horny case with long tendrils at each corner. They fasten themselves by their tendrils to weeds until they are ready to hatch. These egg cases are sometimes found on beaches and are called "mermaids' purses."

Fast-learning Ducks

Ducks can run, swim, and feed themselves a few hours after they leave the egg.

Fast-growing Grasses

Bamboos are giant woody grasses that can reach a height of 115 feet (35 m) and grow at the astonishing rate of 15 inches (40 cm) a day. There are over 1,000 species of bamboo. Most of them grow in subtropical and mild temperate climates.

Building a House

In Asia, entire houses are made of bamboo. Larger stems serve as posts, some are split to make rafters, roofing material, and planks for the floor. The hard outer parts are split off, slit into narrow pieces, and woven into mats. They are also made into lattice-work partitions to separate the rooms.

Eating Rice

Rice is the chief food of almost half of the people of the world. It is eaten in China, Japan, India, as well as in other hot parts of Asia, such as Malaysia and the Philippines. Rice yields more food per acre than any other grain.

Other Uses for Rice

Japanese ferment rice to make a drink called *sake*. It is also used to make alcoholic drinks in India and China. Rice straw, bran, and polish are fed to cattle. The Japanese also make rice straw into hats, matting, shoes, and bags.

322

Baking Bread

Wheat is the grain most widely used for making bread. It was grown as far back as the days of Babylonia and ancient Egypt, and in 2000 B.C. was one of the five sacred seeds that the emperors of China sowed each spring to honor their gods. The United States, Canada, Argentina, and Australia are the main exporters of wheat today.

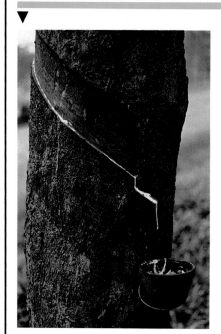

Two Kinds of Rubber

There are two kinds of rubber. Natural rubber comes from *latex*, a liquid that is extracted from rubber trees and then processed in factories. Artificial rubber is made from chemicals in factories.

A Puzzling Name ▶

Monkey puzzle tree is the name given to an evergreen tree whose stiff, arching branches are very closely covered with spiral rows of spiny leaves. It has been said that even a monkey would have difficulty climbing this tree. The correct name for it is the Chile pine.

Cacti are the most curious-looking plants in the world. In shape, cacti may have a number of different forms. They may resemble pipes, trees, barrels, candles, hats, torches, pieces of machinery, or furry caterpillars. There are over 2,000 species of cacti.

Storing Up Water

Cacti grow in dry areas and deserts where they live with very little moisture. As a result, their root systems are different than those of other plants. During the rainy seasons, they take up moisture and store it in the hollow insides of their thick, hard-walled stems.

Plant Protection

Not all cacti have spines. Those that do may have as many as 50,000 on each plant. Spines help the plant by keeping off thirsty animals who try to bite the juicy stems. Some cacti produce flowers, even though they do not flower often— perhaps only once every five years. Flowers are usually large and brilliant in color.

Animals that Look like Flowers

Even though sea anemones may look like flowers, they are animals that are related to coral and jellyfish. They are lovely to look at in colors of red, orange, yellow, brown, gray, and white. If they are uncovered, they look like lumps of jelly. They close up if they are touched.

Strange Animals of the Sea

Sea cucumbers are not vegetables; they are soft-bodied animals that live in shallow water. These creatures are cylindrical in shape and often warty. Most have five rows of tube feet that can be used for walking on seabeds. Tentacles surrounding their mouths are used to gather food. Sea cucumbers can expel their insides and grow new ones. This is probably done to confuse an enemy.

Snakes of the Seas

There are over 50 different species of sea snakes. Unlike land snakes, most sea snakes do not lay eggs. They give birth to small, fully formed young.

Shaving Origins

No one knows exactly when men started to shave the hair on their face, but by 3400 B.C., Egyptians were shaving. The ancient Greeks considered shaving a mark of good manners.

Some Very Hot Springs

Reykjavik, the capital and largest city in Iceland, gets its water from underground hot springs (189°F or 87°C). The water from these springs is led through pipes, supplying hot water to public buildings, houses, swimming pools, and hothouse gardens.

Amazing Ice

Dry ice is solid carbon dioxide. It is colder than regular ice at −109.3°F (−78.5°C) rather than 32°F (0°C). It also does not melt. Instead, it "sublimes"—passes from a solid to a vapor state—without leaving a wet mess.

We Need Our Salt

Salt, or sodium chloride, is an essential part of our diet. Most of the common salt we use today is obtained from underground deposits that were left after the evaporation of ancient seas and have since been covered by mud and sand.

Staying in a Hotel

One of the first hotels to be built in the United States was the City Hotel in New York City. It operated from 1799 to the 1840s. In 1829, the 170-room Tremont Hotel opened in Boston, Massachusetts. It was one of the first hotels to offer private rooms. Previously, travelers had to share a room with strangers.

Trademarks Through the Ages

Many household goods—from matchboxes to cans of food— have trademarks to distinguish products made by one person or factory from those made by another person or factory. They have been used since ancient times. Egyptian bricklayers put their names and symbols on bricks. Craftsmen in ancient Greece always put their names on pottery. The Romans marked their lamps, tiles, containers for eye ointments, and even cheeses.

A Dual Profession

In the 16th century, barbers and surgeons shared the same profession. In those days, barbers not only concentrated on the care of hair and beards. They also practiced surgery, blood-letting, and dentistry.

The History of a Barber's Pole

The barber's pole, which can still be sometimes seen today, was used to advertise a barber's/surgeon's profession. The pole represented a splint that was used to support a broken limb. The red stripe was a symbol of the blood of the damaged limb, and the white stripe represented the bandage wrapped around the damaged limb for protection.

Ancient Permanent Waves

Over 4,000 years ago, the ancient Mediterraneans had their own method for permanent waving, or perms. They set their hair in the style that they wanted with wet clay and sat in the sun until the clay dried. The clay was then crumpled and combed away, leaving the hair permanently waved. Another ancient method was to wrap hair with hot sticks.

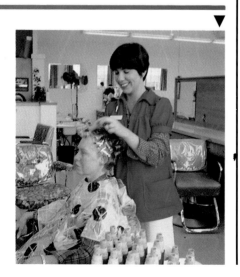

Furniture for Hot Lands

Furniture is often made to suit the climate. In tropical areas, people often sleep in hammocks so that a breeze can pass through the cloth. Rattan furniture is also very popular in hot areas, since air can pass through it. Big, upholstered furniture that many of us have in our homes would be impractical in very hot areas. For one thing, the wood would rot.

Postage Stamp Firsts

Postage stamps were probably the idea of Rowland Hill (1795-1879), a retired schoolteacher who persuaded the English government to adopt his postal system. These first stamps, issued on May 1, 1840 showed the head of Queen Victoria. There were two stamps issued—a penny black one and a twopenny blue one. The name of the country was not printed, since at the time no other country used postage stamps.

Making a Chair Quickly

A small wood chair can be produced from raw timber in less than an hour using automatic machinery.

The Many Kinds of Postage Stamps

Postage stamps were issued by Brazil and by the Swiss canton of Zurich in 1843, by the United States in 1847, and by France, Belgium, and Bavaria in 1849. By 1861, there were about 1,000 different stamps. Five years later, the number rose to 2,500. Currently, there are thousands of different kinds of stamps.

More Innovators

The first supermarket was opened by Clarence Saunders in 1916 in Memphis, Tennessee. The first enclosed shopping mall opened in 1956 near Minneapolis, Minnesota.

A Shopping First

The first department store was opened in Paris in 1850. The first department store in the United States was probably the one opened by John Wanamaker in Philadelphia. The store opened in 1875.

A Very Tall Building

For many years, the Empire State Building in New York City was the tallest building in the world. Today, the Sears Tower in Chicago, Illinois, is the tallest. It is 1,453 feet (443 m) high and has 110 floors. It was built of steel tubes.

A Different Way of Counting

An abacus is a device for doing simple calculations. It has rows of beads on wires that correspond to tens, hundreds, thousands, etc. By moving the beads up and down the wires to represent numbers, you can add or subtract. The abacus is very popular in Asia.

A Very Important Stone

The Rosetta Stone is a black slab that was found in Egypt in 1799. Dating back to about 195 B.C., this stone enabled scholars to translate hieroglyphics for the first time. It bears three inscriptions—one in Greek, one in ancient Egyptian *hieroglyphics*, or picture writing, and one in ancient Egyptian writing.

Talking by Code

Morse code is a code of communication using dots and dashes instead of letters and numbers. *A* is .–., *B* is –..., and so on. When sending a Morse code message over the radio, a dot is indicated by a short sound and a dash by a long sound. The code can be sent by flashing lights, too. Morse code was invented by American inventors Samuel Morse and Alfred Vail in about 1838.

Many Different Languages ▼

There are more than 3,000 different languages spoken in the world today. One half of all the people in the world today speak one of 15 languages. More people in the world speak Mandarin Chinese (387 million) than any other language.

Ever-changing Language

Language is constantly changing as events bring new words into our vocabulary. World War II introduced words such as *blitz, radar,* and *jeep.* Travel into space gave us words such as *astronaut, spaceship,* and *blast-off.* Meanings of words are constantly changing, too. In the game of tennis, for example, a ball striking the net is called a let ball. *Let* in this usage means "stopped." It is an old meaning of this word that is no longer used except in tennis. Today, *let* means "to allow or permit," almost exactly the opposite of what it used to mean.

Languages No Longer Spoken

"Dead languages" are no longer the native languages of any living people. They are understood only by scholars who study them. Examples of "dead" languages are ancient Greek, Latin, Sanskrit, classical Arabic, Gothic, Old Norse, and Old English.

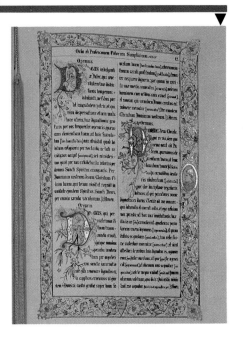

Traveling by Bus

The first bus service was a horse-drawn one that began operating in Paris in 1662. It failed, because the government banned it for ordinary people, restricting it to the wealthy. In the 1820s, a new bus system was developed for all people in Paris. The vehicle was called an "omnibus," which is a Latin term meaning "for all." By 1895, an eight-passenger bus powered by gasoline was built in Germany. The first motor bus ran in London in 1904.

Buses that Bend in the Middle

Chicago and Seattle in the United States and Canberra in Australia are three cities that have *articulated* buses. This means that they can "bend" in the middle when they turn corners.

Practical Double-deckers

The first motor bus was run in London in 1904. It was a double-decker. These types of buses are still used in London, since they are very practical. They have seats for about 70 passengers, whereas single-decker buses can only carry about 50 people.

Natural Protection ◄

Some animals are naturally protected from their enemies because they match the background against which they live. Tree frogs are green, lions are golden colored to blend in with the sandy areas in which they live, and polar bears are white. Other animals can change their color within minutes after they have moved into new surroundings. The chameleon, for example, can become green, gold, brown, or blackish to match its background. Some fish are capable of doing this, too.

Lucky Colors ▼

There are insects whose colors act as a warning to their enemies. Some butterflies and moths both taste unpleasant and are brightly colored so that birds know to leave them alone. The yellow and black colorations of wasps warn their enemies that they sting.

Warning Your Friends ▲

Another type of warning coloration is one that is used among members of the same group to warn others of danger. A rabbit uses the white on its tail as a warning. If a rabbit that is outside its burrow sees or hears danger, it will return to its burrow. Other rabbits, seeing the white of its tail, will follow suit.

Fortunate Resemblance

It is amazing that some animals are able to protect themselves from danger by looking like a poisonous animal. The viceroy butterfly, even though good-tasting to birds, is protected from them because it looks so much like the bad-tasting monarch butterfly.

Mountains Made of Sand

The largest sand dunes are found in the Sahara Desert. These are desert plains covered with sand hills over 500 feet (150 m) high. Even camels have a difficult time walking on these giant slopes of loose sand.

Seif *dune*

Moving Sands

The phenomenon of sand dune movement is not well understood. Some move quickly; others are almost still.

Different Types of Sand Dunes

Regularly spaced, crescent-shaped dunes are called *barkhans. Seif* dunes are long ridges aligned in the direction of the prevailing wind. Australian sand dunes, which are seldom more than 50 feet (15 m) high, are very long and separated from each other by a belt of pebbles. These belts are called "gibber plains."

Noise in the Desert

If a person or animal stands on a higher dune, a downrush of sand may be started. This movement of sand produces a loud roaring noise. Since it is terrifying to hear in the silent and empty desert, natives believe that evil spirits live in sand dunes.

Origins of Oriental Rugs ▶

Oriental rugs are named for the countries where they are made. The main groups are: Indian, Chinese, Caucasian (now part of U.S.S.R. between the Black and Caspian Seas), Turkestan (now divided between U.S.S.R., China, and Afghanistan), Turkish, and Persian (now Iran).

Common Designs

Chinese rugs are usually made with a flower or dragon design on a solid background. Indian rugs usually have a round or oval design in the middle and a smaller border. Persian rugs often have flower patterns or hunting scenes.

The Most Amazing Carpet

The most beautiful carpet ever made was woven for the royal palace of Persia in the 6th or 7th century A.D. Measuring about 84 feet (25.6 m) square, it showed a garden with flowerbeds, fruit trees, streams, and paths. The main part was made of silk, but the gravel paths were made of gold. The flowers, fruit, and birds contained pearls and jewels, and the green meadow on the border was made of emeralds.

The Meaning of Colors

Colors in Oriental rugs have always had definite meanings. White symbolizes purity and a holy life. Black represents errors and mistakes. Red stands for movement and religion. Yellow signifies evil and sorrow, whereas blue symbolizes strength and truth.

Ancient Flags

Flags are so old that no one knows who invented them. They are mentioned in the Bible and all ancient civilizations used them. The eagle, which is still a symbol of the United States, was often used on ancient flags.

A Very Old Flag

The oldest flag still in use is the Danish National Flag, called the *Danebrog*.

White Flag, Red Flag

A white flag is a signal of surrender. A red flag is used as a danger signal.

Flying Flags

There are special rules for flying flags. For example, a flag must be hoisted quickly and lowered slowly. It is flown at the top of a mast (or pole), except when it is flown as a sign of mourning. Then, a flag is flown half-way up the pole, or half-masted. The flag of one country cannot be flown above the flag of another country. They must be at the same height, side by side.

Communicating with Flags

Flags have been used to communicate signals between ships for hundreds of years. In 1817, an international sign book for flag use between merchant ships of different countries was produced. Since 1934, the International Code of Signals has been used. It is printed in English, French, German, Italian, Spanish, Norwegian, and Japanese.

Cultures Around the World

Samurai warriors, who ruled Japan for many years, lived according to a strict code of behavior that ruled their actions in many areas of life.

Charlie Chaplin was perhaps the greatest—and most famous—of all the early movie stars. Much of his popularity came from the way he could show sadness and humor without saying a word.

Peking Man

Evidence tells us that Stone Age people were in China as long ago as 10,000 B.C. Beyond this, scientists discovered what is called "Peking man"—remains of people who lived between 250,000 and 500,000 years ago. All of this suggests that China was one of the earliest places to be inhabited by man.

A Staggering Statistic

The best estimate is that slightly more than one billion people live in China. This means that almost 25 percent of the population of the whole world lives in this one country.

Writing in Pictures ▲

Chinese writing does not use an alphabet. Instead, it has over 50,000 pictures, or characters. Thousands of years ago, these pictures probably were meant to look like the objects they named. Now, however, there is little or no resemblance, and people simply have to learn what each of the pictures means. To make writing even more difficult, many characters can stand for more than one word. To help readers with characters that can be pronounced the same way, writers often add other marks to show exactly which word it is.

A Tough Language to Write

Much of the Japanese language is borrowed from Chinese, just as much of English has been taken from Greek, Latin, and French. Originally, Chinese characters were used by the Japanese to stand for Chinese words. In time, though, the characters were used for Japanese words that meant the same things. This has helped make Japanese one of the most complicated of all written languages, since a written Japanese character can stand for a Chinese word, a Japanese word, or even a particular sound in the Japanese language.

The Boxer Rebellion

The Boxers were an important part of Chinese history, but they had nothing to do with prizefighting. They were a secret society that got together to try to drive Europeans out of China at the end of the 1800s. At that time, Europeans had taken control of most of China, and the Boxers wanted to return rule to the Chinese themselves. Since the groups performed martial arts exercises that looked like shadow boxing to Westerners, the name "Boxers" was given to the members. Starting in 1900, members of these societies rose up and killed Westerners whenever possible. In response, Western governments sent in troops to put them down.

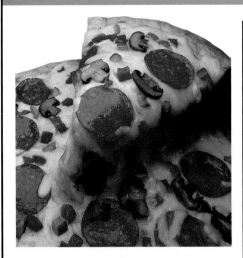

The Travels of Marco Polo

Marco Polo was the first person to bring back first-hand knowledge of life in the Chinese Empire. Polo left for China in 1271 when he was only 17 years old, traveling with his father and uncle. Journeying over land on mules, horses, and camels, they made their way to China. Young Polo wrote about the trip so clearly that even today it is possible to pinpoint exactly where the travelers were and what they did at each step of the way. When Polo returned to Europe after almost 20 years in the Far East, he told people of a world they had hardly dreamed of. Polo's tales of gunpowder, tree-shaded highways, hot-and-cold running water, paper money, oil-based paints, wonderful medicines, and even gold and jewels made thousands of Europeans eager to visit this strange world.

Pizza Pointers ◄

According to most experts, pizza was probably invented in the city of Naples in southern Italy. It quickly spread to other parts of the country, where cooks made it slightly differently. The original pizza, for example, was made from bread dough, olive oil, tomatoes, and mozzarella cheese. In Rome, cooks did not use tomatoes; they added onions and olives instead. Other ingredients were added when Italian immigrants brought pizza to the United States, where the first pizza parlor opened in 1905. Sausage, ground meat, mushrooms, peppers, and even shrimp, pineapple, or oysters are found on American pizzas—all of which would seem strange to the makers of the first pies.

Pasta Eaters

According to one old story, the Italian explorer Marco Polo discovered spaghetti and macaroni when he visited China in the 1200s. But, in truth, people in Europe had been eating macaroni since the time of the ancient Greeks. The best guess is that Polo's discovery helped get people interested again in this age-old dish.

An Amazing Discovery

The Ch'in Tomb is the place where the first Chinese emperor was buried. For over 2,000 years, the grave lay undisturbed. Then, in 1974, archaeologists found an underground room, which contained a replica of an entire army of soldiers and horses. Each was life-size, and no two were alike. Along with this army of 6,000 figures were chariots, tools, and weapons. Three other rooms were also found. These contained another army of chariots, cavalry riders and their horses, and a group of generals to command the forces. Ever since, archaeologists have been exploring this amazing discovery.

The Two Chinas

In 1949, Communist forces under Mao Tse-tung defeated the government of Chiang Kai-shek. Chiang led a group of his followers to the island of Formosa, where they established a new government that still exists today. Meanwhile, Mao's government took control of the Chinese mainland. For many years, many countries refused to do business with Mao's government, and people got into the habit of referring to it as "Mainland" China. The country is also called "Red" China, because, in keeping with Communist tradition, red is the color that symbolized Mao's communist revolution.

Homes in Japan

Traditionally, Japanese houses have been made of wood and rice paper, which is a thin material that really isn't the same as the paper this book is printed on.

The Art of Flower Arranging ▲

The art of arranging flowers, or *ikebana,* is an activity that people spend many years studying and practicing. Since nature is important in Japanese culture, placing flowers in a beautiful arrangement is a way of bringing nature into the home or office.

Birthdays in Japan

In Japan, ages are figured out according to an old system quite different from that used in other countries. In this system, children are automatically one year old when they are born. New Year's Day is also everyone's birthday. This means that a child who is born the day before New Year's Day would be two years old the next day!

Ancient Japanese Customs

The people of Japan's cities live very much like anyone else in the world. Some old-fashioned traditions do continue, however. One of these is the *tatami* mat, a soft bamboo mat on which people sleep. Just as many Japanese homes contain mats instead of beds, the dining rooms have no chairs. Instead, people are seated on the floor with warm quilts hanging from the table to keep a family's feet warm while they eat.

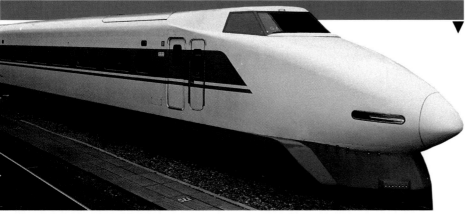

The Fastest Trains

Japan was a pioneer in the use of special high-speed trains. These bullet trains are used to take people back and forth between Japan's biggest cities. They travel at amazingly high speeds, often managing to go 150 or even 175 mph (240 to 280 kph).

◄ Samurai Warriors

For many years, Japan was ruled by nobles and their knights, who were called "samurai." The samurai lived according to a strict code of behavior that ruled how they acted, how they served the noble who employed them, and even how they fought in battle.

The Pygmies of Africa

To scientists, pygmies are any people whose adult males grow to be less than 59 inches (150 cm) in height. The most famous pygmies are those of Africa. In the forests of Zaire, for example, are the Mbuti people, whose lives have been almost unchanged for hundreds of years. Other pygmies live in the countries of Rwanda and Burundi.

The Defeat of the Zulus ▼

Today, the Zulu people live in South Africa. Before this, they were part of a great empire that ruled much of southern Africa. In the early 1800s, the Zulu leader, Shaka, had made his people the most important group in the area. In time, though, white settlers managed to take land and power from the Zulus. Eventually, British army forces defeated the Zulus and broke their empire up into 13 small kingdoms.

Africa's Many Languages ▲

Africa, like many other continents, is home to many different people who speak dozens of different languages. Many of these languages belong to the Khoisan family of languages. Others belong to the Niger-Congo language family. Just because two languages belong to the same family doesn't mean that the people can talk to one another and understand what is being said. After all, English, Italian, and German also belong to the same language family!

A Language Everyone Knows ▶

Because there are so many languages spoken in Africa, people have developed so-called "lingua francas"—languages adopted as common media for trade and general communication. Swahili is the official language of Kenya and Tanzania, as well as throughout most of East Africa. Hausa is the lingua franca of Niger and other areas of West Africa. Similarly, Amharic is the lingua franca of Ethiopia, and Lingala is the lingua franca of central Africa. European languages, such as English, French, and Portuguese also function as lingua francas in countries where they were the languages of former colonies.

The Most Common Language

In Africa north of the Sahara Desert, Arabic is the most widespread language, with some 80 million speakers. In central and western parts of North Africa, Berber is spoken by 7 million people. ▼

Writing It Down

The vast majority of modern African writing systems are based upon the Latin-derived alphabet.

Watch Your Tone!

Many African languages are tonal, which means that they use differences of voice pitch to distinguish the meanings of words—usually two or three pitch levels. For example, in Kele, a Niger-Congo language spoken in Zaire, the expression *alambaka boili* can either mean "he watched the river bank" or "he boiled his mother-in-law," depending upon the tones of the words.

Berber women

343

By Way of Mouth

Many African societies of the past had no written language. Specially selected persons would memorize the traditions, customs, laws, and history of their country, and then orally pass them on to others. Their memories served as their books. Many traditions have been preserved in this way for hundreds of years.

Very Fine Sculpture

The richest sculptural heritage is found in Nigeria. It ranges from small clay figures over 2,000 years old found at Nok to the bronze heads and statues of Ife and Benin, which are considered among the finest bronze sculptures in the world.

Dancing to African Music

Traditional African music, played ▶ on instruments made and often invented in Africa, has become famous for its complex rhythms. African music is meant to be danced to, not just listened to, and many distinctive African dance styles have developed. People all over the world now enjoy African music in the form of jazz, reggae, and others.

◄ Ancient Artwork

Painting and sculpture are ancient traditions in Africa. Rock paintings and engravings made thousands of years ago still survive, dating from the Stone Age. West Africa has produced great traditions of sculpture, which have an immense impact on modern Western art.

Changes in the Arab World ▶

Pressures of the 20th century world have modified traditional Arab values. About 40 percent of Muslim Arabs live in cities where family and tribal ties tend to break down. However, the majority of Arabs who live in small farming villages still adhere to traditional values.

Living Longer

The surge of oil wealth in the 1970s has helped to greatly raise the life expectancy in the Arab world. In the most developed countries like Kuwait, life expectancy has risen to the 70-year mark. It remained nearer 50 years for the larger, less developed parts.

Arab Households

Most Arabs outside the main cities live in a similar fashion. They have little furniture other than carpets and rugs to sit and sleep on and cushions to lean on. When entering a house, a guest will remove his shoes to keep dirt off the carpets, and will sit at the edge of a room. Most houses are divided into two parts. Men visit in the outer part, and women live in the inner part. Cooking is done in the women's part, but the men's part has a fire-hearth where tea and coffee are made for guests.

Religious Practices ▲

Arabs of the 20th century are not exclusively Muslim. Approximately 5 percent of the native speakers of Arabic worldwide are Christians, Druzes, Jews, or animists.

Indian Dress ▶

Many Indian women wear a *sari*, a long piece of cloth draped as a skirt, with one end drawn over the shoulders. Sometimes, a sari is also draped over the head. A tight, short-sleeved blouse is worn under the sari. The manner in which a sari is draped changes in different parts of the country.

Celebrations in India

Festivals and religious pilgrimages are important in Indian life. The festival of Holi, held in the springtime, is especially enjoyable for children. During Holi, people decorate themselves, and each other, with colored powder, which they smear on their faces and clothing. Diwali, the Festival of Lights, comes at the beginning of winter. During Diwali, hundreds of tiny candles glow in the villages.

The Many Languages of India

The different peoples of India speak a great variety of languages. There are about 15 main languages and a far greater number of local dialects. English is widely used and is still taught in schools, but in 1965 Hindi became the official language.

Beautiful Jewelry ◀

India is famous for its arts and crafts. Jewelry is worn more often than in the West, and Indian jewelers are renowned for their fine enamel work on gold, silver, and copper. The best work comes from Jaipur in the state of Rajasthan.

Disintegration of the Caste System

The traditional Hindu Indian caste system has existed for more than 2,000 years. Every Hindu was born into a caste, and some castes were thought to be higher than others and are graded on a scale according to how "pure" they are. There are more than 25,000 subcastes in India, distributed between four broad castes. When India became independent in 1947, the lower castes were granted some political and educational rights, and the "untouchability" or the lowest caste was declared illegal.

Cities and Villages ▲

India has a number of important cities. New Delhi is its capital, Bombay has cotton mills, and Calcutta is the home of jute mills. All of these cities are great industrial centers as well as capitals of states or provinces. The main ports are Bombay, Calcutta, and Madras. However, the vast number of people— 80 percent—live in villages.

Sacred Animals ▲

Hindus believe that all living organisms, including insects, have souls. For this reason, many devout Hindus are vegetarians. Among all animals, the cow is considered most sacred. Other important animals, regarded either as incarnations (a god inside the animal body), or messengers of various gods, are the monkey, serpent, elephant, bull, horse, buffalo, dog, and mouse. Certain birds are also venerated by Hindus.

A Lot of Tea

The largest tea-growing country in the world is India. The biggest weight of Indian tea comes from Assam in the northeast where there are both mountain and valley tea gardens.

Buckingham Palace ▼

Although a duke of Buckingham had a palace built for himself in the early 1700s, it was bought by the royal family in 1761. Since then, it has been used as a home for relatives as well as for the king or queen.

London Bridge is *NOT* Falling Down ▲

Contrary to the famous singing game of "London Bridge is Falling Down," the famous old London Bridge, which dates back over 800 years, never fell down. It was, however, taken apart during the 1960s and moved to Lake Havasu City, Arizona, where it is visited by many tourists every year.

Here in Camelot ▼

For hundreds of years, people in Britain have searched for evidence that there really was a King Arthur. A history book written way back in the 800s mentions an Arthur who won many battles. But the book is also filled with tales of magic and sorcery, so it might not be entirely accurate. Other mentions of King Arthur and the Knights of the Round Table are found mostly in poems and legends. The first mentions of Merlin the Magician and Arthur's childhood do not appear until the 1200s. All of these findings make experts suspicious about whether or not there ever was an Arthur, a Camelot, or a Round Table.

The Legend of Robin Hood ▲

Although there are hundreds of songs and stories about Robin Hood, there is no real evidence that the famous hero actually ever lived. The stories and songs even contradict one another about who Robin Hood was, when he lived, and what he did. So, as far as anyone can tell, Robin and his whole merry band—Little John, Friar Tuck, and even Maid Marian—were just characters in stories and songs.

Funny Food Names ▲

Sausages are a popular dish in many parts of Germany, and German immigrants brought the art of making knockwurst, bratwurst, and dozens of other kinds of sausage with them when they came to the United States. Over the years, one of these sausages was named a "frankfurter," after the German city of Frankfurt. Strangely enough, the hamburger also got its name from a German city—Hamburg.

Feeding the Birds ▲

Even to this day, the guards of the Tower of London take care of the ravens that make their home there. Long ago, a legend began that said that if anything happened to these birds, England itself would come to an end. So, for hundreds of years, guards have fed and cared for these birds, just in case the old superstition might be true.

The Tower of London ▲

The famous Tower of London dates back to the time of William the Conqueror, who took over England in 1066. Since then, many kings and queens have added to the original fort. The different parts of the building have been used as a palace, a prison, a zoo, and, most famous of all, a place where kings, queens, and other nobles were put to death. Today, there are 20 towers in this famous building.

The Greatest Writer of All

Even today, many people believe that William Shakespeare was the greatest writer ever to use the English language. Shakespeare himself, of course, had more humble opinions. Born in a small town, he went to London and joined the theater at an early age. He earned his living as an actor before turning to writing, and he continued taking small parts in his own plays for many years. During his career he wrote comedies, tragedies, and historical plays about the history of England. Except for brief times when all plays were banned, his plays have been put on for almost four hundred years.

The Art of French Cuisine

For hundreds of years, French food was considered the world's best. In part, this was because French cooks took their craft so seriously. It was also because many areas of concern—how bread is made, how things are grown, and so on—are controlled by the government of France. But most importantly, French cooks had an excellent training system that taught them everything they needed to know about cooking and rewarded them with good pay and the respect of people around the country.

Real French Fries

French fries are really one of France's gifts to the world. In France, though, they are called *pommes frites*, or "fried potatoes." And they are just as popular there as they are in America.

Art Capital of Europe

During the 1400s and 1500s, Italy was the capital of the world of art. But, by 1800, Paris, France, was the home of many of the world's most famous artists. All through the 1800s and early 1900s, painters and sculptors went to Paris to study, to look at the many great works of art in Paris' museums, and to be with other painters. Soon Paris was the best place for a painter to work.

Traditional Dress

Lederhosen are part of the traditional dress of Bavaria, a province in southern Germany. These short pants were traditionally made of leather and had suspenders to hold them up. Today, they are worn as costumes for festivals rather than as part of people's everyday clothing.

Changing How People Learn

In 1455, a German metalworker named Gutenberg forever changed how people learn. Before Gutenberg, books were either made by hand or printed from hand-carved wooden blocks that printed a whole page. Gutenberg created metal molds into which he could pour hot liquid metal, in order to produce separate letters. These letters could be arranged and rearranged as the printer wished. As a result, books were easier and cheaper to make—and they became available to more people.

Bullfighting Tips

Bullfighting is not a fight between two bulls. In fact, it really isn't a fight at all. This popular activity is really a spectacle, since the whole idea of the event is for the bull to lose. The bull is fought in a kind of ceremony by many different *toreros*, or "bull men." Some place fancy darts in the bull's shoulders, and the matador eventually kills the bull.

Bullfighting Controversy

Although bullfighting has been a tradition in many countries for hundreds of years, many people think of it as a cruel and terrible sport. Because the bulls suffer pain and death, bullfighting has been against the law in many countries for quite some time. Other countries, however, have not banned it, and it continues to be popular in those areas.

An Ancient Tradition

Although bullfighting is common in many Spanish-speaking countries, it actually had its beginnings far from Spain itself. Pictures on the walls of buildings on the island of Crete show that special bullfights were held there thousands of years ago. Although these were bare-handed contests, they certainly were the first bullfights.

Mona Lisa Smile ▲

The "Mona Lisa" is one of the most famous paintings by Leonardo Da Vinci, an Italian artist of the 1400s. Painted sometime between 1503 and 1506, it shows a young woman in a dark dress. Her strange, half-smile has made thousands of viewers wonder what she might be thinking about.

The Agony and the Ecstasy

Michelangelo was the most famous artist of the Italian Renaissance, a period when art, literature, and music reached great heights. He painted the famous ceiling of the Sistine Chapel in Rome, spending over four years lying on a scaffold hung from the building's ceiling. He was also a famous sculptor, well known for "The Pieta" and "David."

A Wealth of Music

The Russians have a great wealth of traditional folk music, and the *balalaika*, a Russian stringed instrument, was used to play this music from the 18th century. In the 19th century, Russian composers began to compose truly Russian concert music. Among the most famous are Peter Tchaikovsky, Modest Mussorgsky, and Nikolai Rimsky-Korsakov.

Going to School ▲

Education in Russia and other countries in the same region is free and compulsory for children from the ages of 7 to 15 or 16. Modern schools in these countries stress engineering and the sciences, although the arts, particularly music and ballet, are also important.

352

◄Russian Delicacies

The chief item of Russian meals continues to be black bread. Other traditional dishes include cabbage soup (*shchi*) and grain porridge (*kasha*). Specialties of Russian cooking are small meat pies (*pirozhki*), pancakes (*blini*), beet soup (*borsch*), and various forms of sour cream and cream. Caviar, the eggs or roe of sturgeon, comes almost exclusively from the region around Russia and rates as one of the world's most expensive delicacies.

Beautiful Churches

Russian architecture shows best in its churches, which until the 17th century were the most important buildings in the country. Early churches were built of wood. Something of their style later descended to the stone churches, with their square ground plan, tent-like form, and onion-shaped domes. The multi-domed Cathedral of St. Basil is world famous.

Coming to America ▶

After the year 1900, more than 1 million immigrants of all nationalities arrived in the United States every year. Some of these people returned to their homelands after a few years, but the great majority remained in the United States. Most of them settled in big cities such as Boston, New York City, Philadelphia, and Chicago.

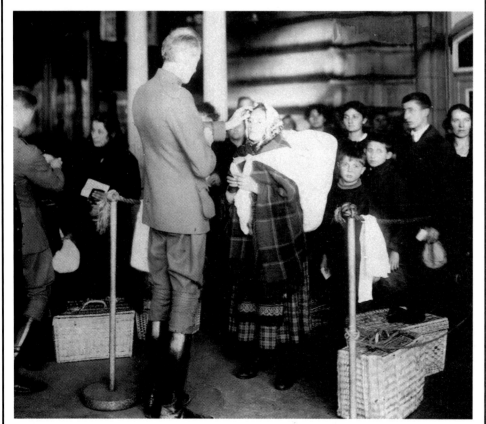

Two Ports of Entry ▲

For more than 100 years, New York City served as the port of entry for most of the immigrants who came to America. Only in recent years has Los Angeles taken over as the chief point of entry to the United States.

Speaking Your Own Language

More than 80 different languages are spoken throughout the neighborhoods of New York City. Among the larger immigrant groups were the Germans, Irish, Jews, and Italians. At one time, the Irish made up one quarter of the city's population. Today, more than 12 percent of the state's population is Jewish, the largest percentage in any state.

A Famous Neighborhood

The Harlem section of Manhattan is the best-known black neighborhood of the United States. Earlier in the century, it was home to a cultural and literary revival called the Harlem Renaissance. A number of artists and writers, including James Weldon Johnson, Claude McKay, Countee Cullen, Langston Hughes, Wallace Thurman, and William Jordan Rapp, were brought to fame.

Speaking Spanish in the United States

Mexicans are the largest Spanish-speaking ethnic group in the United States. In 1980, they officially numbered 7 million. Other members of the Spanish-speaking ethnic group are approximately 1.6 million Puerto Ricans, 600,000 Cubans, and roughly 1 million from other Central and South American countries.

Street scene in Israeli city of Jerusalem.

A Unique City

Los Angeles, with 1.5 million Mexican residents, has the largest concentration of Mexican people in any urban area outside of Mexico City and Guadalajara.

Going to the Land Down Under

Since World War II, more than 3,350,000 immigrants have settled in Australia. Most newcomers came from Great Britain, but large numbers also came from Greece, Italy, Germany, the Netherlands, Poland, and the Baltic States. Others have come from Asia. Because of Australia's policy of helping refugees coming to the country from the politically troubled parts of Southeast Asia, there are now more Asians than non-Asians entering the country.

◄A Highly Developed Country

Over one million Jews from all over the world have settled in Israel since 1948. Many of the Jewish immigrants from Europe, the former Soviet Union, and North America have helped make Israel into one of the most highly developed countries in the world.

Grimm's Fairy Tales ▲

The Grimm brothers were born in Germany in the late 1700s. Since they were very interested in language and the stories that were passed down from person to person, they began collecting these tales when they were young. In 1812 and 1814, they published *Children's and Family Stories,* which included dozens of stories like *Little Red Riding Hood, Hansel and Gretel, Rumpelstiltskin,* and *Rapunzel.* The book made the two brothers famous. One brother, Wilhelm, went on to collect even more fairy tales, while the other, Jakob, spent his time studying the German language.

Singing Down Under

"Waltzing Matilda" was written by "Banjo" Paterson, a writer who created many songs and poems about life on the early Australian frontier. The song was hugely popular, and was sung by Australian soldiers during both World Wars. Ever since, it has been the unofficial Australian national anthem.

The Story of Snow White

Most people know of Snow White from the feature-length Walt Disney cartoon that was released in 1938. However, the story goes back hundreds of years and was part of the first book of fairy tales written by Jakob and Wilhelm Grimm. It probably came from Germany.

Once Upon a Time ▲

In the 1600s and 1700s, a Frenchman named Charles Perrault collected folk tales and rewrote them so that they could be published in a book. Among them were *Cinderella, The Sleeping Beauty,* and *Bluebeard.* The stories have been read to children around the world ever since.

American Fairy Tales

Uncle Remus was a character created by the writer Joel Chandler Harris. In Harris' stories, Uncle Remus was a slave on a cotton plantation in the years before the Civil War. Uncle Remus told stories to the plantation owner's son. Those stories—which were supposed to be by this kindly old man—made Harris famous.

The Adventures of Brer Rabbit

Joel Chandler Harris' most famous tale, *The Tar-Baby Story,* has been enjoyed by children for years. Brer Rabbit is the main character who finds himself in trouble with a lump of tar. Like many of Harris' stories, this one comes from the folk tales told by the African-Americans of his native Georgia.

Folk Dancing▶

In many parts of the world, people celebrate springtime with special dances. Many of these dances are done by groups of young men. In England, Morrice (or Morris) dancers wear white costumes and decorate themselves with ribbons, flowers, and bells. Their dances go back hundreds, even thousands, of years to times when dancing was a way of asking the gods to give the people good crops during the coming summer.

An American Songwriter

Stephen Foster is probably the most famous composer of American folk songs. Writing over 160 songs, he focused most of them on the lives of the black slaves in the southern United States. Among the popular songs that he wrote are "Oh! Susanna," "My Old Kentucky Home," "Beautiful Dreamer," "Old Black Joe," and "Jeanie With the Light Brown Hair."

Songs of the People

Folk songs are traditional songs passed down from parent to child over the years. Many of these songs are about holidays and seasons. Others tell of heroes, adventures, or even people in love. The songs are usually fairly simple because they are meant to be memorized, not written down or performed by professional musicians.

Dancing the Jig

Jigs are dances in which the dancer keeps his or her body up straight, with arms to the side. The dancer then does quick, springing steps. Jigs can be danced by one person, a couple, or even a whole group.

Swing Your Partner ▲

Square dancing is an old American tradition that goes back hundreds of years. The dancers move around in pairs and groups, following the instructions of a "caller," or a member of the band who calls out directions to the dancers. Although square dancing has been done in almost every part of the country, it is especially popular in the West.

A Beautiful Folk Song

◀

"Greensleeves" is one of the most famous folk songs of all, and it has been sung by people for hundreds of years. According to many experts, the person who wrote it was King Henry VIII of England. King Henry, who was famous for eating huge meals and for his many wives, was also an excellent musician. He performed in public often and wrote dozens of poems and songs.

The Adventures of Wild Bill Hickok ◄

James Butler (Wild Bill) Hickok was born in Illinois in 1837. He moved to Kansas after leaving home at a young age, where he served as a peace officer in the town of Monticello. By the time he served in the Civil War, Hickok had a reputation as a successful gun fighter. After the war, he became the deputy sheriff in Abilene, Kansas. There, he ruled with an iron hand, as he did in Hays City, where he also served as sheriff. He became so famous that by the 1870s, he was touring with the Buffalo Bill Wild West Show. Bored with city life, Hickok set out for the Dakota gold fields, where he was killed in an argument over a card game.

Billy the Kid ▼

Born in Brooklyn, New York, as William Bonney, Jr., Billy the Kid was actually one of the most wanted criminals in the West. Before he was shot by Sheriff Pat Garrett, he was said to have killed at least 27 men. Along with his parents, Billy moved to Kansas and, from there, to Colorado. In his early teens, he began a life of stealing, wandering around the Southwest and northern Mexico. He was finally captured in 1880 and was sentenced to death. He escaped and remained at large until he was shot by Garrett on July 17, 1880.

Buffalo Bill ▲

William F. Cody was the famous "Buffalo Bill" of the American West. He was a scout for the army, a buffalo hunter, and Indian fighter. Eastern writers heard of his adventures and filled dozens of pages with stories of his bravery and skill. He won the Congressional Medal of Honor for his work as a scout and helped the army in its many battles against the Plains Indians. In 1883, he organized his first Wild West Show, traveling the country showing people fancy shooting, buffalo hunting, the capture of a stagecoach by bandits, and an Indian raid. The show traveled throughout the world and made Cody one of the most famous men of his day.

357

The Gold Rush

The Forty-Niners were among the most famous groups of pioneers in American history. In 1849, after gold was discovered in California, thousands of people rushed into the area in hopes of getting rich. Although the gold rush created a boom in California, most of the Forty-Niners found little or none of the precious metal.

Stories of the American West

Western novels appeared long before movies. In fact, some of the very first books written in the United States were about the adventures of people living on the frontier. The most famous Western novels were written in the 1850s and 1860s by E.Z.C. Judson, who wrote under the name "Ned Buntline." His books, which sold for a penny or a nickel each, were romantic tales of cowboys, sheriffs, and bad guys. Judson wrote them by the hundreds and all of them were best-sellers.

Telling Tall Tales

Tall tales were stories told from one person to another over the years. As they were passed on, each storyteller added a few details to make the story more interesting. In time, they became quite exaggerated. That is where the name "tall tale" originates. Since they were meant only to entertain people, no one expected them to be very accurate.

American Heroes

The stories of Pecos Bill, Paul Bunyan, and other heroes have been told for generations. Other tall tales grew up around real life people, and the stories we hear about Billy the Kid, Wild Bill Hickok, and Buffalo Bill have become tall tales in themselves.

Paul Bunyan

358

The Grand Ole Opry

The "Grand Ole Opry" (a colloquial way of saying "Grand Old Opera") began as a radio show in the South during the 1920s. It proved so popular that an entire entertainment center was built around it that continues to this day. For over 60 years, the biggest names in country music have appeared on its stage. They perform for the hundreds of people who come to see a live performance and the millions who listen on the radio.

Gene Autry was one of America's favorite cowboys.

Singing Cowboys

Roy Rogers sings to Dale Evans.

The "singing cowboys" were Hollywood movie stars who rode, shot, roped, and sang in the 1930s and 1940s. The most famous ones were Gene Autry and Roy Rogers—both went on to become television stars. Autry also went on to become the popular owner of the California Angels baseball team.

The Golden Age of Radio

The 1920s, 1930s, and 1940s are often called "the Golden Age of Radio." Dozens of different kinds of shows were on the air. Comedies, variety shows, sports, news programs, special events, dramas, and even soap operas kept people gathered around their radio sets for hours at a time.

The Birth of Radio

In 1910, Lee De Forest, one of the pioneers of radio broadcasting, produced the first real radio show. It came from the Metropolitan Opera House in New York City, and it starred the world-famous singer, Enrico Caruso. Within a few years, new equipment was created that could send signals farther away, and radio was on its way.

The Highlight of the Day

Sound effects for radio shows were complicated, and everything from falling rain to footsteps helped people imagine exactly what was happening on a show. Also, people gathered together around the radio, making listening to radio a social activity.

Television Mania ▲

The first TV broadcasts took place back in the 1920s and 1930s. But it took until the 1940s for the television boom to really get started, since TV broadcasting was stalled by World War II. By the late 1940s, there were TV broadcasts along the East coast—between Boston and Washington, D.C. TV spread quickly, and, by 1960, there were about 50 million television sets in use across the country.

A Television First

The first real television broadcast came from the Radio Corporation of America (RCA). The show was a cartoon of *Felix the Cat*, and it was broadcast in 1936. The first regular TV broadcasts were made by NBC in 1939.

Radio Worldwide

Today, there are more radios than ever before, and radio is booming as usual. The former Soviet Union ranks second to the United States, with about 233 million radios—roughly one for every other citizen.

Radio Madness

There are more than 500 million radios in the United States. Can you imagine what would happen if all of them were turned on at the same time?

Brought to You Live ▲

Early TV shows were broadcast live, so the audience was seeing exactly what was happening on the stage or in the studio. Many of the first TV shows were comedies and variety shows, since these could be put on stage easily and without a lot of props and dramatic scenery. Ed Sullivan's *Toast of the Town*, for example, had performers doing their acts on a stage before a live audience. Other shows, like game shows and contests, had simple sets that could be changed quickly, so another show could go on the air a few minutes later. Another kind of show was the live drama show. These often starred young actors, many of whom went on to become important Hollywood stars. The plays were put on live, and viewers often had the feeling they were watching a real play right in their own living rooms.

Early Radio Greats

Some early radio stars were musicians, like Duke Ellington and Guy Lombardo, whose bands had listeners dancing all the time. Others were comedians like Jack Benny and the team of George Burns and Gracie Allen. There were also actors who appeared in the many drama shows and "serials," or shows that brought listeners a new drama each week, exactly the way many TV shows do today.

The early comedy team of George Burns and Gracie Allen was very popular.

Martians Have Landed!

On October 30, 1938, one of the most unusual broadcasts in history took place. At that time, one of the popular radio programs was *Mercury Theater of the Air*, a show of live dramas put together by a brilliant 23-year-old director and actor named Orson Welles. That evening, an announcement about a special broadcast was made, but few people paid any attention. What they did pay attention to was what followed—seemingly "live" news coverage of a landing by men from Mars. Welles' show was so realistic that thousands of people believed that Martians had landed in New Jersey. Several times announcers interrupted to explain that the events were not real, but many people either did not hear or ignored the message. The police and other officials received hundreds of calls, and millions of people got themselves ready for the "Martian invasion."

Origins of Soap Operas

Since radio's daytime dramas were often sponsored by companies that made soap and detergent, the name "soap opera" evolved. The programs were not very different from the soaps of today, and, in fact, some of today's TV soaps actually began on the radio many years ago.

Television's Most Memorable

Two events on TV were probably the most memorable. The first took place just two days after President John F. Kennedy was shot to death in Dallas, Texas. On November 24, 1963, the man accused in the shooting, Lee Harvey Oswald, was murdered as police were taking him from one building to another. The scene was witnessed by millions of people who were watching the news event live on their TV sets. The other event was far more pleasant—the sight of the first American astronauts to step on the moon. This took place in July 1969.

Pioneer of Motion Pictures

Thomas Edison, the man who invented the light bulb, the phonograph, and other great inventions, was also one of the pioneers of motion pictures. His first motion picture machine was called a kinetoscope. It ran a loop of film about 50 feet (15 m) long. These strange machines allowed one person to look at pictures of moving people and scenes. By 1896, Edison had created a kinetoscope that projected pictures onto a screen. Edison's first movie on a screen had scenes from a boxing match, a dancer, and pictures of waves rolling onto a beach.

Making Them Laugh

In the early days of movies, a director named Mack Sennett created many comedies that kept people rolling with laughter. The films featured bathing beauties, slapstick humor in which people threw pies in each others' faces, and a group of comic police officers who always fell and tripped their way across the screen. The police chases became so popular that the name "Keystone Kops" (after "Keystone," the name of the company that made the pictures) became a household phrase.

Early Movie Stars

By 1912, movies were popular enough for people to have favorite actors and actresses. One of the first of these stars was Mary Pickford (left), a young girl with long blonde hair. By 1918, Pickford was so famous that she had a one-million-dollar contract. Other big names in the early days of movies were Douglas Fairbanks (Mary Pickford's husband), Buster Keaton, and Gloria Swanson.

An Early Winner ▲

Charlie Chaplin was perhaps the greatest—and most famous—of all the early movie stars. Dressed as a tramp, with his broken-down hat, baggy pants, and twirling cane, he was a figure recognized by millions of people. Much of Chaplin's popularity came from the way he could show sadness and humor in his comedies. This made "The Tramp," as Chaplin's character was called, one of the best loved people in the entire world.

The First Televised Debate

In 1960, John F. Kennedy and Richard Nixon debated each other on television, marking the first time candidates for president met in this way on TV. The event was important to the election, too. Because Kennedy was a young man with a brilliant smile, Nixon appeared less attractive. Later, many people believed that this caused him to lose the election.

The First TV Star

Many people lay claim to the title "first TV star," but the one who probably deserves this honor was Milton Berle. His show, *The Texaco Star Theater*, went on the air in 1948 and remained one of the country's biggest hits until 1956. At one time, Berle's shows attracted 80 percent of the TV audience. His comedy acts made millions laugh each week.

Most Popular Shows

In 1985, 1½ billion people tuned in to watch the "Live Aid" concert given to help the victims of hunger in Africa. So far that is the biggest audience ever to see a single event on TV. The most popular series ever was *I Love Lucy*. In its most popular season—1952-1953—67.3 percent of the viewing audience tuned in, according to the Nielsen rating.

Three Big Networks

The three big TV networks all have names that are abbreviations for their full names. CBS, for example, stands for Columbia Broadcasting System. NBC stands for National Broadcasting Company, and ABC stands for American Broadcasting Company.

For the First Time in Color

The Marriage was the first network series to be regularly telecast in color. It was first shown by NBC in 1954.

A Television Regular

The Honeymooners, starring Jackie Gleason, got started as one of many skits on Gleason's variety show. The characters were so popular with the audience that it was made into a show of its own.

Hollywood Legends

During the 1930s, movies were America's most popular kind of entertainment, and the giant studios of Hollywood made many films each month. Big-name stars could be counted on to bring in an audience, and actors like Gary Cooper, Clark Gable (right), Marlene Dietrich, Katharine Hepburn (far right), and Cary Grant became familiar to everyone in the country.

The Age of Hollywood Spectaculars ▲

Hollywood spectaculars began with a director named D.W. Griffith. Griffith's *The Birth of a Nation* (above), which first appeared in 1915, is often said to be the greatest silent movie of all. In another picture, *Intolerance,* which he made in 1916, Griffith made a mile-long model of the city of Babylon. The model was so huge that the cameras had to be taken up in balloons in order to get pictures of the scene.

A Movie First ▲

The first real movie, *The Great Train Robbery,* was actually a Western. It was made in 1903. Later, Westerns starred "Bronco Billy Anderson," the first cowboy hero, and William S. Hart, an actor who always portrayed a cowboy who seemed bad but always turned out to have a heart of gold.

The New Age of Sound

"You ain't heard nothin' yet" were famous words spoken by Al Jolson, the star of *The Jazz Singer.* This was the first silent picture with some musical passages and a few sentences of spoken dialogue. Jolson's words were a warning to people that movies would never be the same as they were in the days of "silent pictures."

What Makes Jazz Special ▼

Jazz has its roots in the music that slaves brought to North America from Africa. Over the years, this music changed tremendously. By the early 1900s, brass bands in New Orleans were playing a special kind of music that became known as "Dixieland." This music soon became popular all over the country, and by the 1920s, jazz was played and loved by millions of people. Jazz has changed a great deal since then, although it still has its roots in the African music from which it began.

King of Jazz ▲

Louis Armstrong was probably the greatest jazz trumpet player of all time. Born in 1900, he began playing in bands at an early age, and by the 1920s was a legend among both musicians and music lovers. By the time of his death in 1971, he had become the symbol of jazz and American music for millions of people all over the world.

We're Just Country Folk

Country and western is the music of the American countryside—the South, the Midwest, and even the cowboy lands of the West. It began with the ballads that people brought to the South from England. Over time, the music changed, as people heard the fiddle music of the Cajuns of Louisiana and the blues of the African-Americans of the South. Today, country and western music is a big business, but its songs are still about people who live in America's farms and small towns.

365

Sgt. Pepper's Lonely Hearts Club Band

In 1967, The Beatles presented the world with an unusual record called "Sgt. Pepper's Lonely Hearts Club Band." Hugely popular, it was one of the first Rock 'n' Roll albums to be more than just a collection of individual songs. Instead, The Beatles thought of the record as a whole, with each song linking up with the others to give listeners several key ideas.

The Woodstock Generation

In August 1969, almost half a million young people came to Bethel, New York, for one of the first great Rock Music Festivals, called the Woodstock Music and Art Fair. For an entire weekend people listened to the biggest names in rock, danced, had fun together, and made themselves famous as "the Woodstock generation." Many other festivals were later held, but none was as famous as the Woodstock festival.

The End of an Era

When The Beatles broke up their group, the musicians drifted their different ways. Drummer Ringo Starr became an actor, while also performing on his own. George Harrison performed on his own as well. Paul McCartney founded another band, called "Wings." John Lennon, who was the writer of many of the group's most famous songs, was murdered outside his New York City home in 1980.

Feeling It Inside ▶

Although jazz has been around since the beginning of the 1900s, no one has really ever been able to say exactly what it is. For some people, jazz includes everything from Dixieland music to blues and music that sounds almost like Rock 'n' Roll. It is a kind of music that began among African-Americans during the late 1800s. To musicians themselves, jazz is very personal. As one musician once said, "If you don't feel it inside you, it isn't jazz."

We Call It Rock 'n' Roll

Many people date the beginning of Rock 'n' Roll to the early 1950s and disc jockey Alan Freed. Instead of playing the "pop" music that most people in his audience usually listened to, he started playing rhythm and blues of black artists over the air waves. To the surprise of everyone but Alan Freed, people all over the area began to tune in, and soon young musicians all over the country were starting to play music like the sounds coming from Freed's show. Within a few years, Rock 'n' Roll had become America's newest and most popular kind of music.

The Rolling Stones appeared on the Rock 'n' Roll scene in the early 1960s.

The British Invasion

In the early 1960s, rock music was changing in Great Britain, and British musicians kept alive the spirit and sound of early Rock 'n' Roll and of rhythm and blues. Many British groups of this era wrote their own music. When groups like The Beatles and The Rolling Stones brought their music to the United States, young people responded. Soon, dozens of other British groups appeared on the music scene. For a while, it seemed as if every big name rock group was from Britain.

Beatlemania! ▲

The Beatles, as almost everyone knows, were Paul McCartney, John Lennon, Ringo Starr, and George Harrison—four young men from Liverpool, England, who took the music world by storm during the 1960s. To this day no one really knows exactly what made the Beatles so popular. But, by 1963, "Beatlemania" had swept much of the world. By 1963, they were a major success in Great Britain, and their tour of America the next year made them the most popular group in the world. Until the group broke up in 1971, everything about them—haircuts, way of dress, and ideas—was copied by young people all over the globe.

Rock 'n' Roll Oldies ▶

By 1956, Rock 'n' Roll already had a set of superstars. One of the first was Chuck Berry, a rhythm and blues guitarist whose singing and playing style was so full of energy that it had teenagers all over the country moving and dancing. One of the blockbuster groups was Bill Haley and the Comets. Their hit song, "Rock Around the Clock," which was released in 1955, was the anthem of Rock 'n' Roll for quite a while. But the most important early rock star was Elvis Presley. Presley's amazing voice and famous swiveling hips made him the most popular singer in the United States for many years.

INDEX

A